Owning the Street

Urban and Industrial Environments

Series editor: Robert Gottlieb, Henry R. Luce Professor of Urban and Environmental Policy, Occidental College

For a complete list of books published in this series, please see the back of the book.

Owning the Street

The Everyday Life of Property

Amelia Thorpe

The MIT Press
Cambridge, Massachusetts
London, England

This book was set in ITC Stone Serif Std and ITC Stone Sans Std by New Best-set Typesetters Ltd. Printed and bound in the United States of America.

Library of Congress Cataloging-in-Publication Data

Names: Thorpe, Amelia, author.
Title: Owning the street : the everyday life of property / Amelia Thorpe ; foreword by Davina Cooper.
Description: Cambridge, Massachusetts ; London, England : The MIT Press, [2020] | Series: Urban and industrial environments | Includes bibliographical references and index.
Identifiers: LCCN 2020002966 | ISBN 9780262539784 (paperback)
Subjects: LCSH: Automobile parking. | Urban parks. | Public spaces.
Classification: LCC HE336.P37 T46 2018 | DDC 388.4/74—dc23
LC record available at https://lccn.loc.gov/2020002966

10 9 8 7 6 5 4 3 2 1

For Sonia, Margot and Penelope

Contents

Foreword by Davina Cooper   ix
Acknowledgments   xv

Introduction   1

Part One: A PARK(ing) Movement?

1   From PARK(ing) to PARK(ing) Day   29

PARK(ing) on Mission Street • San Francisco and the world • Beyond the Rebar story • Sydney • Montréal

2   Moving Things Along   79

A compelling idea • A PARK(ing) movement? • PARK(ing) as a vehicular idea • The aesthetics of PARK(ing): legality and vehicularity

Part Two: Property and the Performance of Legality

3   PARK(ing) Law: Pluralism and Performance   97

PARK(ing) in a niche • PARK(ing) in a larger legal landscape • Parks and positivism • Performing PARK(ing) law

4   Properties of PARK(ing)   131

Proper language • Ownership • A sense of ownership: belonging • Renting space • Rights to the city: property and participation in the planning process

5   Building Ownership   157

Labor • Personhood • Relational theories of property • Grounding ownership in space • Play, pleasure, and love

6   **Performing Property**   193

Ownership and participation • Ownership and legality • Ownership and privilege • Sustaining ownership

Part Three: Politics and Possibility

7   **Products of PARK(ing)**   221

Changing the city • Changing one's place in the city: commoning • Changing possibilities: prefigurative practices • Undesirable impacts?

Postscript   257

Notes   267
Index   315

Foreword

This intellectually insightful, deeply textured book demonstrates the contribution innovative small-scale activities can make to understanding law and social politics. The book brings together three important themes: everyday legalities and legal consciousness; property and ownership; and prefigurative or commoning projects. Its focus is PARK(ing) Days—the temporary take-up of, usually metered, road spaces intended for cars as places in which to install a handkerchief park (or parklet) for people. Amelia Thorpe's book explores the history and contemporary practice of PARK(ing) Days, from their San Francisco origins in 2005 to their widespread presence some years later. In 2011, 975 parks were established in 162 cities across thirty-five countries. A brilliant idea that circulated globally, picking up the sediment of tried-out ideas as it traveled, the miniature spaces of PARK(ing) Days use token objects (turf, plants, seating) to establish a recognizable parklike place in which activities from shared meals to conversations, reading, and craftwork can take place. As Thorpe describes, participation can mean "sitting on a chair or stretching out on lawn or carpet, playing a game of pinball or corn bag, watching a performance, adding to a chalk drawing, repairing their bike, joining a yoga class, petting an animal, reading a poster, sharing a drink or a barbecue."

At the heart of PARK(ing) Days is the symbolic disruption of the naturalized dominance afforded to private cars in public space. Taken-for-granted ways of dividing and ordering city space are challenged and restaged as streets get claimed and remade for collective and shared activities. Through PARK(ing) Days, customary ideas of cars as mobile, agentically forceful entities, and recreational parks as defined fixed spaces, become inverted. Instead, recreational parks became the mobile entities, brought into being through the functional conversion of street spots. Thus PARK(ing) Days become park-making days, with cars discursively and practically excluded. Temporarily demobilized, cars get "parked" outside of the reanimated human uses of the space, while people become "parked" within newly recast recreational zones. Interviewees in the book describe how PARK(ing) Days create unfamiliar tactile relationships to tarmac, and new seated proximities to road traffic. Unlike the individualized, often competitive, sometimes hostile and antagonistic relationship of cars and car drivers to parking spaces in conditions of limited availability, where other road users become a (potential) threat to accessing a sought-after spot (and so getting out of the car), PARK(ing) Days emphasize sharing and collaborative uses. Against a zero-sum relationship in which one user's take-up of a space denies its use to others, PARK(ing) Days rely on participation and the value of multiple bodies engaged in diverse uses. Acting as if curbside, car-sized spaces have the potential to meet important, insufficiently met needs, and by using the space, importantly, to address such needs, from taking blood pressure to performing same-sex marriage, participants legitimate such uses, if temporarily, within shared outdoor spaces.

This coming into being through being done is a recurring theme that I return to. Yet, as the book describes, PARK(ing) Day, as a creative political project, also generates other outcomes. The book describes its contribution to a shift in urban policy and design toward pedestrians and cyclists, its role in supporting the more permanent establishment of handkerchief parks, the city imagery it inspires, its building of community ties, and, perhaps most fundamentally, the collective agency it expresses, manifesting a public freedom to take back and repurpose common spaces. Yet the book is also attentive to those moments in which PARK(ing) Day fails to support progressive democratic imaginaries, to ways it can enact, if unintentionally, regressive social relations and exclusions—from stoking house price escalations associated with communal, arty, green and grassy neighborhoods to alienating disadvantaged communities who experience its recreational pleasures as irrelevant or trivial.

Exploring these different dynamics and concerns, the book contributes to many different discussions. One of the most striking is its contribution to property scholarship. The book is situated within a body of work concerned with everyday manifestations of property both formal and informal. In the development of PARK(ing) Day spaces, officially recognized forms of property intrude in discussions and, sometimes, generate conflict over whether a right exists to use street parking spaces for carless activities. While parking without payment in an identified bay or zone is a penalty offense, in the absence of any formal specification, it often remains unclear whether payment alone makes the allotted space legally available for other (lawful) activities. For many participants, as the book describes, parking meter payment forms an essential enabler of a right to license the space for a meter-defined time. Acting as if this is what the parking meter does, participants claim an economic agency, asserting—and so *animating*—the bilateral character of an exchange typically supressed by standardized contractual forms. In the case of bus and other public transportation tickets, the person paying has no expected entitlement or capacity to vary the terms of the arrangement. If they identify the conditions and price of the offer as unacceptable, their only option is to walk away. PARK(ing) Day participants enact the user's right not only to shape the terms of the transaction but to take control by repurposing or redirecting what tickets do.

In this way, the meter as a legal act of payment authorizes the pop-up park in a relationship variously read as legal, illegal, a mix of both, or as sitting outside legality's terms. At the same time, *informal* relations of ownership structure and intrude upon this economic transaction. Tying social ownership to belonging (rather than merely belongings) and to a constitutive, formative relationship between different kinds of bodies, spaces, and things, the book explores how PARK(ing) Day expresses and gives support to social ownership as a relationship of attachment and connection to place. PARK(ing) Day expresses an ownership-making of the city anchored in its residents. It is a relationship which also allows people to represent space in both a descriptive and custodial sense. Here, remaking the space becomes a way of speaking for it, articulating its interests, needs, and imagined future in conditions where the space belongs to its communities, while they, in turn, are held (together) not only by the pop-up space but also by their assumed entitlement to declare it.

These reciprocating relationships of belonging, however, can also prove fraught. As the book discusses, social ownership claims may be more elastic and positive-sum than formal property relations, but social ownership can still be animated by exclusion—whether from acts of disavowal by participants or from the terms of attachment itself, which may generate alienation, disconnection, or nonbelonging in others. How this plays out has a racialized and economic character—evident in the case of privileged residents who assert a countervailing social ownership over certain street spaces. Here, nonparticipants oppose a pop-up park popping up near them by asserting a trumping relationship of belonging. Police and other public authorities contest claimed entitlements to create a park, restaging the distinction between legal and illegal by *acting as if* the metered park is illegal. Thus, claims of illegality can also be performative, making an activity prohibitive through its practically effective denial. The book describes how this has led participants, particularly institutional ones such as universities, to attempt to lock in their right to establish a temporary parklet in advance, in turn tacitly confirming the doubtful status of the activity.

Throughout, the book emphasizes the importance of adopting a questioning approach, attuned to the risks as well as the possibilities of prefigurative micro-innovations. At the same time, the capacity of PARK(ing) Days to support more inclusive and horizontal relations between people and their city, to generate property for personhood in-relations-of-community (to amend Margaret Radin's striking phrase), is an important theme. So too is the relationship between ownership and pleasure.

Joy is typically linked to ownership through a relationship of consumption—what people do with the things they own. While creating commercial goods can be pleasurable, and while PARK(ing) Day is also enjoyed by participants and those passing by, including through the virtual passing by that social media offer, the pleasures discussed in the book foreground the satisfactions which come from creating. Here, pleasure is linked to ownership through the mediating work of, well, work. Amelia Thorpe pays attention to the historically tenacious problems of anchoring ownership in labor, given its ties to the exploitation of resources through their conversion and appropriation. Yet, along with a "here first" approach—captured in the early morning city drive to get a sought-after metered spot—labor becomes a significant source of social ownership in the PARK(ing) Days discussed. At the same time, and drawing on Sarah Keenan's account of subversive property, the pleasures of performing an ownership that powerful others may deem marginal, precarious, or disorderly is striking, resonating with experiences in other contexts of pleasurable transgressions and reappropriations. In contrast to the ongoing work of guardianship or stewardship with its relations of responsibility, the pop-up park—with its echoes of Bey's Temporary Autonomous Zones and Foucauldian discussions of heterotopia—emphasizes the invention, creativity, and improvised uncertainty of the startup. As one participant remarks, explaining why he did not want to know too much about relevant PARK(ing) Day laws, "just the knowledge of them I think kills some of the magic about these things that just pop up into space."

The thrill or charm of the sudden unexpected emergence, encased in the minor life of socially inventive things that come and go, poses important questions about urban and public governance. What is the place of public bodies, such as city councils and national governments? And how do their roles and responsibilities differ from those of grassroots actors? On finishing my read of this book, I am left with the reflection that if it is primarily the responsibility of public bodies to manage and sustain more permanent collective goods, including the parks and pedestrianized commons which PARK(ing) Days enable and prefigure, then what grassroots actors rightly contribute may often be something else, namely the creation and expression of inspiring, critical, democratic alternatives. As PARK(ing) Days illustrate, participants draw on imaginative thinking, art and craft techniques, and a wily, playful approach to politics to trace relations of responsibility and ownership, demonstrating what these relations *could be like*. Sometimes these urban rehearsals of a hoped-for future endure; sometimes counterinstitutions emerge to take up responsibilities when statutory bodies have failed adequately to do so. And sometimes, grassroots creativity simply moves on.

Davina Cooper

Acknowledgments

First, I am immensely grateful to the architects, artists, activists, and many others who so generously and openly contributed to my research. *Owning the Street* is far richer thanks to the information and ideas they shared and, particularly, to the questions they asked.

Thanks are due also to the Bourke Street community for putting together our park in Redfern, especially Lydia Ho, Davida Sweeney, and Vanessa Trowell.

Owning the Street has benefited greatly from the advice, critiques, and support provided by many friends, colleagues, and commentators, including Davina Cooper, Sarah Blandy, Nick Blomley, Helen Carr, Dave Cowan, Hanoch Dagan, Eve Darian-Smith, Alexandra Flynn, Nicole Graham, Doug Harris, Kurt Iveson, Sarah Keenan, Antonia Layard, Stewart Macaulay, Morag McDermott, Mark Purcell, Carol Rose, Susan Silbey, Marie-Eve Sylvestre, Frank Upham, Mariana Valverde, and Estair Van Wagner. Particular thanks are due to Desmond Manderson and Tim Bonyhady for their invaluable advice, generous guidance, and incisive critiques during the doctoral research on which this book is based.

I am extremely fortunate to be surrounded by brilliant colleagues at UNSW. In particular, I would like to thank Kathy Bowrey, Marc De Leeuw, Ros Dixon, Michael Handler, Fleur Johns, Daniel Joyce, Vicki Sentas, Nofar Sheffi, and Monika Zalnieriute, who provided sage advice and support at various stages, and especially Bronwen Morgan, who was unfailingly enlightening and encouraging.

I would also like to thank my hosts in Montréal and in San Francisco: the Faculty of Law at McGill University, particularly Kirsten Anker and Hoi Kong, and the Centre for the Study of Law and Society at UC Berkeley, especially David Lieberman. Thanks also to Jewel Angeles, Yvonne Hong, and Elisha Laurentis for their transcription of the interviews, and to my father Andrew for his rigorous proofreading (and everything else!).

I am greatful to Beth Clevenger, Bob Gottleib, Anthony Zannino, Matthew Abbate, and the team at the MIT Press for their support, suggestions, and work in publishing this manuscript. I am grateful also for the work and feedback provided by the editors and reviewers of journals in which earlier verisons of some of this material have been published: the *Law and Society Review* ("Pop-up Property: Enacting Ownership from San Francisco to Sydney," 52 [2018]: 740–772), the *Journal of Law and Society* ("'This Land Is Yours': Ownership and Agency in the Sharing City," 45 [2018]: 99–115), and *Social and Legal Studies* ("Hegel's Hipsters: Claiming Ownership in the Contemporary City," 27 [2018]: 25–48).

Finally, to Lee, my most treasured interlocutor, and to our girls, Sonia, Margot, and Penelope, my constant inspiration: thank you for traveling with me to visit parks around the world, for your invaluable insights, and for waiting patiently for me to get this done (but not too patiently; thank you also for the times you pulled me away to play). I love you to the moon and back.

"Oh, now it's possible! We can do things in the city!"
Jérôme Glad, Montréal

Figure 0.1
PARK(ing) Day, Rue Saint-Hubert, Montréal, 2015. Image: Amelia Thorpe.

Introduction

On the third Friday in September 2015, the proprietors of Librairie Paren-thèse, a bookstore on Rue Saint-Hubert, Montréal, stepped into the park-ing space outside their store. Framed by strings of colored bunting, they furnished the space with AstroTurf, a hammock, a table and chairs, and sets of chess and Scrabble. On the adjacent footpath (sidewalk) they placed a chalkboard reading "prenez une pause" ("take a break"). There was no charge or purchase required to take up the invitation, and no signage or promotion for the bookstore. Elyse and Jonathan, the young couple behind the Librairie, then spent the afternoon moving between the street and the store—resting in the hammock, playing games, reading and talking to vari-ous people who joined them in the pop-up park. At the end of the day, they packed up and returned the parking space to its former condition.

Farther down the street, four other parking spaces were remade into similar sites inviting pauses, play, and social interaction, adding to more than 200 across the city. Beyond Montréal, parking spaces in other cities were also transformed. Among many others, the transformations included: a series of seven wedding vow renewal ceremonies in Pittsburgh, Pennsyl-vania;[1] in Singapore, a row of hammocks, a fish curry lunch, and a pair of brightly painted pianos;[2] vegetable gardens, play spaces, and potted plant installations in Madrid, Spain;[3] in Almaty, Kazakhstan, a chalk mural;[4] grass, games, and picnic blankets in Lagos, Nigeria.[5]

This international appropriation of parking spaces was part of PARK(ing) Day, an event that has taken place every year since 2006. Initiated in San Francisco by Rebar, then a fledgling design collective, the event's organiza-tion is extremely loose. A how-to guide and a Creative Commons license were provided on the parkingday.org website, along with photos of other parks, and a set of Google maps on which participants were encouraged to pin the locations of their contributions. Beyond a request not to put parking spaces to commercial use, participants can make of the day whatever they choose.

PARK(ing) Day starts with a small intervention in a specific space, but very quickly becomes a more general claim about rights in and to the city. PARK(ing) Day is explicitly framed as legal. Paying a meter, Rebar argued, amounts to taking out a lease over the space, and while most "lessors" use this to store a car, the space could also be put to other uses. In this novel rereading of everyday regulation, PARK(ing) Day raises questions about the nature of law. How do rules develop over time? Who participates in the making of law? How is it that a social understanding about law can take effect in the world and become "real"?

Drawing together a wide range of debates—about the kinds of changes necessary to increase environmental sustainability, economic resilience, and social inclusion, about agency and belonging in contemporary cities, and about the connections between property and power—PARK(ing) Day provides a vivid example of the connection between belief and action, the dynamic nature of legal interpretation, and the social embeddedness of legality. Through PARK(ing) Day, a global event, this book examines how local, specific and personal understandings about belonging, ownership, and agency intersect with law to shape the city. The analysis offers insights into the ways in which people construct a sense of ownership over space, how those constructions interact with legal notions of property, and the consequences of those relationships for understandings of the city and the place of people within it.

At the heart of this book are claims about property and legality. While Rebar was not the first to appropriate parking spaces for alternative uses, they were uniquely successful in their intervention: no other example has been taken up by so many people, in such a wide range of places, or sustained over so many years. Rebar's invocation of legality is central to that success. PARK(ing) Day draws on law, disrupting established understandings and driving debates forward; it also works to sustain it. By constructing pop-up parks, participants make material and discursive claims about legality, and those claims in turn contribute to the ongoing constitution (and sometimes reorientation) of the laws that shape the city.

The invocation of property law is particularly significant: a key part of the appeal of PARK(ing) Day is its connection to property. Analysis of PARK(ing) Day provides important insights into the nature of property, highlighting complex and co-constitutive relationships between formal property rights, informal ownership, and belonging. Beyond conceptualizing property, PARK(ing) Day shows that ownership is crucial in understanding how rules are applied on the ground. The inherent openness of law to multiple interpretations means that legal actors must look beyond official texts when making determinations about legality; informal ownership is often central in such determinations when it comes to city streets. PARK(ing) Day helps to explain the nature and importance of various forms of ownership; it can also help to build it. Using words like "profound" and "transformative," participants suggest that PARK(ing) Day can itself be productive of ownership. For many, participation in the event changed their relationship with the street and the city, working as a form of commoning to nurture shared interests and identities, a prefigurative practice opening up new and unexpected possibilities for intervention in the city.

Cars in the city

PARK(ing) Day connects to a wider questioning of the place of cars in contemporary cities, flowing from a recognition that the orientation of urban space around private automobiles over the past century has created a host of social, economic, and environmental burdens.[6] From the oil crisis of the 1970s to global climate change, automobility is a key contributor to some of the world's most wicked problems.[7] More immediately, cars create an everyday and extreme danger, with a toll of deaths and injuries on a scale comparable only to war.[8] Other concerns include health impacts from local air pollution and sedentary lifestyles,[9] congestion and the increasing costs of building and maintaining roads and associated infrastructure across ever-widening expanses,[10] and a vast array of local, regional, and global environmental impacts.[11] Equity and environmental justice are important cross-cutting issues, since vulnerable and marginalized communities bear a disproportionate share of the burdens of car-centric development.[12] As Gregg Culver argues, "the hegemony of the private automobile and its spaces has constituted a slow and geographically diffuse, but steady, hor-rific, and expanding human-made catastrophe."[13]

Increasing awareness of these and other impacts has prompted a range of scholarly, advocacy, and policy proposals to reorient development away from cars. Alongside others, these include: new urbanism,[14] transit-oriented development,[15] complete streets,[16] and Vision Zero,[17] as well as grassroots initiatives like Critical Mass,[18] Reclaim the Streets,[19] Ciclovía[20] and Better Block.[21]

PARK(ing) Day is interesting among these in its use of the parking meter. Unlike the technologies at the heart of other strategies to reduce car use—technologies that restrict the ability of cars to drive, and certainly to drive fast, on city streets—the parking meter played a key role in facilitating the spread of car-centric development.

Until the start of the twentieth century, streets were widely understood as shared spaces for public use: by traveling pedestrians, streetcars, horses and carriages, but also by street vendors, children, neighborhood gath-erings, and other forms of social exchange.[22] Cars were generally seen as unwelcome and dangerous interlopers, consuming scarce space for far less efficient private use, and causing many thousands of deaths and injuries in the process.[23] The rapid increase in car ownership in the 1920s was hotly contested, with pedestrians, parents, policy and business organizations organizing to restrict their use of city streets.

Instead of banning cars from central areas and forcing people to use pub-lic transport, as some had proposed, the decision to regulate cars through parking meters *increased* their use: ensuring turnover of parking spaces greatly increased capacity, and the new revenue stream created municipal support.[24] The result, as John Jackle and Keith Sculle explain, was a process in which "increased parking create[d] insatiable appetite for more parking, leading to the wholesale destruction of traditional city landscapes and to the creation of new and highly wasteful suburban places."[25] PARK(ing) Day is distinctive in its inversion of this tool of automobility: after decades of enabling car-centric development, the meter becomes a tool for its critique.

DIY urbanism

PARK(ing) Day is perhaps the most recognizable example of the increas-ingly prevalent phenomenon of "DIY," "guerrilla," "adaptive," "pop-up," "everyday," or "tactical" urbanism: the shipping container bars, pallet seats, pavement chalk, and knitted bike racks that are now familiar in cities around the world.[26] Advocates describe this as a "quicker, lighter, cheaper" alternative to conventional planning, one that enables citizens to contribute to the development of their cities in meaningful and positive ways.[27] In contrast to the technocratic, top-down approach that dominated planning and development for much of the last century, or to the carefully choreographed forms of engagement that have emerged more recently, DIY urbanism is promoted as much better able to incorporate the multiplicity of publics and public interests that constitute contemporary cities. Connecting to scholarship on the power and potential of the everyday,[28] some see in DIY urbanism the potential to enact the right to the city, perhaps even a new urban politics and in turn a new kind of city.[29]

To others, practices like PARK(ing) Day merit much less celebration. DIY urban interventions are now regularly deployed by activists and communities, yet these groups invariably engage from a position of privilege: the vast majority are white, educated, equipped with cultural if not financial capital.[30] The capacity for intervention in public space, and especially for intervention without negative consequences, is not universally shared, particularly not by marginalized and vulnerable groups like undocumented migrants and indigenous and ethnic minorities. Instead of achieving the right to the city, critics see DIY urban interventions as highlighting its absence, emphasizing stark disparities with respect to who actually owns the city and who has the right to make use of urban space.[31]

Beyond privileged creatives, DIY urban interventions are also increasingly being deployed by state planning authorities, professional placemakers and businesses—including large corporations like Coca-Cola and BMW. Small-scale, informal interventions like PARK(ing) Day in that context are dismissed as too trivial to counter the powerful interests that drive development in contemporary cities. Far from inclusive or progressive, DIY urban interventions can be understood as one more tool that has been co-opted by big capital, one more contributor to processes of gentrification and real estate speculation.[32]

PARK(ing) Day has not been the focus of these critiques. In contrast to larger and longer-lasting DIY interventions, particularly those with a commercial element—things like pop-up beer gardens, restaurants, swimming pools, and art projects—most critiques of PARK(ing) Day center instead on its lack of impacts. Yet many participants are aware of and concerned about the potential for the event to have negative consequences, and many struggle to work out how best to engage in this context. There is a recognition, particularly among those who have been involved in PARK(ing) Day over many years, that interventions in public space are highly charged, and require careful attention to the complexities of the local context.

Participatory planning

PARK(ing) Day is significant in the context of concerns about the involvement of citizens in contemporary city-making processes. The adoption of DIY or tactical techniques by professional planners reflects the influence of the "collaborative turn" from the 1990s, and a general commitment to participation as essential for democratic values such as legitimacy, accountability and effectiveness in governance, as well as better planning outcomes.[33] Yet it is reflective also of an ongoing failure to engage the public in meaningful ways. Perhaps because there is little evidence that the emphasis on participation has brought with it any real increase in citizen influence, public participation remains reactive and largely oppositional (resisting proposals for highways, public housing, or other controversial developments).[34] When it comes to developing the more constructive visions necessary to guide future development, professional planners regularly lament the fact that participation rarely extends beyond a small group of "usual suspects."[35]

PARK(ing) Day provides a stark contrast to such apathy and opposition. PARK(ing) Day is now entering its fifteenth year. Most of the original participants have long ceased being involved, yet PARK(ing) Day continues to attract new participants, to capture the imaginations of the people who happen upon a tiny, temporary parking space park on the street, and the many more who see images and video footage of parks online. The idea remains compelling.

For Elyse and Jonathan, the young couple who run Librairie Parenthèse, PARK(ing) Day was unlike anything they had ever done before. Neither had any expertise or experience in planning or related activities; Elyse commented that the city would not be interested in her ideas, because she is "not qualified."[36] Elyse and Jonathan are not typical among the participants in PARK(ing) Day (many of whom do have some experience or expertise in design or planning), but nor are they unusual. A very wide range of people get involved in the event, motivated by many different aims and aspirations. The activities with which participants fill their parking spaces are similarly varied: some are very elaborate, some simple, some highly political, some playful, some meticulously designed, some makeshift.

What is it about the event that draws in people like Elyse and Jonathan who had previously paid little or no attention to planning processes? What do they get out of their participation? How might this relate to other forms of city-making?

These are the questions at the heart of this book. The origins of this research lie in my longstanding commitment to public participation in the process of city-making and, as a former planner and current member of a planning authority, my firsthand frustration with the way in which this is undertaken in practice. Far too often, citizens are relegated to the role of objector, and then derided as obstructive NIMBYs seeking to protect their private (property) interests at the expense of the public good. My aim in examining PARK(ing) Day was to understand a practice through which citizens contribute constructively to their cities, to learn what draws them in and what comes of their contributions.

Property in the city

Particularly significant in thinking about these questions is the way in which the event is framed. PARK(ing) Day is grounded in a claim about property. By paying a meter, Rebar explained, participants take out a short-term "lease" over the parking space, acquiring a property right that enables them to remake the space, at least for the duration of their "rental."

The idea that private property rights are generative of more social and sustainable approaches to city-making is novel. From NIMBY mums and dads to global development corporations, there is a large literature suggesting that property owners use the planning system to pursue their interests with little regard for wider consequences.[37] Property is frequently portrayed as having a negative influence on urban development, blamed to various degrees for a very wide range of problems: from urban sprawl and environmental destruction to the current housing crisis, from racial segregation and colonial dispossession to the privatization and securitization of public space.

PARK(ing) Day may be read in contrast to many of the narratives about the role of property in contemporary cities. Yet in its reliance on a lease and, particularly, the claim that such a lease gives participants the right to do whatever they wish with the parking space, PARK(ing) Day can be read as exploiting loopholes to pursue activities at odds with those determined through collective, democratic planning processes. Not unlike the real estate investors who are so often critiqued for their profit-focused manipulation of the rules through which cities are shaped, PARK(ing) Day might thus be viewed as another example of enclosure, more competitive and individualistic than progressive or inclusive.

My initial approach was very much along those lines: PARK(ing) Day enables the already (relatively) privileged to expand their claims over the city. Even fleeting assertions of exclusive control over public space, regardless of social context and collective planning decisions, are difficult to reconcile with my commitment to processes through which cities might be made more socially and spatially just. I began this project with a series of case studies, of which PARK(ing) Day was just one; my aim was to contrast this rather libertarian activity with other, more equitable and ethically oriented interventions.

Analysis of the way in which people actually understand the event, however, reveals a more nuanced role for property. Far from enclosure, the pop-up parks constructed on PARK(ing) Day are much more likely to be rooted in relationships of social and material connection, efforts not to take but to give. Examination of PARK(ing) Day was for me a profoundly hopeful experience, and the shift from critical example to central case study reflects this. From my initial position of skepticism, I came to appreciate the contradictions and complexities of the event, its entanglement with a wide range of social and environmental struggles, and the degree to which it is animated by care and commitment. While the idea of the "lease" provides a catchy point of entry, the property that is most significant for PARK(ing) Day is more often an informal and deeply relational sense of ownership.

For Elyse and Jonathan, the decision to get involved in the event followed from their motivation for opening the store two years earlier. It was part of a desire to be more connected to and to contribute more to the local community, and motivated by strong feelings for the street:

We moved into the plaza because we loved it . . . it's really a part of the Montréal story. Yes, it's part of our culture . . . we want to revive [the street] . . . it's like saving an old couple who were once in love and then one tries to recover the first years? Yes, it's a bit like that, our sense of *appartenance*, it's to try to revive this street.[38]

While less typical in their backgrounds, Elyse and Jonathan are typical in the sentiments of connection and contribution they express: the vast majority of participants are drawn to PARK(ing) Day by a desire to give back, make a place better; feelings of personal connection and emotion are often mentioned.

A sense of ownership is in many ways an open term, a matter of subjective and shifting social and material relationships connected to identity, community, belonging (in Montréal, the French *appartenance*), and place attachment—terms that are themselves open and connected in turn to other concepts.[39] A sense of ownership might relate to the street, the neighborhood, or even the city as a whole. A sense of ownership is not a matter of legal title, or at least not merely a matter of such title; rather, it indicates a moral or social feeling of entitlement and perhaps responsibility toward a particular place. A sense of ownership focuses more on voice and influence than on the exclusive control that is paradigmatic of private property.

A sense of ownership is important in drawing people in to PARK(ing) Day and in how others respond to the appropriation of parking spaces for other uses; developing and strengthening ownership is also one of the most significant benefits that people derive from their engagement. The importance of a sense of ownership is consistent with the literature on informality, which suggests that informal ownership may be more important to outcomes on the ground—to who decides how particular places are used—than formal property rights.[40] This project goes further, however, arguing not simply that feelings of ownership can prompt people to act in ways that thwart or constrain the application of formal property rights. A sense of ownership is significant for legality at a deeper level, and should itself be understood as a form of property.

To discuss informal ownership alongside a lease might be challenged as eliding significant differences between them. Yet while a sense of ownership is not the same as a lease or other conventional forms of property, neither is it entirely different. The "lease" here is more than a trick or a Trojan horse.

Even in its most conventional forms, property is a complex concept.[41] There is a long-running debate between theorists who argue for an understanding of property as a bundle of separable, severable rights or "sticks," its difference from other rights a mere matter of degree, and those who claim instead that there is something particular or essential about property, typically framed around the right to exclude as the definitive core or essence of property.

While that debate continues, a growing number of scholars have moved away from attempts to define property in such a thinglike way. Rather than focusing on the rights associated with ownership as self-contained, this scholarship focuses instead on the role that property plays in society, accepting it as socially constructed, contingent, and contextual.[42] For some, the socially constructed nature of property is a normative conclusion. In the US, "progressive property" scholars draw on normative claims to challenge the strong influence of economics on property.[43] What is needed, they argue, is a more explicitly political approach, paying greater attention to the "plural and incommensurable values" that property serves, and the social relationships it shapes and reflects.

Sociolegal scholarship has been important in extending these normative claims, offering a fuller understanding of the ways in which property is indeed materialized in the here and now. Robert Ellickson's examination of disputes between ranchers in Shasta County, California, provides an early demonstration of the complex connections between property and its place in the world: law operates with and within social understandings about property.[44] More recent studies have extended Ellickson's insights, showing that rights are more complex than rules.[45] Among these, Carol Rose has been particularly influential in her claim that property is at heart a matter of persuasion, of various and variable ways in which people make up their minds about the scope of proprietary rights and, importantly, seek to persuade others to do the same.[46]

Perhaps the most sustained empirical examination of the practices of property can be found in the work of Nicholas Blomley.[47] With examples ranging from contemporary struggles over gentrification to colonial displacement and enclosure, from urban gardening to early modern surveying, Blomley presents a rich and provocative picture of property as "definitionally, politically, and empirically heterogenous."[48] Particularly interesting is Blomley's call for an understanding of property as performative, in the sense that claims about property help to constitute the things and relationships that they describe.[49]

Claims about property build upon earlier claims, repeating and rearticulating claims made in other places and at other times. Significantly, Blomley explains, the performances through which property is enacted extend beyond the official actions more typically associated with property law, such as passing legislation, deciding cases, or registering titles. Property depends also on performances that are more humble, and more diverse. Like other areas of law, property takes effect in the world through everyday activities like fence painting, hedge trimming, removing graffiti, or paying council taxes.

There are multiple forms of property, and, when it comes to city-making, private property may not be the most important. Adding to calls for a refocusing of attention away from private ownership to enable a fuller and more meaningful conception of property,[50] analysis of PARK(ing) Day emphasizes the interactions between different forms of property, and their mutual and co-constitutive role in shaping the urban environment.

In illuminating the dynamic and socially entangled nature of property, analysis of PARK(ing) Day provides new insights into questions that have long troubled property scholars: What is the source of property rights, and why do others respect them? What are the connections between property, power, and agency? PARK(ing) Day is rich also with relevance for more contemporary and politically pressing questions: how do formal and informal understandings of property intersect, and what impacts do those understandings have on the development of suburbs and cities?

The tension in Rebar's use of the lease in PARK(ing) Day, as something that can be read in both progressive and conservative directions, is one that lies at the heart of property. With its connections to wealth and power, property is both deeply desired and fiercely contested. Beyond its implication in the challenges facing contemporary cities, property is blamed also for a much wider range of problems: from the exploitation of workers to the exclusion of minorities, from the dispossession of indigenous peoples to the entrenchment of gender inequality and, more recently, vast environmental degradation.[51] Yet property is also highly valued, connected to powerful human needs for autonomy and identity, belonging and community.[52]

On top of longstanding critiques about the forces of neoliberalism and globalization, the concentrations of property in a rapidly shrinking proportion of society have attracted heated responses. In contrast to the more direct and dramatic challenges posed by actions like squatting or the Occupy movement, PARK(ing) Day questions the workings of property in more subtle ways. Yet, while the conversion of parking spaces into temporary parks may seem far removed from either the theories or the challenges that animate property discourse, they provide important insights about its nature. As Andres Van der Walt has argued, there is much that can be gained by approaching property from the margins.[53]

Reading for difference

PARK(ing) Day stands as both a celebration and a critique of ownership. In line with the work of scholars such as Blomley and Sarah Keenan, my aim is not to highlight flaws or to propose reforms to property, but instead to seek out the "cracks" in dominant understandings. As John Law and John Urry argue, social inquiry and its methods are productive: they do not simply describe the world as it is, but also enact it.[54] As scholars, we have a responsibility to think about the worlds we want our work to help bring about.

This project is very much motivated by that responsibility. While recognizing the important role of critique, my aim is not "to confirm what we already know—that the world is full of devastation and oppression."[55] PARK(ing) Day is in many ways an easy target: for its brevity, its lack of tangible outcomes, the privilege of its protagonists, its potential connection to gentrification and to the marketization of the creative class. But would this take us closer to the kind of world we want?

We know that social and economic power shape who participates in the diverse range of activities through which claims and counterclaims are made on city streets—not just playful experiments like PARK(ing) Day, but daily struggles for survival by more vulnerable groups like unlicensed vendors, windscreen washers, day laborers, sex workers, and panhandlers. Structural imbalances are again apparent in PARK(ing) Day and must not be ignored, but they tell only part of the story.

Significantly, a focus on structural imbalances may not be the most productive or progressive part of the story to examine. There is a very real risk, as scholars like J. K. Gibson-Graham explain, that an emphasis on naming and shaming can naturalize and further entrench forms of dominance and oppression, obscuring more hopeful forms of difference that might point the way to more just alternatives.[56] As Kurt Iveson urges, scholars must do more than critique; we must "identify, nurture and participate in ongoing collective efforts to make different and more just kinds of cities through the practice of critical urban theory."[57]

Just as Gibson-Graham has sought to generate new economic possibilities by "reading for difference rather than dominance," in studying PARK(ing) Day I hope to foreground the multiplicity of property and of city-making practices, and as such to perform the political task of valorizing a wider range of possibilities.[58] While there is much that pop-up parks do not do, or do not do consistently (particularly with respect to questions about gentrification, race, and privilege), this should not overshadow the contributions that PARK(ing) Day does make (particularly with respect to the environment: in the face of political inertia despite the growing climate crisis, PARK(ing) Day suggests that small-scale citizen actions can make a difference). Drawing on critical property scholarship but also literature on commoning, the right to the city, and prefigurative politics, my aim is not to evaluate PARK(ing) Day (and certainly not to defend it against critique), but to examine how participants themselves understand the event, and how this might point toward more progressive cities.

Methodological approach

Within the broad tradition of sociolegal studies, this project examines the way in which law and property are understood and enacted at the local level. There are many texts on property theory, and cases where judges discuss various concepts of property that they then enforce as law. However, these provide only a partial picture of the way property is enacted and maintained in the world. As Blomley argues, "Empirically speaking, we simply do not know enough about lay conceptions and practices of property."[59] Qualitative, empirical research provides a direct sense of how people understand property and how this in turn affects (and is affected by) their contributions to the urban environment.

To understand the ways in which people engage with law and property in their interactions with PARK(ing) Day, the study uses in-depth, face-to-face interviews as well as site visits with photo-ethnography and background research on participants and contexts. This fine-grained, qualitative approach is crucial in gathering the detail and nuance necessary to understand how law and property are enacted in the world. My goal is to understand how participants themselves understand and engage with the theories and discourses of property and, in turn, how those understandings shape and are shaped by engagement with property in the world.

In line with calls from George Marcus and others for a multi-sited imaginary to enable examination of the circulation of always-fluid cultural meanings, objects, and identities,[60] my research spanned multiple cities and countries: San Francisco, where PARK(ing) Day began in 2006; Sydney, a city that PARK(ing) Day reached relatively early but where the event remains quite small; and Montréal, a city where PARK(ing) Day was not taken up until late, but which quickly grew to become home to the world's largest PARK(ing) Day. In considering examples of PARK(ing) Day from different times and places, my aim was not to undertake comparative research. These are not full case studies for detailed comparison, but rather a selection of different sites to reveal a range of attitudes and opinions so as to enable reflection on the ways in which ownership matters in contemporary cities.

I spent PARK(ing) Day in 2014 in Sydney, visiting two parks (the only two I was aware of). In Montréal I visited several sites suggested by participants (community gardens, parklets, pop-up villages, festivals, public art, local and state government offices, *éco-quartiers*, green laneways) between July and September 2015, and on PARK(ing) Day visited 14 parks around the city. Research in San Francisco was conducted between August and December 2016, and again included visits to several sites recommended by participants (particularly parklets and the Market Street Prototyping Festival). On PARK(ing) Day in 2016, I visited 11 parks around San Francisco. In 2017, I participated in PARK(ing) Day by building my own park, back in Sydney.

I conducted semistructured interviews with 84 people involved in PARK(ing) Day and related activities. Participants were identified through the parkingday.org and montrealparkingday.org websites and the Sydney Parking Day Facebook page, as well as blogs, social media, and online searches. Invitations were sent to participants from a range of different professions and organizations, and to people who had engaged at differing times: some who had participated multiple times, some just once, some recently, some earlier. A snowball referral method and ongoing investigation yielded additional potential participants. I interviewed more people in

Montréal (38) than Sydney (24, including one based in Melbourne) or San Francisco (22, including two based in New York), the higher interest among participants in Montréal perhaps reflecting the popularity of the event at the time.

Recognizing the risk of bias in this kind of recruitment, I made selections between potential participants so as to maximize diversity. Interview participants included built environment professionals, computer scientists, small business owners, school and university students, teachers, community workers, engagement professionals, journalists, and officials from state and local government. Subjects were generally professionals, but included a range of ages (from tertiary students to adults approaching retirement) and of ethnic and socioeconomic backgrounds. While participants varied in socioeconomic status, all of the people I interviewed had jobs or were studying; all lived in a house they either owned or were renting. Participants were not asked about their ethnicity, but during our conversations some did note that they or their parents were born elsewhere—including Southeast Asia, the Indian subcontinent, Latin America, Africa, the Middle East, and both Eastern and Western Europe. I interviewed more men (51) than women (33).

Efforts to maximize diversity were of course constrained by the relative homogeneity of the kinds of people who participate in PARK(ing) Day. My research was not designed to gather or to interrogate the demographics of participants, and the fact that PARK(ing) Day is not a coordinated event or movement makes it difficult to work out who is involved (or how to contact a more diverse range of people). Anecdotal evidence and studies of other kinds of DIY urbanism suggest that participants are more likely to be white, able-bodied and relatively privileged, and often male.

The interview design was informed by previous studies of legal consciousness and legal geography.[61] Participants were asked about how they came across PARK(ing) Day, what they thought about it, why they decided to get involved, what they did, and how they thought it went. Open-ended questions were used to start, with participants asked to "tell the story" of what happened. These were followed by more questions about a wide range of details: the advice and resources available and used in the event, coordination with other PARK(ing) Day events, site selection, responses from others, social media and publicity, the experience of being on the street, impacts of the event after the day, dealings with police and other officials, the laws applicable to the event, and hopes and plans for the future. Law, property, and ownership were not targeted until late in the interviews, allowing themes to emerge from more open questions.

Interviews were structured around a loosely consistent set of questions. The questions were tailored prior to each interview based on the interviewee's particular background and context. For example, some participants had already discussed their interventions online or in the media, so questions responded to those discussions. Questions were also varied during the interview, with some added or skipped according to participants' responses. The questions were reviewed after each interview, and this in turn informed future refinements to the sequencing and wording of questions.

Interviews were intended to provide an insider perspective that was open-ended, flexible, and, at least initially, nonjudgmental. The research was inductive, iterative, and reflective, following the patterns and relationships revealed by participants. Data collection was refined through progressive focusing, with adjustments to examine concepts or relationships that emerged through the research process.[62] For example, questions about participants' opinions on the planning system were dropped during later interviews, while new questions were added about social media and connections to parks in other countries.

The interviews lasted between 30 minutes and 2.5 hours. Most ran for a little over an hour. In some cases I interviewed two or three people together; those interviews tended to be longer (they were also lots of fun, with a strong atmosphere of excitement and celebration as participants shared memories of the event). Venues for interviews varied. Most commonly, I interviewed people in their workplaces. Sometimes we met at a café or bar, and a few participants took me to places they wanted to talk about—I conducted two interviews in the Jardins Gamelin in Montréal, for example. Some interviews were conducted by phone or video conference. In a few cases I met participants at their homes, or they came to mine. This often meant interviews were punctuated by children, families, or flatmates, and those interruptions were frequently productive, leading to discussions about priorities, possibilities, and personal values.

Transcripts were coded thematically using nVivo software. Coding and analysis approximated the grounded theory approach set out by Kathy Charmaz, but with attention given to the potential for the refinement of existing theories as well as theoretical discovery.[63] The data and the field were revisited as certain theories emerged as particularly relevant, with the four-year duration of research enabling the tailoring of later interviews to evolving theoretical refinements.

Recognizing my role as a producer—not merely an objective gatherer—of data, I sought to engage the subjects of my research through collaborative methods.[64] I began and ended interviews by asking participants if they had any questions about me or the project. As a result, interviews were often followed by discussions about my findings and preliminary analysis; in a few cases the conversation continued, including sharing drafts of my research. This feedback was extremely helpful in increasing the accuracy, the subtlety, and the depth of my findings.

Participants' understandings of PARK(ing) Day were the primary focus of my research, and their data was accordingly central. Other perspectives provided important insights to supplement this, particularly those of people from municipal authorities and state government agencies, and from local community organizations. Two groups with important perspectives on PARK(ing) Day were difficult to recruit: members of the public who saw and perhaps interacted with pop-up parks, and officials responsible for the regulation of parking spaces. As regards the first group, spending time in and around parks on PARK(ing) Day provided very valuable information about how the event is received by outsiders. By visiting parks on PARK(ing) Day, I was able to observe and sometimes talk to passersby. Constraints of ethics approval meant I could not quote or directly reference these people, but the insights gained from these interactions were important to my analysis. Significantly, passersby were more diverse than participants in formal interviews, with an evidently much greater range in age, ethnicity, and socioeconomic status. The passersby I spoke to and observed included children and elderly people, tourists and recent migrants, and people who were homeless and unemployed. Most of these were people who had stumbled upon a park; yet some were in the process of taking tours around the city to visit multiple parks. Most people knew nothing about PARK(ing) Day, some knew it well.

With respect to police, rangers, and others responsible for the enforcement of laws on the street, I was unable to get even this kind of information. I saw a few officials during my observations on PARK(ing) Day, but I did not see any interact with participants in the event, and I did not get to speak to any myself. My inability to interview police was largely a result of police policy, and despite my sending multiple emails, making numerous calls, and completing lengthy request forms. For official perspectives, the research relied on secondary sources—interviews with other officials (planners, sustainability and community development officers), media and social media (including photos and video footage of interactions with police), and participants' accounts of their interactions with officials.

Collection of visual material was an important part of the research. PARK(ing) Day is a visual event; participants place a high priority on documenting and disseminating images of pop-up parks. Many participants sent me copies of photographs or video footage in preparation for our interview, even though I did not request or even suggest this. During interviews, photographs played an important role. When I met participants in their workplace they often took me to their computer to show me photographs and drawings of the event; when I met people elsewhere they often brought printed material or a laptop to enable us to go through their images. Some participants drew little sketches to explain things as we went. Like the photographs, these depicted both participants' own interventions and those by others. Several participants sent further material after we met: USB drives loaded with images, links to Dropbox and Flickr streams, blogs and articles discussing the event. Again, these were often unsolicited and unexpected. Images are central also for others who engage with PARK(ing) Day: much of the commentary centers on photographs, often without much explanatory text. Understanding PARK(ing) Day necessitates engagement with its images.

The images should be read as more than illustrations or supporting evidence for the text, or for my authority and authenticity as a researcher. As Sarah Pink explains, photographs interact with, cross-reference, and produce meaning in relation to other elements in the text.[65] Parks are often complex assemblages, drawing together (with various degrees of success) and dependent upon the parking meter, the footpath, the roadway, surrounding cars, trees and street furniture, the weather and the local atmosphere, planned and unplanned interactions within the space, passing pedestrians, cars and cyclists, plants, animals, games, and much more. In providing images my aim is to invite you, the reader, to engage in the process of making sense of these elements and the interactions between them.

Interviews, site visits, and photoethnography were supplemented by examination of scholarly texts, cases and legislation, reports and policy documents, print and online media. Online and social media were particularly important: given the relatively small scale and informal nature of PARK(ing) Day, the event has not attracted much academic commentary, yet there has been considerable discussion in various online fora, including websites, blogs, social media such as Facebook and Twitter, and comments posted onto reports by mainstream media. These sources provided important insights into the way in which people understand and interact with legality in PARK(ing) Day. As Eve Darian-Smith argues, "to rehumanize law we have to pay attention to the myriad of in-between legal spaces through which people create meaning, such as website chatrooms . . . , visual media in films and television, archival documentation, [and] judicial rhetoric reinforcing particular codes of morality and ethics."[66]

Consistent with earlier studies of legal consciousness, I was struck by the richness of the data.[67] While there were some overarching concerns (for example, a widespread unease about the privatization of public space and the complicity of private property in such processes), attitudes did not coincide with categories such as age, gender, professional qualifications, institutional affiliation, or level of involvement with PARK(ing) Day or related activities. The kinds of claims that people make about property cannot be explained simply by the kind of person making them. Participants understand property in diverse and even contradictory ways, reflecting the degree to which sociocultural and legal understandings are always and already entangled.

The insights into understandings of property revealed through the study show that PARK(ing) Day—a playful, informal, and in many ways everyday event—is richly informed by theories and discourses of property. Beyond procedural or rights-based theories, the ways in which participants discuss the event suggest that property draws strength by being embedded in social life and social action. Consistent with the claims made by Rose, Blomley, and others, the discourse of PARK(ing) Day reflects social understandings of property. Yet it also goes further: PARK(ing) Day works performatively to constitute and legitimate a certain idea of property as immanent in social relations. In doing so, it sustains the relevance of that language across a much wider range of debates in and about contemporary cities.

Chapter organization

The book is divided into three parts. The first, chapters 1 and 2, provides the history and context of PARK(ing) Day. This part is detailed and quite descriptive: readers interested primarily in what PARK(ing) Day tells us about property, ownership, and participation in contemporary cities may wish to skip ahead to part two.

Chapter 1 traces PARK(ing) Day from its origins as a brief and playful installation in 2005 to its development into an international event that continues today, giving an overview of the event as a whole as well as its particular trajectories in San Francisco, Sydney, and Montréal. PARK(ing) Day has grown and evolved since its first iteration, incorporating a wide range of aims and achievements, complementing and connecting to many other networks and campaigns. Tens of thousands of people have participated, in San Francisco and comparable cities in Europe and North America, but also in cities not usually associated with urban activism—cities including Ahmedabad, Guangzhou, Budapest, and Jakarta.

Chapter 1 also puts PARK(ing) Day in context, setting out some of the many precursors for the event. From conceptual and performance art to TV shows, from playful and spontaneous citizen interventions to political demonstrations by transportation and public space activists, the appropriation of streets for purposes other than car parking has a long and rich history. PARK(ing) Day stands out among these in its scale and scope. No other example has been taken up by so many people, in so many places, over such long periods, or to further such a wide range of causes.

What is interesting about PARK(ing) Day is not simply the geographic reach or temporal duration of the event, but the fact that these have been achieved almost accidentally. The first pop-up park was intended as a one-off installation that would last for just two hours. Far exceeding the hopes and even the imaginations of its instigators, that installation proved inspirational. PARK(ing) Day responded to that interest—with little expertise and even a degree of reluctance from Rebar—and an openness to impromptu collaboration remains a key feature of the event. Participants have dropped in and out over the years, Rebar itself has long stepped back from coordination, and since 2014 Rebar no longer even exists. Despite this, PARK(ing) Day continues, and continues to attract new participants.

Chapter 2 centers on definition. The large scale and scope of PARK(ing) Day have prompted commentators to describe it as a movement, yet this label fails to capture its loose and varied nature. PARK(ing) Day has no explicit agenda or message beyond creating a space for citizen engagement. The pop-up parks produced on the day are often intended to convey messages about sustainability and social justice (from reducing waste and recycling, to protecting biodiversity and local waterways, to promoting urban agriculture and food sharing, to finding noncommercial ways to socialize and connect with others, to expanding infrastructure for pedestrians, cyclists, and car-sharers), but these are far from unifying themes.

Yet PARK(ing) Day is more than simply a series of ad hoc installations. If not a movement, then what is it? Connected to this, how can we explain why PARK(ing) Day has been so much bigger, wider-reaching, and longer-lasting than its various precursors? PARK(ing) Day can be understood as what Gregor McLennan and Thomas Osborne define as a "vehicular idea": a simple and yet malleable concept that works to set things in motion.[68] PARK(ing) Day emerged from the right place (San Francisco, California), at the right time (when the place of cars in cities was increasingly subject to question, and when social media was just taking off), and it was effective in moving things forward. PARK(ing) Day was not the product of committed ideals or principled theory, but instead a tool that could be adopted and adapted to further a wide range of causes.

Law lies at the heart of this vehicularity: Rebar's invocation of the lease engages and empowers a very wide range of participants. Significantly, it does so in a way that creates a disjunction or, in the language of Jacques Rancière, a *dissensus*: a new way of looking at things.[69] A key part of what makes PARK(ing) Day so successful is its disruption of established interpretations. Rebar's claim that the meter creates a lease provides a basis for the event that is accessible and easily understandable, connecting to important contemporary issues but also offering a new perspective from which to approach them.

The second part, chapters 3 to 6, examines the legality of PARK(ing) Day. Chapter 3 considers the role of law in general; chapters 4, 5, and 6 focus specifically on property, the ways in which PARK(ing) Day draws on and is animated by a range of proprietary concepts.

I begin in chapter 3 by examining how PARK(ing) Day makes use of law. Many different legal analyses have been applied to the event: Rebar's initial interpretation involving a niche or loophole, their more catchy presentation of a lease, and a range of efforts by officials and by participants to fit the event into various regulatory processes. While law has been important for many commentators in describing the event, this chapter provides the first effort to engage seriously with the statutory context of PARK(ing) Day.

PARK(ing) Day does not involve a lease, but the laws that do apply are difficult to describe with precision. Taking a plural and performative approach, and drawing particularly on the work of Hendrik Hartog, Lon Fuller, and Robert Cover, I argue that the legality of PARK(ing) Day is best understood as a matter of excess, an example of what Cover calls the "too fertile forces of jurisgenesis."[70] Amongst many possible interpretations of the law at stake, PARK(ing) Day depends on participants believing in their right to reclaim the parking space in this way, and on the lack or inability of people with differing views to challenge those installations. The successful installation of parks relies on legal claims that are constructed and enacted physically as well as discursively, and those enactments of law themselves help to bring purported legalities into being.

PARK(ing) Day highlights the multiplicity and the slipperiness of property, and I begin chapter 4 by setting out the multiple forms of property at play: the specific property right of the lease, the broader category of property, the not-quite-synonymous concept of ownership, and finally an informal sense of ownership. I focus particularly on defining a sense of ownership, drawing on Davina Cooper's work on property practices to conceptualize this as an emergent form of property: a relationship of belonging that comes to be strengthened through various authoritative practices. A sense of ownership can be understood as more than belonging, but not (yet) property.

In the second part of chapter 4 I move to the work that these concepts do in PARK(ing) Day, beginning with the concept of property. Inspired by the work of conceptual artist Gordon Matta-Clark, a desire to push the boundaries of property was an important motivating idea for Rebar. Property was invoked explicitly as a device through which to rethink links between power, voice, and agency in shaping the city. Property has been an enduring concern for subsequent participants, in line with growing interest in ideas of a right to the city. Connecting what might seem a frivolous activity with deeply felt human needs, and with heated contemporary debates about cities and the place of people within them, property is central to PARK(ing) Day.

In chapter 5 I argue that the property claims made in PARK(ing) Day are deeper social claims about ownership. This chapter centers on the understandings of those invoking property, and highlights the ways in which ownership claims and ideas about property are mutually constitutive. In the process of building a park, feelings of ownership are often strengthened. To explain this, participants draw on concepts that are well known in property scholarship: ideas about property arising from labor and rewarding effort, from the expression and development of personhood, and from relationships with others. This resonance between popular understandings and property theory reveals a complex relationship between folk and more technical conceptions. PARK(ing) Day suggests that property theory is sustained by and deeply entangled with values and with feelings.

Consistent with Cover's claims about the fertility of jurisgenesis, participants describe other sources too: spatial and material factors, as well as play, pleasure, and even love. In contrast to the imagined histories of labor-based appropriation, examination of the ways in which people construct ownership in PARK(ing) Day provides a thicker, richer story. As Cooper argues, property is developed and sustained through multiple practices. For participants in PARK(ing) Day, various descriptive and justificatory approaches do not compete, but work together to produce a sense of ownership.

In chapter 6 I argue that conceptual claims about ownership are themselves implicated in and built by their enactment in the world. Extending the conceptual work in the previous two chapters, I move here to performance, showing how various forms of property and legality work together to give effect to the claims about law made on PARK(ing) Day. Whether these claims are successful depends on their context. This is clearly apparent in the responses that parks generate among the wider public and, particularly, among officials. Examination of the cases in which participants interact with police and other officials suggests that ownership exerts a powerful influence on the legality of parking spaces. The high level of discretion involved in regulating the installation of parks in parking spaces—an activity that is not expressly prohibited, but to which many regulations could be applied by an unsympathetic official—means that legal actors must look beyond the text of relevant rules to determine how they should be applied.

Performances of property in PARK(ing) Day depend upon social constructions of ownership for their success. Like property, those constructions are
often tied to privilege: informal ownership may be more attainable than
private property, but it is by no means open equally to all.

The final part, comprising chapter 7 and a postscript, considers participants' own reflections on the event, examining what participants take
away from PARK(ing) Day and how this might relate to other forms of
city-making.

While PARK(ing) Day spans just one day each year, a belief or hope that
it might have more lasting consequences is an important driver of engagement. In discussing their hopes when approaching the event, participants
often emphasize physical and policy changes: traffic calming, city greening
and amenity improvements, new and expanded forms of citizen engagement. On reflection afterward, however, many find that the impacts that
are most significant turn out to be more abstract and more affective.

Building a park on PARK(ing) Day can be a moving experience, prompting participants to rethink the city and their place within it. Participation
in the event can be understood as a form of commoning, an effort to prioritize a sense of shared life and collective responsibility over the instrumental, individualized rationality of neoliberal governance.[71] The parks
built for PARK(ing) Day might be small in scale and short in duration, but
they enable participants to materially test and demonstrate alternative possibilities. That process can be transformative, catalyzing policy and physical changes—notably, the creation of more permanent "parklets" in San
Francisco and many other places—as well as inspiring and empowering
participants to contribute to the city in other ways. PARK(ing) Day has had
important impacts in providing a new language with which to discuss public space in contemporary cities, in shifting perceptions about what might
be possible, and, perhaps most significantly, in shifting participants' understandings of their capacity to effect change in the city.

Chapter 7 concludes by reflecting on participants' thoughts about the
potential for less positive impacts to arise out of PARK(ing) Day. While the
small scale and short duration of parks built for the event means they are
generally seen as too tiny to make a difference, PARK(ing) Day has not
escaped critique. Particularly when coupled with other forms of DIY urbanism, some participants were concerned that PARK(ing) Day might (unwittingly) contribute to processes of gentrification and displacement, enclosure

and uneven development. Good intentions are not enough: there is a need for very careful engagement with context and potential consequences to understand how (and whether) these kinds of interventions can contribute to more just kinds of cities.

In the postscript I reflect on my own experience building a park in 2017, and on the significance of the event. PARK(ing) Day goes well beyond Rebar's initial claims about the property rights obtainable by paying the parking meter. Through its performance over the years in cities far from San Francisco, PARK(ing) Day reveals a deeper contingency within property relations, and within law more generally. At a time when opportunities for protest are increasingly limited, PARK(ing) Day presents a form of intervention that is at once more open and more contained.

Part One A PARK(ing) Movement?

Figure 1.1
"PARK(ing)," Mission Street, San Francisco, November 2005. Image: Andrea Scher.

1 From PARK(ing) to PARK(ing) Day

From its inception, PARK(ing) Day was an international event. Before PARK(ing) Day, however, there was a one-off event called PARK(ing): a far more modest exercise intended to last just two hours. PARK(ing) Day grew out of PARK(ing) almost accidentally, responding to an enthusiasm far exceeding the expectations of its creators. Over the years since that initial installation, PARK(ing) Day has evolved to incorporate a wide range of aims, aspirations, and achievements, connecting in diverse and shifting ways to many other networks and campaigns.

While well-narrated, that trajectory from a small installation to a worldwide event tells only part of the story. Rebar was not the first to appropriate metered parking spaces for uses other than the parking of cars; precursors can be found as early as the 1930s. Within days of the installation of the world's first "Park-O-Meter" in Oklahoma City, locals were making use of the meter to legitimate other activities in the newly regulated space. In the decades since, others have been similarly inspired, drawing on the meter to explore other possibilities for city streets. The idea can be traced to the meter itself.

1.1 PARK(ing) on Mission Street

PARK(ing) Day grew out of an event called PARK(ing).[1] In 2005, members of the art collective Rebar paid a San Francisco parking meter for two hours one Wednesday in November. Rather than park a car, Rebar used the space instead to create a park by laying out turf, a tree, a bench, and signs inviting passersby to share and enjoy the space (figure 1.1).

Rebar had formed just one year earlier. Its only built work was a tongue-in-cheek installation conceived for an art magazine, *Cabinet*. As part of a themed issue on property, the editors had purchased a remote piece of New Mexico scrubland, site unseen, through eBay. They named this "Cabinet-landia." Matthew Passmore, a lawyer with a background in conceptual art, was inspired by this to propose a "Cabinet National Library," which he offered to build on a small part of the land.[2] The editors accepted, and Passmore traveled with three friends to install the library, a filing cabinet set into the landscape.[3] The Library was conceived and installed by Passmore and his friends as a loose art collective; the name Rebar came later, the (perhaps unexpected) success of the project prompting the search for a label through which to claim credit for their work.

Back at his day job as a lawyer in San Francisco, Passmore recalls looking out of his office window at a postal van moving in and out of various parking spaces along the street.[4] He imagined making a time-lapse video in which cars and vans would come and go, and amongst these the parking spaces would be occupied occasionally by other uses, an art gallery perhaps. Over beers in their local bar, Passmore shared the idea with another Library contributor, John Bela, as well as Blaine Merker, who was studying landscape architecture at UC Berkeley with Bela at the time. Bela and Merker had also been thinking about parking spaces, inspired particularly by work on everyday reclamations of the city by writers such as Michel de Certeau and Pierre Bourdieu.[5] Together, Passmore, Bela, and Merker became excited about alternative possibilities for parking spaces, and sketched out various options: an aquarium, an office, a sleeping space, a peep show (figure 1.2).[6]

After confirming that the San Francisco Traffic Code did not expressly prohibit uses other than car parking, Passmore, Bela, and Merker swapped a few emails exploring the idea further. Playing with the rules on parking fitted well with the group's interest in testing alternative uses of public space and, particularly, doing so by pursuing niches rather than more conventional forms of advocacy or protest. Conceptual artist Gordon Matta-Clark, the subject of then-renewed interest through *Cabinet*'s Spring 2005 "Odd Lots" issue, provided important inspiration.[7]

After a month or so, the group decided to proceed. They settled on a park as the new use to which the parking space should be put: something that would highlight the contrast between the installation and the usual use of the space, but also something that would meet a local need.[8] Further preparation included a few emails, more discussions over beers in a bar, and

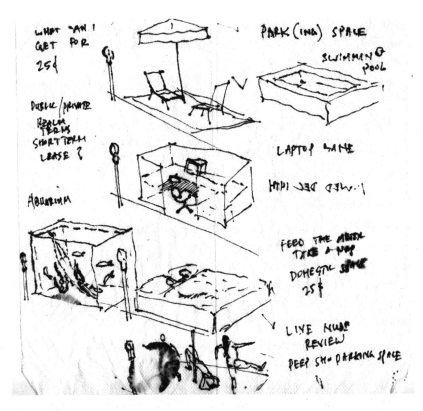

Figure 1.2
Ideas for a parking space, sketched on a napkin in the Latin American bar, 2005.
Image: Rebar.

around $200 worth of materials.[9] The main preparatory task was scouting for a suitable site. Bela had a city map showing areas underserved by public space; this provided an initial range. In selecting a parking space within this range, the group wanted a site that was sunny and with a good vantage point from which to observe and document the park. Rebar chose a site in the SoMa (South of Market) District, an area with which they were familiar: Merker walked past the site on his way to work every day; Passmore had grown up a few blocks from Mission Street and as a child used to go to the cinema there.

On November 16, Rebar rolled out their park at noon. They then left, moving to their planned vantage point in a parking garage across the street. From there, with the help of friends, Rebar filmed and photographed the event. Beyond its documentary use, moving away from the site was important also for the operation of the event. Rebar's aim was not to be artists interpreting the work for visitors, but to create a park for public use.[10]

Rebar was unsure how people would respond to the park. Passmore recalls:

> We were fully expecting to be arrested or to engage with the police. We had sort of written notes for like what we were going to say to the police about how we're working in the public interest and we're going to not only clean up this parking space, but we're going to sweep the whole block before we go, and just leave it better than we found it, you know? And that we're not here to cause trouble or to hurt anybody, and that actually the park is open for anybody, for all.

Some people took little notice, passing by with indifference. Others were more curious, several ventured in and "found a place to sit and took a place to enjoy the novelty of cool grass and shade. Some of the strangers enjoyed some unplanned social interaction by exchanging a few words with each other; others took the occasion to rest or read."[11] Passmore's fears about hostile officials proved unfounded:

> The police didn't care [laughs]. I think we saw one police car drive by and I don't even think they noticed us.

After two hours, the end of the time purchasable through the parking meter, Rebar packed up and returned the space to its former condition. A few weeks later, Passmore's wife Andrea Scher posted photos of PARK(ing) on her blog, which had a relatively large following of around 10,000 readers. That post was picked up by a number of high-profile design sites, as Passmore explains:

> From there it just went just viral in a matter of like a week or two. It got onto *BoingBoing* . . . and then from there it just, I mean suddenly it was on everything, you know. People were like "Oh my God, I saw you on *Archinect*," you know, all these big design and architecture blogs ran with it.

By mid December, as many as four million people were visiting Rebar's website in a single day.[12] The images proved inspirational: requests soon came from people wanting to create parks in their own cities.[13] Within six months Rebar had received hundreds of inquiries.[14]

Many of the requests were invitations to Rebar to come and replicate PARK(ing) in other places. This was tempting, but Rebar decided to take a different approach. Inspired by the booming San Francisco tech community, they treated PARK(ing) as "open source" and applied a Creative Commons license.[15] Rather than present themselves as experts, Rebar offered their experience for others to use in deciding how to go about building parks themselves. The PARK(ing) template came with two provisos. First, that people credit Rebar for the idea, and second, that they don't use the space for commercial purposes.

Parks began to appear in other cities. In May, the Santa Monica Recreation and Parks Commission built a park.[16] In January, a group called Rename Your Files built one in Trapani, Sicily. After carefully laying turf on a sand base, they set out potted trees, benches and posters about Rebar's event, and tables with food for a celebratory party. In June, John Gilbert Architects built a park in Glasgow, Scotland as part of Architecture Week, a simple installation with AstroTurf, potted plants, and deck chairs (figure 1.3).[17]

Figure 1.3
Paul from John Gilbert Architects enjoying the sunshine in the park installed for Architecture Week in Glasgow, June 2006. Image: John Gilbert Architects.

Initially, Rebar provided advice in personal emails, but as the requests kept coming this became more of an exercise in cutting and pasting text. This in turn prompted Rebar to make the information more widely available. Modeled loosely on an IKEA manual, Rebar produced a simple step-by-step guide that could be downloaded free of charge from their website.

With requests still coming, Rebar decided to organize an event that would focus this energy and interest. Coordinating an international event was not something that Rebar had considered in 2005 and, for Merker at least, it was an enterprise entered into somewhat reluctantly. Merker recalls a conversation with Bela:

> JB was saying, you know, "We're getting all these enquiries about this, we need to create a manual. . . . We need to make sure people do this right. We need to give them instructions." . . . He was trying to convince me to help him on the manual and I was like "Dude, I'm so busy." . . . I'm not really a joiner, I was excited to do this stuff with friends, and I liked doing projects, but I wasn't trying to become part of a group, and especially not a group that required a lot of commitment to being a member.

1.2 San Francisco and the world

Rebar began planning PARK(ing) Day in the summer. Recognizing that this was going to be something that people from all over the world would want to do, their idea was to maximize the impact of the growing number of parks by coordinating them on a single day.[18]

Friends and colleagues in San Francisco provided important support. Andrea Scher, Denise Sauerteig, and Amy Seek, then partners of Passmore, Bela, and Merker respectively, were key collaborators, actively involved in planning and implementing the event. Public Architecture, a San Francisco-based charity working to promote pro bono and social impact design, helped by sharing their contact list and hosting an information session. More formal support came from the conservation nonprofit Trust for Public Land. As with Public Architecture, this partnership arose out of personal connections: Bela had done some work for the Trust, and Trust staff member Brady Moss had helped film the 2005 PARK(ing) installation.[19] For the Trust, which had recently started increasing their efforts around urban parks after years of working primarily outside of cities, PARK(ing) presented an ideal advocacy tool to highlight the need for greener cities.[20]

Rebar also had support from the City of San Francisco. Among the many people who contacted Rebar in response to the first PARK(ing) event was Marshall Foster, Director of City Greening in the mayor's office. Foster invited Rebar to meet, and explained that both he and the mayor liked the idea and would like to see it grow. Foster was adamant, however, that PARK(ing) should remain unsanctioned in order to retain its impact. While he did not want to make it a City project, Marshall said that the City would talk to the police and make sure that it could happen.[21] In a more public show of support, Mayor Gavin Newsom allowed his personal parking space outside City Hall to be turned into a park.

The first PARK(ing) Day was set for September 15, 2006.[22] Rebar wanted a date close to the equinox, a time when the climate would be fairly amenable in most cities around the world.[23] Friday was chosen as a "regular" day for maximum impact, as Rebar explained: "This kind of thing isn't as effective or magical on a weekend. Fridays also allow businesses to participate, and many companies choose to dedicate the day to it, designing and building a PARK as a team-building activity or as a way to give back to the community."[24]

Rebar focused on planning PARK(ing) Day in San Francisco and internationally, while the Trust focused on promoting the event in other cities across the US. As well as distributing guides and holding information sessions, Rebar distributed posters for groups to place on their parks, and prepared maps and flyers to explain the event to people on the day. The Trust played an important role in organizing social media and online support for the event. This was new territory, making use of resources that were only beginning to attract attention. Matthew Shaffer, who worked in marketing and communications for the Trust, joined and learned to use Facebook expressly for PARK(ing) Day.[25]

On PARK(ing) Day, Rebar recreated its 2005 park in five different locations. Transported from site to site by bicycle with the help of a team of volunteers, Rebar called this a "Temporal Distributed Network of Public Open Space."[26] The Trust for Public Land built a park outside its office on Montgomery Street, and another 16 parks were built across the city by community groups (including the San Francisco Bicycle Coalition, Plant*SF, Friends of the Urban Forest, the Neighborhood Parks Council), architecture and design offices, a coffee shop, and more informal groups of students, artists, and activists.[27] Parks were also built in other cities, including Berkeley,

Figure 1.4
"Dahlia Park(ing)." Potted dahlias in wheelbarrows ready for soil to be shoveled in around them, set out in in Mayor Newsom's parking space outside City Hall, San Francisco, 2006. Image: Jane Martin, Plant*SF.

Cleveland, Manhattan, and Milwaukee in the US, Manchester and London in the UK, and Rio de Janeiro, Brazil. Altogether, at least 47 parks were created on the first PARK(ing) Day.[28]

Many of the parks were much like the 2005 PARK(ing) installation: turf, potted trees, and seating were common features. Some were more experimental. At the mayor's invitation, landscape architect Jane Martin worked with Mike Farrah, senior advisor to Mayor Newsom, and her group Plant*SF to remake Mayor Newsom's parking space (figure 1.4). Martin and her collaborators laid out a set of wheelbarrows representing each of the City's districts, each with a potted dahlia (the city flower). Passersby were asked to shovel soil into the wheelbarrows to facilitate planting of the dahlias. These were delivered to supervisors of the relevant districts at the end of the day.[29] Other new ideas included a free WiFi hotspot, a lemonade stand, a stormwater demonstration garden, a seed giveaway, and a beach.[30]

Typically, parks were located in areas well known to participants, often outside the offices of the groups involved. Visibility was also important. Merker asked his girlfriend, Amy Seek, to choose a location in the main retail district:

We wanted the visibility downtown because we felt like the thing had more impact if it was right in the face of folks, you know, and it was in the heart of retail culture. And so yeah, Amy had this idea to do the lemonade stand and I . . . remember telling her she needed to go be in a more visible location. We were just afraid people wouldn't see, we wanted people to see it, you know?

PARK(ing) Day was well documented by participants, but also by others outside the event. Filmmaker Clarence Eckerson Jr. was visiting at the time and spent the day collecting footage. Eckerson describes the experience:

I'll never forget being in Oakland visiting a friend and learning that PARK(ing) Day was happening the following day. I got up early, jumped on the BART with my camera and went looking for all the spots inspired by Rebar, a unique & awesome art and design studio in San Francisco.

What a day. I never had so much fun as an in-the-moment filmmaker. I shot for almost 8 hours straight and by the end was exhausted and nearly dehydrated. But as I saw the energy and the diversity of the spots—and the underlying message in Rebar's mission—I knew I had to churn out a film fast. 36 hours later the above film debuted on-line. It was easily our most popular film for the next two years.[31]

*   *   *

For PARK(ing) Day in 2007, CC Puede provided health checks and food for migrant day laborers (figure 1.5). Centered on Cesar Chavez Street, one of the more dangerous streets in San Francisco, CC Puede (their name a play on the "Sí, se puede" (yes, we can) cry of Cesar Chavez's farm workers union) was a group focused mainly on traffic calming. Like many other PARK(ing) Day parks, CC Puede's park was motivated by concerns about safety: a young girl had recently died in a traffic accident at the corner at which they built their park, and the group had previously held a rally there to mark and protest her death. For PARK(ing) Day, however, their installation embodied other concerns too, particularly with respect to the day laborers who congregated in the area. While the gathering of day laborers in public places has attracted opposition in some communities,[32] CC Puede used PARK(ing) Day to recognize the *jornaleros* as part of the community, and to try to help them meet their needs.

CC Puede's park spanned three spaces. In one, volunteer nurses offered free health checks in a makeshift clinic. Drawing on the nursing expertise of one of the group's members, this was well received, and the waiting area (equipped with chairs and magazines) was frequently busy. The next

Figure 1.5
Park created by CC Puede on Cesar Chavez Street, San Francisco, 2007. This included a makeshift health clinic with free checks provided by nurses, a picnic area with a barbecue, and a fruit and vegetable "market" with produce from Veritable Vegetable (the Veritable Vegetable truck can be seen at the edge of the photo). Image: Steve Rhodes.

provided a picnic space, including a barbecue and perhaps the best-laid sod of any park: many of the day laborers worked in landscaping, and were quick to offer advice and assistance to the relatively inexpert members of CC Puede as they set up for the day.[33] Like the clinic, the barbecue was provided primarily to meet the needs of the day laborers; it was also an effort to connect to the adjacent steakhouse. A third space offered fresh fruit and vegetables in a truck provided by organic produce distributor Veritable Vegetable, part of an ongoing campaign by some of the group's members to improve the quality of food available in local stores.

The intervention was so successful that CC Puede recreated the park in 2009, including an upgraded health clinic with privacy screens. Again this was popular. When barbecue supplies ran out, a passing pedestrian topped them up with *nopales*, another effort to respond to the tastes and needs of the day laborers (figure 1.6). Years later, Passmore still sees these as some of the best parks ever created for PARK(ing) Day:

Figure 1.6
Barbecue provided by CC Puede in 2009, including *nopales* donated by a passing pedestrian. Image: Steve Rhodes.

> They were giving out free food and then giving basic health care, and taking people's blood pressure, talking about diet to this community that has no access to healthcare in this country, right? These are probably entirely undocumented workers looking for informal work by the hour, for a day. Totally disenfranchised and no access to healthcare, so I thought it was just, number one it was so well-tuned to its location. And number two providing this critical unmet need, right? You think about, like, sure a park is fun and there's unmet needs for parks all over, but I feel like CC Puede really got that concept of what is missing in our neighborhood. What would be a neighborhood benefit, you know? So yeah, that's one of my all-time favorites.

CC Puede's park was one of more than 200 installed in over 50 cities worldwide in 2007.[34] Turf and potted plants continued to feature prominently, but the parks were increasingly diverse. Dinner parties, games from Scrabble to croquet, dog parks, massage parlors, paddle pools, libraries, WiFi hot spots, seed giveaways, and urban micro-farms were also installed.[35] Parks were changing in form and style, but also in ambitions. Like CC Puede, a growing number of participants were engaging more directly with the wider political significance of public space.

The event was most visible in San Francisco, where 57 parks were built, and in other cities where the Trust for Public Land were active: Los Angeles (45) and New York (25). With smaller numbers, other cities hosting parks included Washington, Miami, Salt Lake City, St. Louis, St. Paul, Tampa, and Chicago. Outside the US, PARK(ing) Day reached cities including London, UK; Utrecht, the Netherlands; Barcelona and Valencia, Spain; Munich, Germany; Rio de Janeiro, São Paulo, and Belo Horizonte, Brazil; Toronto, Canada; Melbourne and Brisbane, Australia; and Vilnius, Lithuania.[36]

Rebar prepared for the 2007 event by distributing updated how-to information on their website, and again holding community organizing sessions. The third Friday in September was confirmed as a permanent date. The Trust for Public Land continued as a partner, promoting the event across an increased number of offices around the country. Public Architecture also took on an expanded role as a more formal partner in the event, including hosting a skill-sharing session and coordinating a map to encourage people to tour various parks across the city. Liz Ogbu, an architect with Public Architecture, describes their contribution:

> That was the first year that there was a dedicated map of all of the parks around the city. We created a flyer to educate people about what PARK(ing) Day was, and try to get people to start crowd sourcing their location so we could say that you could almost do a tour if you wanted to of all the PARK(ing) Day set-ups.

Public Architecture had been investigating the potential for parking spaces to become "sidewalk plazas." This was part of an open space strategy the group was developing in response to shifts in the local area: as industrial uses moved out, the SoMa district was becoming a residential area, and the lack of green space was increasingly apparent. Public Architecture had been working with the city and had succeeded in obtaining a grant, but progress was slow. In this context, PARK(ing) Day was exciting for its potential to help move the strategy forward:

> [We] had already been thinking of it as this long-term thing, so PARK(ing) Day was interesting because we were running into a lot of red tape with the City to push it forward. And so PARK(ing) Day became this thing of like, Oh, that's an interesting idea, if you could do it in a sort of guerrilla fashion, maybe that would be a way to spark interest. (Liz Ogbu)

Treating the day as an opportunity to do a full-scale mock up of their strategy for Folsom Street, where the Public Architecture office was located,

Ogbu set up parks related to adjacent businesses. These included parks themed around a beauty school (offering massages, hair and makeup sessions; figure 1.7), a leather shop (a "muscle bar"), and a laundromat/café/comedy club (a community table), as well as a bike repair stop. Ogbu and Public Architecture volunteers provided most of the materials, did much of the installation, and also helped to keep the parks staffed throughout the day.

The Black Rock Arts Foundation joined as another partner for PARK(ing) Day in 2007. This included an $8,000 grant, enabling the construction of a "Parkcycle," a "human-powered open space distribution system" built in collaboration with kinetic sculptor Reuben Margolin.[37] Topped with grass and a shade tree, the Parkcycle was built on an old boat frame and equipped with solar-powered electric brakes, padded seats, and three sets of pedals. On PARK(ing) Day, Rebar pedalled the Parckcycle to visit some of the 57 parks installed around San Francisco. Sasha Wizansky, one of the participants in the first PARK(ing) installation in 2005, documented this beautifully—including triumphant images of the park, its steel base sparkling in the sunshine outside City Hall (figure 1.8).

Rebar was also growing. Further collaborations with the Black Rock Arts Foundation, as well as other organizations including local gallery Southern Exposure and Danish studio Droog Design, were producing a growing body of work. Projects included *EnCannment*, a performance exhibition in summer 2006, *Commonspace*, an 18-month project exploring privately owned public spaces by holding a series of events to test how public the spaces really were (including Balinese monkey chanting, kite flying, and a "nappening," in which office workers were invited to book 20-minute slots in a "safe and comfortable indoor snoozing environment"),[38] the *Panhandle Bandshell* (a performance space made entirely from recycled materials including 65 automobile hoods, hundreds of computer circuit boards, and 3,000 plastic water bottles)[39] and *Bushwaffle* (a series of "playful personal inflatables" deployed in cities including Paris, Amsterdam, and San Francisco).[40]

While Rebar's work remained centered on "niches," gaps, or loopholes in the tradition of Matta-Clark, they were gaining increasing attention among both practitioners and theorists of urban design. By 2008, Rebar was receiving regular inquiries, including an invitation to participate in the Venice Architecture Biennale in 2008. For the Italian Pavilion, Rebar

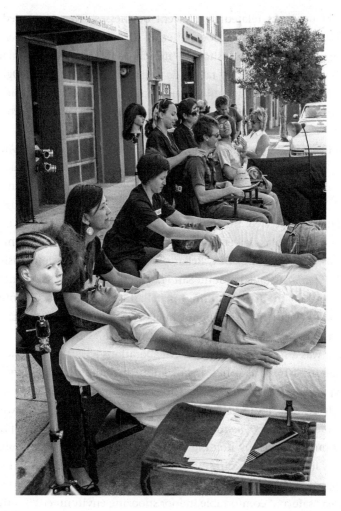

Figure 1.7
Park created by Public Architecture in partnership with the San Francisco Institute of
Esthetics and Cosmetology, Folsom Street, 2007. Image: Steve Rhodes.

Figure 1.8
Rebar touring PARK(ing) Day by "Parkcycle" with artist Reuben Margolin, San Francisco, 2007. From left: Reuben Margolin, Blaine Merker, John Bela, Matthew Passmore. Image: Sasha Wizansky.

showed video footage of PARK(ing) Day around the world, set into a turf-covered wall. Rebar also presented their *Panhandle Bandshell* in the American Pavilion.[41]

PARK(ing) Day expanded significantly in 2008. Around 600 parks were created, spanning 100 cities and 13 countries. This was despite the absence of Rebar, who were in Europe for the Biennale in Venice and then for ExperimentaDesign in Amsterdam. After releasing an updated "PARK(ing) Day Assembly Manual" earlier in the year and hiring a press company to put out media releases, Rebar left much of the organization to others. Merker commented at the time: "We're receding into the background. . . . It's nice in a way."[42]

Many branches of the Trust for Public Land in other cities helped to coordinate local events, and several other groups took on coordinating roles. In Philadelphia, for example, the Center for Architecture and Design partnered with the Philadelphia Parking Authority, the American Institute of Architects in Philadelphia, Community Design Collaborative, and Charter High School for Architecture + Design to organize PARK(ing) Day across the city, with 25 parks in 2008.[43]

In the Australian city of Brisbane, café owner Morgan Daly and urban designer Yen Trinh coordinated PARK(ing) Day in 2008. After building a single park outside Daly's coffee shop in 2007, the two were inspired to organize a larger event. Trinh and Daly produced posters and a locally focused how-to guide, and distributed these along with links to Rebar's materials and information about previous parks, as well as a registration form to help coordinate participants on the day. They provided extensive local information including prices and contacts for useful resources (such as witches' hats, rope barriers, turf, plant rentals, furniture rentals, and recycling services), design ideas to help with planning, talking points to use on the day, links to related events, and information about local parking rules and planning policies. They organized workshops and local meetings in various parts of the city for six months leading up to the event, as well as various "tours de park" on the day. The two also negotiated (unsuccessfully) with Brisbane City Council to arrange approval for the event. Alongside Trinh and Daly, Nicole Sully, a lecturer in architecture at the University of Queensland, had her students participate in PARK(ing) Day as a formal assessment task: 78 students built 19 parks on the UQ campus.[44] With 47 parks, Brisbane declared itself the third largest city for PARK(ing) Day in 2008.[45]

With the diversity of parks growing again that year, PARK(ing) Day was increasingly known as a platform (or vehicle) that could be adopted by a very wide range of causes. In San Francisco, Jay Bolcik and Michael Borden were married in a park outside their home in the Lower Haight district, attracting significant media attention to the debate around Proposition 8, a proposal to ban gay marriage as part of the election in California that year.[46] Several other parks featured social and environmental messages, such as the "forest" of plastic water bottles in which participants were invited to drink water from a ceramic jug to encourage people to reduce their use of plastic; a human-powered paddleboat generating electricity to demonstrate how much more power it takes to light an incandescent bulb than a compact fluorescent; and a native nursery constructed with recycled bamboo, donated shade cloth and hay bales, as well as more than one hundred hanging plants and a range of native animals.[47] Many parks focused on local communities, with activities designed to encourage people to connect and to share—games including bocce, mini golf, and Scrabble, libraries, and giveaways of home-grown vegetables.[48]

As in previous years, many participants in 2008 were designers. Some, such as San Francisco offices INTERSTICE Architects, David Baker + Partners, and BAR Architects, built parks for the second or third time. Community groups also featured prominently, including the San Francisco Bicycle Coalition, the Neighborhood Parks Council, and SPUR (the San Francisco Bay Area Planning and Urban Research Association) which had been involved from the start. Several small businesses also joined in the event, particularly cafés and bike shops.

*   *   *

INTERSTICE Architects built a number of forests for PARK(ing) Day. Researching the parking space outside their office in preparation for the first PARK(ing) Day in 2006, they discovered the building had been constructed over a creek. Their first park was an attempt to recreate this: potted reeds and a paddle pool were laid out over blue tarpaulin sheeting to recreate the creek; a bridge with a bench was constructed over this for people to walk across, sit in, and enjoy the temporarily restored creek. INTERSTICE continued the forest theme the next year, recreating the forest outside their office with bamboo, pebbles, a bridge, and a bench. In 2008 they moved a little further afield, working with local environmental organizations Flora Grub and SF Native Rescue to build the native nursery (described above) on a slightly more prominent site nearby.

In 2009 INTERSTICE took the idea further, expanding in scale and scope to create a Forest on Foot (figure 1.9). This was a set of 12 large trees, carried in pots with specially constructed handles that threaded into bamboo poles to make it easier for volunteers to share the load. Over the course of the day, these were arranged in five different locations around the neighborhood, along with 24 folding chairs. The timing and configurations responded to their locations: two rows of chairs along a central bench at lunchtime outside the local restaurant, semicircular rows outside the bookstore where a reading was held, an S-shape creating two spaces for informal conversation. Community partnerships and relationships were crucial: not just in deciding which spaces to choose, but particularly in moving between them. Each

Figure 1.9
Forest on Foot, San Francisco, 2009. Image: INTERSTICE Architects.

tree required two people to carry it, so numerous volunteers helped out along the way (figure 1.10). This was a deliberate strategy, as INTERSTICE principal Zoee Astrachan explained: "that was to make more people come to us, we were going to take the parklet to them."

This evolution in scale and ambition, and particularly in efforts to take the event to a much wider section of the community, was a strong theme in 2009. In the lead-up to PARK(ing) Day that year, Rebar launched an online DIY planning network and blog, a Facebook site, and a Twitter account. They produced an official T-shirt, running an international competition to select the design. The winner was Maki Kamaguchi from Madrid, Spain, selected from several hundred entrants.[49] Rebar also released a PARK(ing) Day Manifesto and an updated manual, still modeled on an IKEA catalogue (figure 1.11). Unlike the earlier guide, the new manual had to be purchased (for $6.99, or together with the Manifesto for $9.99), with funds going to help with costs of running the event.[50] These changes were prompted in part by the departure of the Trust for Public Land, a result of the shift in economic circumstances in 2009.

Figure 1.10
Staff and volunteers transporting elements of the Forest on Foot around the Mission District, San Francisco, 2009. Image: INTERSTICE Architects.

PARK(ing) Day continued to expand. In 2009, there were over 700 parks in 140 cities and 21 countries. In 2010, there were 800 parks in 183 cities and 30 countries. In 2011, there were 975 parks in 162 cities and 35 countries, including China, Colombia, Hungary, India, Indonesia, and Mexico.[51]

PARK(ing) Day is generally undertaken as a grassroots activity, loosely coordinated and with no identifiable leader. In some places, the event has been promoted more formally. Several community organizations have worked to facilitate engagement by sharing information and ideas, encouraging other participants, or seeking support from city authorities. Others, like the American Institute of Architects and AILA Fresh (the student and graduate group within the Australian Institute of Landscape Architects), have run competitions to encourage and celebrate innovative park designs. Several universities have been involved, either informally (as at the University of Technology Sydney, where students were involved through clubs and the university sustainability office) or as part of formal programs (as at the University of Queensland, or at San Francisco State University,

PARK(ing) Day
Assembly Manual

and Streetscape Intervention Toolkit

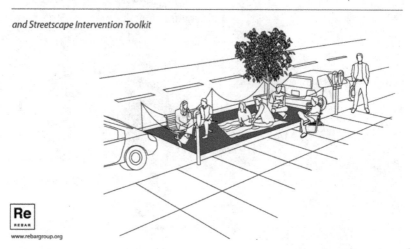

Figure 1.11
PARK(ing) Day Assembly Manual, 2009. Image: Rebar.

where design students have been required to create parks for the past
10 years).

PARK(ing) Day has even become an institutionalized event in some
places. In the Australian city of Adelaide, for example, local design organizations worked with the city council to promote and manage the event.[52]
This included a formal process in which sites were identified where people could construct parks, all located around a small number of central
city blocks. Participants were asked to register to build a park two weeks
before the event, and also to comply with rules regarding timing, number
of participants, bollard positioning, and other matters. The City supported
a competition for the best installations, bringing in high-profile international judges such as Charles Landry. This was entered—and invariably
won—by large companies (the global architecture office Woods Bagot won
three years in a row).[53] Other public authorities, from Singapore to Iowa,
have also become promoters of PARK(ing) Day, establishing various procedures and competitions to regulate the event.[54]

After 2011, Rebar stopped keeping track of the number and distribution of parks. This was because, they explained, "many people (mostly lazy

journalists) are only interested in numbers, and not the qualitative effect of the project and its impact on cities around the world."[55]

Rebar's shift was reflective also of shifts in the office. Participation in the Venice Biennale and then ExperimentaDesign in Amsterdam gave Rebar two weeks of "being professional," and this inspired them to pursue more paid commissions.[56] In 2009 Passmore left his day job as a lawyer to lead the establishment of the Rebar office. Bela and Merker soon followed, and from 2010, when Bela obtained his certification as a landscape architect, the office began to undertake a greater range of work. Increasingly, Rebar focused on larger projects.

Rebar continued to support PARK(ing) Day after 2011, but less intensively. They maintained the parkingday.org website, put out press releases each year, and produced an updated PARK(ing) Day Manual and Manifesto in 2011. In the spring of 2014, Rebar itself came to an end as the founders separated to pursue different projects. Passmore launched Morelab, a public art practice focused on public space. Bela and Merker launched Gehl Studio, the American office of Copenhagen-based Gehl Architects, one of the most established and influential international urban design practices.

Merker and Bela remain supportive of PARK(ing) Day but, as directors of an international design office, devote very little time to the event. Passmore continued for several years to maintain a web presence, and in 2016 set up a crowdfunding drive in an effort to produce a book documenting the event. Passmore's work with Morelab, however, has limited his capacity, and there has been little progress on the book project.

Yet the event continues.

*   *   *

In 2016, WRT Planning + Design used PARK(ing) Day as a way to engage with their San Francisco neighborhood. They began by holding a "happy hour" to encourage others in the area to engage, which led to two other groups joining: Techshop, part of a small, national group of membership-based, open-access, DIY workshops, and Studio O+A, an interior design firm across the road. After regular Wednesday planning meetings over the next month, they each transformed one parking space: WRT created a "curb café" (figure 1.12) providing free coffee and lemonade (donated by the local WholeFoods Market) and encouraging passersby to enjoy their drinks amongst potted plants, on seating made from reclaimed timber (reflecting a growing interest within WRT in fabrication and the impacts of making

Figure 1.12
"Curb café" created by WRT for PARK(ing) Day on Howard Street, San Francisco, 2016. Image: Amelia Thorpe.

things). A few steps along the street, Techshop provided a park bench and potted tree, a resting space shared with a flock of timber pigeons. Across the road, Studio O+A set up a desk on which staff worked outside. Carpet samples were used to create a sitting space, also framed by potted plants, which was used for much of the day by a sleepy dog.

These were all installed on Howard Street, at the time a four-lane, one-way street on which traffic moved at high speeds. Located south of the SoMa district and north of the Tenderloin, Howard Street was occupied by a mix of businesses and social and other housing, in close proximity to a large homeless population and support services geared toward them. With fast traffic, few trees, and no cafés or shops oriented to pedestrians, Howard Street did not encourage much lingering or social interaction. The shade, seats, bright colors, and conversation provided in the three parks created quite a contrast, helped by beautiful sunny weather: people stopped and engaged with the new public spaces. The curb café was particularly popu-lar, attracting a wide range of people, including parents and children who enjoyed the balloons, and homeless people grateful for the free refreshments. Throughout my observation there was a very strong sense of celebration, with people laughing, moving, and talking excitedly about ways the street could be improved on a more permanent basis.

There were at least 15 parks installed on PARK(ing) Day in San Francisco when I visited in 2016. Others included a purpose-built giant plywood pinball machine, a forest of balloons, and a miniature pier constructed from recycled plastic bottles. There were also several more "traditional" parks, with plenty of turf, potted plants, and borrowed, recycled, or repurposed seating. Common across the parks were efforts to engage the public. Several featured giveaways, including cookies, fruit, coffee, and cold drinks (typically homemade or donated by local businesses). Games were popular, including a giant Jenga set, corn bag throwing, and board games such as Guess Who and checkers. Like WRT and their collaborators, others sought more purposeful contributions from passersby, providing chalk, pens, and other equipment for people to share their ideas for the street and the city.

Most of the parks built for PARK(ing) Day in 2016 were located near the site of Rebar's first park, around the SoMa and Mission districts, or in the North Beach area. There were also some more central parks, including one near Union Square and one close to the busy intersection of Howard and 2nd streets.

Many were built by architects and landscape architects. Other participants included students, a branding agency, a real estate services company, and a carshare company. Some were first-time participants, though typically at least one group member had been involved before. At least three of the participants in 2016, BAR Architects, WRT Planning + Design, and the San Francisco Bicycle Coalition, had also created parks for the first PARK(ing) Day in 2006. Despite these longstanding connections, most participants from these organizations were new to the event, taking part for their first or second time. BAR Architects, for example, is a large office, with almost 100 architects; none of the team who put together the 2016 park had been involved more than three years previously. Many participants did not know the history of PARK(ing) Day: how long it had been running, that it began in San Francisco, how far afield it had traveled. Many had not heard of Rebar.

1.3   Beyond the Rebar story

The story of PARK(ing) Day as an evolution from the 2005 PARK(ing) installation is one that has been repeated many times. Invariably, these accounts refer to histories provided by Rebar, or to other sources drawing heavily on them. These accounts put Rebar front and center. While Rebar was undoubtedly central, a fuller picture of PARK(ing) Day must recognize the important contributions made by others in San Francisco and beyond: people like Andrea Scher, Amy Seek, Denise Sauerteig, Matthew Shaffer and the Trust for Public Land, Liz Ogbu and Public Architecture, Andres Power and the City of San Francisco. Historical precedents should also be acknowledged, as more recent commentators have argued: Mike Lydon and Tony Garcia point to "parking meter parties" held in Hamilton, Ontario in 2001;[57] Robin Abad Ocubillo argues that San Francisco artist Bonnie Ora Sherk's experimental installations of the 1970s form the first major precedent for contemporary parklets.[58]

While the idea of creating a park in a parking space is unusual, it is one with a long history. Two days after the installation of the world's first parking meter in Oklahoma City in 1935 (patented as a "Park-O-Meter," with an hourly rate of one nickel), the *Tulsa Tribune* reported alternative uses of the newly regulated space.[59] In one, two couples set up a folding table and chairs, then played a game of bridge. In the other, a local rancher tied his horse to a parking meter, explaining that it was cheaper than a livery stable.

By the 1980s, the use of parking spaces for purposes other than storing cars could be seen on national television. The opening sequence of the sitcom *Bosom Buddies* shows Peter Scolari paying a meter (figure 1.13), then relaxing with Tom Hanks on lawn chairs in the parking space (figure 1.14). This high-profile reclamation may be indicative of a wider embedding of the idea in popular culture. While not systematically documented, there are many examples in which people have taken over parking spaces for brief or longer periods. Jeff Ferrell, for example, describes how he and a local activist in Berkeley were inspired by an abandoned sofa, moving it into the roadway to encourage sitting rather than driving.[60] Ferrell compares this to an example in Montréal, documented in the magazine *Car Busters*, in which a couple were similarly inspired to take over a parking space when they saw a sofa awaiting the rubbish truck.[61] They placed the sofa on the edge of the

Figures 1.13, 1.14
Stills from the opening credits of *Bosom Buddies*, 1980.

road, sat down and enjoyed engaging with people passing by for the next few hours—perhaps one of many other examples of similar, small-scale and largely unnoticed reclamations of the street.

Others gained more attention. The work of conceptual artist Bonnie Ora Sherk is one of the most-cited precedents for PARK(ing) Day. In the early 1970s, Sherk produced *Portable Parks I-III*, a series of installations featuring turf and other items.[62] First on an elevated freeway, then on concrete islands next to a freeway off ramp, and finally by closing off a whole street, Sherk created a series of temporary parks on California roads (figures 1.15 and 1.16). As the installations progressed, they became increasingly participatory, deploying various items to engage passersby: trees, picnic tables, straw bales, farm and zoo animals (including live cows, chickens, and a llama). In 1974 Sherk established Crossroads Community (the farm), a seven-acre ecogarden/art/education space in the traffic medians under a freeway overpass in San Francisco. The project lasted six years, until 1980 when it was transformed into a public park.[63] Perhaps inspired by PARK(ing) Day (Sherk was herself involved in PARK(ing) Day, as part of the CC Puede group), Sherk revisited the idea in 2012.[64] For the Getty's Pacific Standard Time Performance and Public Art Festival that year, Sherk collaborated with curator Karen Moss and graduate students at Otis College to install *Portable Park IV* at the Santa Monica Place Shopping Center.

Sherk was one of several artists working in the roadway during the 1960s and 1970s.[65] In her 1970 survey of Bay Area art practice, Brenda Richardson described a tendency to "take to the streets," explaining this as "oriented towards more or less political or environmental concerns" and "significantly more relevant to people (including many of the artists involved) than the traditional art channels of museums, galleries and collectors."[66] The Chicano art collective Asco, for example, staged a number of performances on the streets of East Los Angeles. In *First Supper (After a Major Riot)* (1974), Asco members Patssi Valdez, Gronk, Harry Gamboa Jr., Willie F Herrón III, and Humberto Sandoval shared a Christmas Eve meal in a traffic island, sitting in costumes at a table and chairs and surrounded by props (figure 1.17). The island was part of Whittier Boulevard, the site where police had opened fire on anti-Vietnam protesters three years earlier.

In the 1990s, David Engwicht led several experiments in Australia and North America to counter what he described as a psychological retreat

Figures 1.15, 1.16
Portable Park ll. Performance installation from series *Portable Parks l-lll*, Mission/Van Ness offramp and adjacent concrete islands, Highway 101/Otis Street, San Francisco, California. Detail showing Sherk talking with California Department of Transportation officials while petting cow. Images: ©1970 Bonnie Ora Sherk.

Figure 1.17
First Supper (After a Major Riot), 1974, Harry Gamboa Jr., from the Asco era. Image: ©1974, Harry Gamboa Jr.

from the street (figure 1.18).[67] While Engwicht began with a focus on traffic calming through street engineering, his emphasis shifted over time to street parties and social gatherings in which residents formed new friendships that led in turn to more time chatting and playing on the street. As he explains, "The speed of traffic on most streets is determined to a large extent by the degree to which the residents have psychologically retreated from their street. This means that working with people's perceptions of their street and creating social infrastructure may be more effective in slowing traffic than building speed bumps."[68] Some of Engwicht's more playful activities included developing a folding throne with which he set out on a world tour, temporarily reclaiming sections of the Champs-Élysées, Times Square, and other famous streets.

Closer in time to Rebar's first PARK(ing) installation, there were many comparable projects. In September 2000, Transportation for Liveable Communities Hamilton held a "Parking Meter Party" in the Canadian city of

Figure 1.18
Street party hosted by David Engwicht in Henry Street, Brisbane, 1996. The party was
held to celebrate the 34% reduction in traffic speeds achived in the first week of a
"Traffic Reduction Treaty" pilot program in partnership with Brisbane City Council.
Image: David Engwicht / Creative Communities.

Hamilton, Ontario at the end of a march to celebrate what they dubbed
"World Car Free Day" (figure 1.19). Offering to supply the change for parking meters, the group invited people to join the next party in July 2001:
"Bring some grass (the kind you sit on), a lawnchair, food, drums, soap
bubbles, boombox, sidewalk chalk, and your sense of adventure," and
promised that the parking spots would "magically transform into liber-
ated car-free spaces."[69] Transportation for Liveable Communities Hamilton hosted a number of parties, each with an environmental and anti-car
emphasis (figure 1.20). The September party, for example, was held near an
Esso station, and participants handed out flyers encouraging people to boy-
cott the Esso corporation. While this targeted environmental activism differed from Rebar's approach, there were strong parallels to PARK(ing) Day
in the explanation of the event: "Parking meters provide cheap party rental

Figure 1.19
Paying the meter at the first Parking Meter Party held by Transportation for Liveable
Communities Hamilton, Ontario, 2000. Image: Andrew Curran / TLC Hamilton.

space (50 cents an hour in downtown Hamilton) and are readily available
on city streets all over North America. Unroll a bit of sod for texture and
some green and crank up the boom box. Pull up a chair, play a game of
chess, have a glass of lemonade. Enjoy the streets!"[70]

In 2002, Steve Rasmussen Cancian began installing "outdoor living
rooms" in Oakland and Los Angeles.[71] Working with local residents, Rasmussen Cancian used discarded sofas to provide outdoor seating and tables
in low-income neighborhoods where city-funded improvements were
scarce, progressing to purpose-built furniture in later installations. These
were initially removed by city authorities, but later received official support.[72] In Los Angeles, Mayor Antonio Villaraigosa joined in to help with
the construction of one bench.[73]

In the UK, Ted Dewan was also reclaiming the street for more sociable
uses. As part of a broader program of "road witching" or "folk traffic calming," Dewan placed life-sized stuffed dolls with witches' hats for heads on
various streets to slow traffic.[74] Dewan takes a broad definition to "road
witching," and "witches" need not be involved. Dewan's website provides

Figure 1.20
Poster for Parking Meter Party designed by Gord Pullar for Transportation for Liveable Communities Hamilton, 2001. Image: Gord Pullar / TLC Hamilton.

links to other projects—including PARK(ing)—as examples of the practice, and some of his own activities have strong parallels to PARK(ing) Day. In 2003, Dewan arranged a sofa, side tables, reading lamps, and a (broken-down) TV on a carpet in Summertown, Oxford.[75] Others contributed magazines, games, children's toys, and a functioning TV, allowing the group to watch the tennis at Wimbledon (figure 1.21).

Closer to Rebar's installation, San Francisco architect Jane Martin was developing sidewalk landscapes to facilitate the greening of city streets.[76] Martin initially wanted to convert part of the footpath near her building

Figure 1.21
Beechcroft Living Room, assembled by Ted Dewan and residents of Beechcroft Road, Oxford, 2003. Image: ©Ted Dewan.

into a garden. Frustration with the regulatory process led Martin to establish Plant*SF (Permeable Landscape as Neighborhood Treasure in San Francisco) and to work with the city to develop a new sidewalk landscaping permit. These proved popular: between 2006 and 2009, the City of San Francisco received over 500 applications for sidewalk landscaping permits.[77]

Chicago-based artist Michael Rakowitz's *(P)LOT* installations provide a particularly strong parallel to PARK(ing). Using PVC pipe and tent poles, Rakowitz reworked standard car covers to create tents in which a range of activities could be undertaken. These were deployed in parking spaces in Vienna, Austria in 2004, in Trento, Italy in 2005, and then in a traveling exhibition from 2005 to 2008. Rakowitz's interest was in questioning the way in which public space is allocated, and in using the payment of parking meters to provide legitimacy for alternative forms of civic participation. The similarity between Rakowitz and Rebar's language is striking:

> (P)LOT questions the occupation and dedication of public space and encourages reconsiderations of "legitimate" participation in city life. Contrary to the common procedure of using municipal parking spaces as storage surfaces for vehicles, (P)LOT proposes the rental of these parcels of land for alternative purposes. The acquisition of municipal permits and simple payment of parking meters could enable citizens to, for example, establish temporary encampments or use the leased ground for different kinds of activities, such as temporary gardens, outdoor dining, game playing, etc.[78]

Rakowitz's installations were less public than Rebar's parks. The parking space is hidden by the cover, making it hard for others to join or even see what is happening inside. Like Rebar, Rakowitz conceived his tents as one of many possible interventions that could be deployed in parking spaces. The tents were presented as a pilot rather than an end point: "A first initiative for this re-dedication is realized through the conversion of ordinary car covers to portable tents for use as living units or leisure spaces. Ranging from a common sedan to a luxurious Porsche or Lexus, the tents enable a broadcast of desire within the marginalized space of need."[79]

Just before Rebar's first PARK(ing) installation, Transportation Alternatives held a "parking squat" in Williamsburg, Brooklyn, New York, in October 2005.[80] The group offered free bike parking and encouraged people to meet and chat in the space, in an effort to prompt reflection on the use and allocation of public space in the city.[81] In 2006, a group of livable streets advocates staged further squats in Park Slope, Brooklyn.[82]

Like Rakowitz's installations, Transportation Alternatives' squats used vehicular forms to create a gathering space for people (figure 1.22). Car-shaped silhouettes and orange cones provided a barrier, inside which people sat on various chairs (including lawn chairs like those in *Bosom Buddies*), playing games, reading newspapers, and relaxing in the sunshine. Playing on the toy car brought along by his son, one of the organizers of the Park Slope event commented on his blog, "New York City regulations say that metered, curbside parking spaces are only to be used for the storage of vehicles. This kid made sure the rules were being followed."[83] Flyers provided information about the event and its aims (figure 1.23); a sign closely resembling an official street sign proclaimed "Public Space Reclamation in Progress."

Figure 1.22
Parking meter squat, 7th Avenue and 1st Street, Brooklyn, New York, Transportation
Alternatives, 2006. Image: Aaron Naparstek.

Rebar's PARK(ing) Day far exceeded any of these—or any of the other
multitude of DIY urban interventions that can be found in contemporary
cities—in its reach. Some of these precursors were undertaken multiple
times; some, like Plant*SF's sidewalk landscapes, were taken up by many
others. Yet none were adopted on anything like the scale of PARK(ing)
Day, for such sustained periods, or with such momentum. None gained
anything like the media attention attracted by Rebar. It was not until the
advent of PARK(ing) Day that many of these earlier activities became more
widely known, or that commentators like Lydon and Garcia or Abad Ocubillo began to seek out precursors. Rebar themselves were unaware of any
prior examples, even local and relatively well-documented precedents like
the work of Sherk.

This lack of visibility is apparent in the claim by Transportation Alternatives to be the "true" originators of the idea (and the number of blog

Figure 1.23
Flyers for parking meter squat, Transportation Alternatives. Image: Aaron Naparstek.

posts about PARK(ing) Day with an addendum acknowledging this at their request).

> Truth be told, the event actually started in Brooklyn, New York (http://parkingdaynyc.org/about), but the name came from the Rebar group. On October 25, 2005, a handful of New Yorkers associated with Transportation Alternatives (http://www.transalt.org/) squatted down in a parking spot, offered free bike parking, and a place to meet friends and strangers alike, and this encouraged people to begin to question the concept of charging money for the use of public space and dedicating so much public space to cars.[84]

Transportation Alternatives, like Rebar, were not the first to repurpose a parking space for uses other than parking a car. Like parking meter parties, road witching, *(P)LOT*, and the many other comparable activities preceding it, however, Transportation Alternatives' parking squat is clearly distinguishable from PARK(ing) Day in its reach, scale, and longevity.

1.4   Sites of study

Among the many possible sites that could be used to examine PARK(ing) Day, Sydney and Montréal are useful as examples that are similar in many respects to San Francisco and to each other—relatively global cities in Western liberal democracies, with populations of several million creating significant challenges for city planners. In all three cities, parking is contested, and planning policy has been directed increasingly toward reducing car use. Again, in all three cities these policies are supported generally, but not universally. Sydney and Montréal are also different in interesting respects. Sydney is a city that took up PARK(ing) Day relatively early, but one in which the event has remained small in scale. Montréal was quite late to take up the event, but very quickly grew to become home to the world's largest PARK(ing) Day.

Sydney

PARK(ing) Day reached Sydney in 2008, two years after the first PARK(ing) Day and one year after the event was first undertaken in Australia (parks were built in 2007 in Melbourne and Brisbane). Two groups participated in the event. One was a group of students from the University of New South Wales (UNSW) led by James Patterson, then studying environmental engineering. The other was a group of professional planners and engineers from the Sydney office of international consultancy group Arup, led by Safiah Moore, then a graduate planner in the office.

Patterson and his friends Angela Johnstone, Eytan Rocheta, Adrian Emilsen, and Tessa Dowdell heard about PARK(ing) Day when Streetfilms' PARK(ing) Day film showed in Sydney as part of the Bicycle Film Festival in 2007. They were immediately taken with the idea and set about planning their own event. On PARK(ing) Day in 2008 they got up early and loaded the ingredients for a park—turf, trees, milk crates, picnic blankets, bollards, and balloons—into rented bike trailers and the back of a car (the plan had been to rely entirely on bikes, but the turf was heavy and the ride was at least thirty minutes). They cycled across the city to King Street, a busy commercial strip in the inner west suburb of Newtown. Finding two vacant parking spaces side by side in a sunny, prominent part of the strip, they stopped. After quickly checking in with the adjacent business, they began setting up. They laid down plastic sheeting, then the grass,

Figure 1.24
PARK(ing) Day installation by James Patterson, Eytan Rocheta, and friends, King Street, Newtown, Sydney, 2008. Image: Adrian Emilsen.

trees, and a perimeter fence. Suddenly, there was a little park on the road (figure 1.24). They sat down, and people started approaching them. Almost instantly, there was a "really good vibe."[85] There were children and strollers, and people excited by the reallocation of space from cars to people. Some brought contributions to the park: a small bench, food to add to the picnic. Patterson and his friends handed out leaflets explaining what they were doing, and a young filmmaker recorded the event.[86]

While the park was very much in the model of Rebar's earlier parks in its form, it differed in the response it generated from officials. The group had followed Rebar's guidance in preparing their park, looking up legislation and even printing extracts of relevant provisions. These proved ineffective when an objecting ranger called the police, however: the police insisted that the park was unsafe and must be removed.

Arup's park was more elaborate and less controversial.[87] Moore heard about PARK(ing) Day from a colleague, who suggested she could do it with

Figure 1.25
PARK(ing) Day installation by Arup, Circular Quay, Sydney, 2008. Image: Safiah Moore, Arup.

the backing of the office. Arup's provision of support and resources for her to participate in PARK(ing) Day, Moore explains, was perhaps intended as encouragement for her to pursue a longer-term career with the firm. Building on their then-current Libraries of the Future project, Arup collaborated with a City of Sydney library for their park (figure 1.25). This was installed not in a parking space, but on the forecourt of Customs House, a prominent site in the heart of the central business district, adjacent to Circular Quay (a busy train, bus, and ferry interchange) and close to major landmarks including the Sydney Opera House. Developed around a theme of productivity, the park demonstrated ways in which the space could be more productive. Hay bales, potted plants laden with fruit and vegetables, fresh fruit giveaways, and chickens borrowed from Moore's parents' backyard were used to engage people in ideas of food productivity. WiFi was provided as a gesture toward work productivity, and two Arup-branded smart cars were stationed next to the park, highlighting a less productive use of the space (and the company behind the intervention). Passersby were invited to write their wishes for the city and to hang these on a tree. Arup's park attracted many visitors, with overwhelmingly positive responses.

Sydney's first two parks were thus quite different in their origins, their resources, their aims, and the responses they generated. They also differed in their trajectories. Patterson and his collaborators did not participate in PARK(ing) Day again, but Moore led the installation of Arup parks for all but one of the eight PARK(ing) Days between 2008 and 2016. The Arup office has provided around $5,000 in support each year, with about $600 spent on materials and the rest on staff time (which Moore estimates covers around half of the time actually spent on the event).

Arup's later parks have been built in parking spaces, generally located near their office in the Rocks, wherever the closest available parking spot could be found on the day. These have included a "sanctuary," created by screening a parking space on all four sides with bamboo and playing bird-songs inside; a "creativity show and tell," with Arup products including a "pocket habitat"; a "window into the future" where people were invited to write on glass doors and windows about what they would like to see in the city; a digital library with an XBox motion detector; a soundscape, where people were invited to sit on milkcrates and experiment with soft-ware developed by Arup's acoustic team to remix everyday sounds, from bells to boiling kettles; and a set of boards displaying alternative futures for Barangaroo (a major redevelopment site near Arup's office), against which people where invited to take pictures. Arup's 2016 park was an effort to engage the housing affordability debate, a major issue in Sydney.[88] Moore and colleagues provided maps and figures about the growing housing crisis, along with a cardboard "home" on which passersby were invited to write their views on the issue.

PARK(ing) Day has attracted additional participants in subsequent years, though no more than a handful in any one year. Invariably, parks have been located in inner-city areas: Paddington, Surry Hills, Pyrmont, Ultimo, Newtown, and the central business district. More than half of Sydney's 30-plus parks have been installed by built environment professionals. Planners, engineers, landscape architects, urban designers, and architects have participated as part of professional offices, typically in collaboration with one or two neighboring offices.

Figure 1.26
PARK(ing) Day installation, Australia Street, Newtown, Sydney, 2013. Safety was a key concern (perhaps because Carle worked for the council, or because the park was located very close to the local police station), so hay bales and soft hit posts were used to provide a prominent border for the park. This was filled with plants, pallet furniture, and activities to entice people (particularly young people) to spend time in the park: wooden toys, craft activities, and a water pump. Image: Steve Webb.

Built environment professionals have also been involved more informally, participating outside of work. The volunteer organization Architecture for Humanity has built parks on two occasions. Jonathon Carle, a planner working at the City of Sydney, coordinated a PARK(ing) Day installation near his home in Newtown in 2013, working with neighbors and local businesses including Black Star Pastry, Rosie Boylan Headwear, and Edible Kids Gardens (figure 1.26). Carle's aim in building the park was to encourage the council to find a more permanent solution to urban design problems in the area, particularly a shortage of footpath space near a busy intersection outside a popular group of small businesses (especially Black Star Pastry). The council responded positively, encouraging Carle to participate again the following year (and even providing funding to support this).

As in San Francisco, certain elements have proved consistently popular in Sydney's parks: turf, potted plants, hay bales, and pallet seating. Many have included efforts to engage passersby more actively, either in play (from chess to ping pong), or in more directly planning-focused activities (surveys, blackboards, small notes on which to write ideas about the city generally, or about particular planning proposals). To accompany the park on Australia Street, Jonathon Carle produced postcards explaining what a parklet is. On the back of the card, people were asked if they would like to see one installed there, and if they had any other feedback on the idea. Another more playful intervention created a set of cardboard cars that traveled around several parking spaces through the course of the day, ending up as a longer-term installation in an art gallery.[89]

It is difficult to be sure how many parks have been built in Sydney. There has been little coordination; participants rarely pin their parks on the PARK(ing) Day website and are often unaware of parks built by others. There have been some efforts to address this. The Surry Hills not-for-profit arts organization Object put out a "call to action" in 2010, distributing information and advice about the event in an effort to encourage people to participate.[90] In 2013, planning consultant John O'Callaghan set up sydneyparkingday.com, a Facebook page, and a Twitter account to try to coordinate participants and encourage others to join in. O'Callaghan had participated in PARK(ing) Day in 2011 while working for Paddington place-making consultancy Place Partners, and was keen to see the event grow in Sydney. This proved difficult, however, and even with many calls and flyers sent across his personal and professional networks, O'Callaghan found it hard to expand the event. O'Callaghan still maintains the Facebook page, though there is very little activity on this, and the website is now defunct. Moore and her colleagues at Arup have also discussed setting up a map to encourage people to visit multiple parks on PARK(ing) Day, but so far have not pursued this.

The biggest year for PARK(ing) Day in Sydney was 2014, when at least six parks were built across the city. Two new participants joined the event that year: North Sydney Girls High School (NSGHS) and an inner-city university, University of Technology Sydney (UTS). Led by art teacher Karen Profilio, PARK(ing) Day at NSGHS was a major undertaking. The students had

Figure 1.27
PARK(ing) Day installation by North Sydney Girls High School, David Street, North Sydney, 2014. Image: Karen Profilio.

been planning for the event since 2013, working in teams on logistics, risk management, design, and documentation. With the support of the local council and an arts grant, NSGHS closed off a whole section of the street. They filled this with art installations themed around the Chinese heritage of many of the students (figure 1.27), music performances, free food, and small paintings as gifts for passersby, and held classes and a staff meeting in the space.

The UTS event was coordinated by Seb Crawford of UTS Green, an organization promoting sustainability across the university. Working with academics in architecture, landscape, and real estate, Crawford helped a small group of students to borrow pallets and beanbags to build their park, which was well used by staff, students, and other passersby.

NSGHS did not participate again, largely because the date fell during school holidays in 2015 (this was partly a problem of confusion, thinking PARK(ing) was held on the same calendar date each year, rather than the more variable third Friday of September). UTS Green did participate again in later years. In 2015 and 2016, Crawford enthusiastically explained,

PARK(ing) Day was much more of a student-run initiative. The students arranged to borrow several potted plants (tall eucalypts, smaller flowering natives), and again borrowed beanbags and rugs for people to sit on. In 2016, the third Friday in September fell unusually early, which meant the date was during UTS's study break. Several students who had participated in previous events were still keen to be involved, however, and decided to participate off-campus. Working largely independently of UTS, the students put together a citrus-themed park by the beach at Bondi. This included potted trees and a lemonade stand, the proceeds of which were used to pay the parking meter. Guitar performances by the students aimed to encourage people to linger with their lemonade.

Montréal

While PARK(ing) Day in Sydney was closely related to the San Francisco event—directly inspired by images and footage of Rebar and other participants in San Francisco—the connection between Montréal's PARK(ing) Day and San Francisco's was less direct.

PARK(ing) Day didn't reach Montréal until relatively late, with parks first built in 2011. Much like in Sydney, the first PARK(ing) Day in Montréal was small; I found evidence of only two parks. Both were created by community-based environmental organizations, the Groupe de Travail en Agriculture Urbaine (Work Group on Urban Agriculture, GTAU) and VertCité (GreenCity). Neither of Montréal's two 2011 parks received much publicity, and many of the participants of later years were unaware that these had taken place.

For GTAU, part of the larger Collectif de Recherche en Aménagement Paysager et Agriculture Urbaine Durable (Research Collective on Landscape Planning and Sustainable Urban Agriculture), PARK(ing) Day was an opportunity to raise awareness about sustainable urban food production. Described as a "day of horticultural occupation," GTAU's park included many potted plants, food giveaways, and a table and flyers with information about urban agriculture.[91]

VertCité, the *éco-quartier* (eco neighborhood) for the borough of Saint-Laurent, engaged in PARK(ing) Day as part of its program of promoting various local environmental initiatives. Almost every borough in Montréal includes an *éco-quartier*, typically with two or three staff employed to encourage and facilitate community actions around recycling, composting, street greening, and other community-based environmental initiatives. Saint-Laurent is one of Montréal's largest and most ethnically diverse boroughs and, unlike many of the sites where PARK(ing) Day first appeared in Sydney, San Francisco, and other cities, Saint-Laurent is not located in the inner city.

Although PARK(ing) Day was novel in Montréal, a related event, En Ville Sans Ma Voiture (In Town Without My Car), was well established in 2012. Following a 1998 French initiative, which in turn expanded across Europe and beyond, Montréal had been participating in En Ville Sans Ma Voiture every year since 2003.[92] This involved closing parts of the downtown area to traffic for one day in September, and in many years for several days, with additional traffic closures in parts of other inner city areas. Performances, displays, and other activities were undertaken to animate the street, and businesses invited to set up displays on the footpath. En Ville Sans Ma Voiture was organized by the public transport authority (Agence Métropolitaine de Transport, AMT), in partnership with other city and provincial agencies. The day was preceded by several months of community education and awareness-raising around the social, economic, and environmental costs of car use, and supported by a budget of around $300,000.[93]

In 2012, the Conseil regional d'environnement de Montréal (regional environment council, CRE) began promoting PARK(ing) Day. For the CRE, an umbrella organization representing more than fifty environmental groups, PARK(ing) Day fit well with their campaigns around urban sustainability. Daniel Bouchard, who led PARK(ing) Day for the CRE, had not heard about Montréal's 2011 parks when he decided to get involved. Instead, Bouchard had been reading Donald Shoup's book *The High Cost of Free Parking* and came across pictures of parks in other cities. In contrast to En Ville Sans Ma Voiture, Bouchard saw in PARK(ing) Day a far more accessible way to engage the public in thinking about the allocation of public space.

Once the CRE became involved, PARK(ing) Day grew rapidly. The CRE's connections in Montréal made it easy to attract participants, as Bouchard explains:

> Because we're an umbrella organization of maybe 50 or 60 organizations . . . it was easy for me to say, ok we want to use public space, who is interested? I called the *éco-quartier*, I called different groups and people say yes. The noise and the *bruit*, start to go in every direction, and we made the biggest PARK(ing) Day in the world the next year.

The CRE worked also with a newly formed organization, the Association du Design Urbain du Québec (Urban Design Association of Quebec, ADUQ) to promote PARK(ing) Day. ADUQ was established by a group of young designers with the aim of promoting urban design, strengthening links between practitioners, and increasing the quality of urban interventions in Montréal.[94] ADUQ set up a competition for PARK(ing) Day, providing an incentive for creativity and originality among participants, as well as encouragement for people to visit multiple parks. Several prizes were offered: a Facebook prize (for the park receiving the most "likes"), a public prize, and a participation prize, as well as a $400 jury prize.[95]

More than 60 parks were built across the city in 2012, created by more than 35 organizations.[96] As in Sydney, many participants were architects, planners, or designers. Yet parks by built environment professionals accounted for less than a third of those installed in 2012. Many more were by community, nongovernment, and nonprofit organizations, typically with an environmental focus. Many others were semigovernment organizations, including *éco-quartiers* and transport agencies.

Many different parks were built in 2012; several were elaborate and interactive. The CRE's own park was a beach on the street. Taking up three parking spaces near the old port of Montréal, this included sand and paddle pools, as well as potted plants, deck chairs, and a ping pong table. Other parks included: a resting space, with mattresses and eye masks; a greenhouse; playgrounds for children; yoga classes; bike repair stops; an urban farm, with live goats, cows, donkeys, and an alpaca; and a performance in which two clowns strung their laundry on a line. There were also simple parks much like Rebar's first installation, featuring turf, seats, and potted plants (figure 1.28).

Prize-winning parks included a hockey rink, a mini golf course, an installation in which people were invited to cover cars with graffiti, and another in which hundreds of toy cars were set out in neat, white-lined rows. The jury prize went to IBI-CHBA (a large design firm, now known as Lemay) for "Plante ta ville" (Plant your city). This began with a wire frame around the parking space, with plants in recycled tin cans laid out inside, along with furniture made from recycled pallets and building materials. People were invited to choose a plant and hang it onto the frame, so that the park was progressively greened during the course of the day (figure 1.29). On the footpath nearby a seed dispenser (resembling a gumball machine) offered

Figure 1.28
PARK(ing) Day, Arrondissement Villeray–Saint-Michel–Parc-Extension, 2012. Image: Ville de Montréal.

Figure 1.29
Participants hang potted plants, creating a green screen around the parking space as part of the PARK(ing) Day installation by IBI-CHBA, "Plante ta ville," Rue McGill, Montréal, 2012. Image: Chloé Charbonnier.

free seeds, with paper bags marked "Prenez, Plantez, Admirez, Partagez" (Take, Plant, Admire, Share) and "On vous remercie de semer la bonne nouvelle" (Thank you for sowing the good news).

The CRE's PARK(ing) Day campaign very quickly expanded well beyond the scale of any of its previous campaigns. In 2013, the CRE set a target of 200 parks, and succeeded in beating this with more than 250 across greater Montréal.[97] More than 200 parking spaces were turned into parks again in 2014,[98] 2015,[99] 2016,[100] 2017,[101] and in 2018,[102] far exceeding numbers in any other city and establishing Montréal firmly as the site of the world's biggest PARK(ing) Day.[103]

As in Sydney, in Montréal PARK(ing) Day is concentrated in the inner areas of the city. Most parks have been located on the Île de Montréal, and most of these in inner areas. Yet parks are also built in other locations across the city—in 2016, parks were installed in 16 of Montréal's 19 boroughs.[104]

Groups with a sustainability focus continue to build a large proportion of parks, as do built environment professionals, but PARK(ing) Day extends beyond these groups. Schools, universities, and community organizations have built parks (figure 1.30), as have several small businesses, from dentists to dance teachers, bike shops to bookshops, small bars to shopping centers.

> I don't know at this point if it's momentum or inertia, like if it's gaining speed or slowing down? But it seems to be going strong every year and it seems to be prevalent in the cities that I keep an eye on. So it doesn't look like it's going to disappear any time soon. (Alan Chen, Montréal)

Twelve years after Rebar's first installation, and more than 70 years after the first use of the meter to legitimate activities other than the parking of cars on city streets, PARK(ing) Day remains a captivating concept. How long PARK(ing) Day will continue remains unclear.

> I'd like to think that it would eventually go away because it's not necessary anymore, but we're a very long way from that. But that's what I'd sign up for. (Jane Martin, San Francisco)

> I don't think Parking Day will be an event that will be replayed forever. I know there will be an end to that, I don't know if it will be in a few years or, I, I couldn't say that. (Félix Gravel, Montréal)

Ideas about public space, citizen participation, and the place of cars in cities have shifted significantly since 2005, so that many of the claims made

Figure 1.30
Sébastien Adam teaching a class on urban psychology during PARK(ing) Day in 2017, Collège Rosemont, Montréal. Image: Caroline Nioucel, Collège Rosemont.

in PARK(ing) Day are now less controversial (and perhaps even passé). Pop-up and DIY-style urbanism are ubiquitous in many places, a standard tactic used by all sorts of businesses and other organizations, the subject of guidebooks, masterclasses, and university courses, and supported by a growing number of professional placemakers.[105] Far from subversive, temporary appropriations of public space are regular occurrences in many cities.

PARK(ing) Day is seen by some as unnecessary in that context, prompting commentary such as "Why We Don't Need PARK(ing) Day Anymore."[106] In interviews, some participants also thought that the event was becoming superfluous, at least in some cities:

> It does seem like it's slowed down a little bit. . . . The ideas are still being exchanged, from city to city. There still is this kind of enthusiasm around nitty-gritty street design changes . . . but yeah, I don't know, so many of these ideas have been

mainstreamed. I think that's part of it, you know? It's like it's not punk-rock anymore. It's pop culture. (Aaron Naparstek, New York)

In most cities, it appears that interest in PARK(ing) Day is waning. In San Francisco, numbers are far lower than they were ten years ago; in Sydney participation has also dropped. When I began the project, knowing most about its trajectory in San Francisco and in Sydney, I assumed it was coming to an end, imagining after ten years that I would be able to tell the story from start to finish. But Montréal contradicted this, and it remains possible that people in other places could still take up the idea, or that new people could begin to engage in cities where earlier participants have since moved on.

Figure 2.1
"Shifting the Paradigm," PARK(ing) Day design by Maki Kawaguchi, 2009. Image: Rebar.

2   Moving Things Along

There are many known precursors for PARK(ing) Day, and a deeper search would probably extend that list. While PARK(ing) Day is in many respects like these earlier appropriations of parking spaces, it is also fundamentally different: PARK(ing) Day is well into its second decade, with parks created in hundreds of cities, by thousands of people. Unlike its precursors, PARK(ing) Day is often described as a movement.

Such a label is misleading, however, in its implication of a shared identity or overarching objective. In trying to explain the event and, particularly, how it has been so much more captivating than its many (often very similar) precedents, Gregor McLennan and Thomas Osborne's work on vehicular ideas is helpful. Like other vehicular ideas, PARK(ing) Day can be understood as a problem-solving device, not an expression of principles, ideals, or theoretical commitment but an open-ended and highly temporal tool that serves to catalyze reflection and debate, and in turn to make way for other ideas. PARK(ing) Day works as a vehicular idea because it connects with broader shifts in approaches to cities and the relative places of people and cars within them, but also because it is available for appropriation and extension.

Central to the vehicularity of the PARK(ing) idea is its invocation of legality. Unlike its precursors—especially those with more aggressive names like "parking squats"—PARK(ing) Day makes no explicit challenge to the governance of urban space. PARK(ing), Rebar claims, is not out of place. The activity, like the term, is presented as an everyday one, with just a small shift: parentheses around the "ing," accommodating a park instead of a car, but not outside of what the road rules prescribe. Consistent with Jacques Rancière's notions of aesthetics and dissensus, a key part of what makes PARK(ing) Day so successful is its engagement with—and disruption of—common sense.

2.1 A compelling idea

> We saw a film about PARK(ing) Day from the States by the people who first came up with the idea and then how it was spreading there and . . . we were all just like, wow! That's really cool. We should do that. (James Patterson, Sydney)

PARK(ing) Day captures the imagination. Just as images and footage of Rebar's initial installation very quickly prompted people in other cities and countries to build their own pop-up parks, the people I interviewed were often inspired to get involved in PARK(ing) Day simply by seeing photos or hearing stories about earlier instances. Many participants described wanting to take part as soon as they heard about the event.

> I loved the idea and . . . I was really compelled to do it to see what the impact would be. (Amy Seek, San Francisco)

> I heard about it then, back in 2010, and for me I guess at that point I was really inspired by PARK(ing) Day and all I wanted to do was do it here in Sydney. (John O'Callaghan, Sydney)

> I've seen in maybe Google image like some place that they use the space to do something and say oh [clicks fingers] that's a good idea. Probably we should do it. (Daniel Bouchard, Montréal)

> PARK(ing) Day is quite famous in its own respect I guess. We heard about it, I don't know, it was just a thing and we were like, we should do this thing! (Alan Chen, Montréal)

> I'm not really sure where I heard about it first. Somewhere on the internet, you know? Doing that thing. But it was a few years ago and I wanted to make it happen (Karen Profilio, Sydney)

PARK(ing) Day also inspires considerable effort. Participants spend weeks or even months planning to install a park, meeting with friends and colleagues multiple times to discuss possible ideas and how best to execute them, perhaps seeking donations or support from local businesses, drawing options or even mocking up full-scale trial versions, encouraging people to come along on the day, and often planning how best to maximize their exposure through press releases and social media.

It got pretty intense . . . it was quite a significant time commitment, and I kind of got a bit obsessed with it. . . . I can do it once, maybe twice, but I couldn't do it again. (Jonathon Carle, Sydney)

The time and resources involved are often much more than people anticipate. Architects, planners, and urban designers from the Sydney office of SJB spent weeks collecting used coffee cups, then propagating plants inside these in preparation for PARK(ing) Day in 2012. For their park, they constructed a timber frame onto which cups were set to form an organic sculpture. The plants were placed into these, ready to be selected and taken home by passersby.

At North Sydney Girls High School, preparations began more than a year before the event, building up to a huge effort on the day. Karen, the head teacher, recalls "it was all a bit overwhelming . . . we all worked really hard." For many participants, the labor involved in PARK(ing) Day is substantial.

Others describe similar or even greater efforts. INTERSTICE Architects have participated in PARK(ing) Day nine times. The whole office is involved, including principals Zoee Astrachan and Andrew Dunbar and their seven or so staff, and preparations are extensive.

We spent a lot of resources doing it. Every year we upped the ante, upped the ante, upped the ante, upped the ante. . . . I love having this whole office turn upside down, forget to answer the phone calls while we are making our installations. You know, we waste an awful lot of time doing that, and everyone gets paid to do it. (Andrew Dunbar, San Francisco)

Participants go to considerable lengths to make their parks happen, including all-nighters, taking time off work, corralling friends and family to support the event. In most cases, PARK(ing) Day requires quite a bit of effort.

You basically had to get there at some ungodly hour of the morning in order to make sure that nobody was parking there, because you couldn't reserve the spot overnight. So it was a long day from what I remember. (Liz Ogbu, San Francisco)

Looking back it was pretty, pretty crazy, we went to a lot of effort. . . . I remember we cycled, I was living in Kingsford at the time like just near [UNSW] and we cycled over to Newtown . . . twice I think to pick up the big bike trailers . . . bloody massive ones, which were wild, like really hard to ride with because they were really too heavy for a bike. . . . It was really heavy to be carrying turf and all

the stuff but, but we just did and we cycled slowly . . . it took us a while and then
we eventually got there. (James Patterson, Sydney)

I remember being in excruciating pain trying to help lift lemon trees. I had broken
my pelvis and . . . I was still in a lot of pain. But yeah, it was such an exciting day.
And I took the day off work, which is quite a big deal. (Amy Seek, San Francisco)

Far more than the comparable activities that were undertaken on city
streets prior to its inception—parking meter squats, parties, road witching—
PARK(ing) Day inspires people who see it to get involved, and to undertake
the work necessary to bring more parks into being. What is it that gives
PARK(ing) Day such power and purchase?

Rebar is of course central to the PARK(ing) Day story, but the event must
be understood also as propelled by the power of the idea itself. Rebar later
tried for several years to develop something similar, as Merker explains:

We've never, no one's ever been able to really repeat that exact thing. I think we
spent years trying to find, we did a lot of really cool projects that were very participatory, but nothing that has ever been quite like that.

2.2   A PARK(ing) movement?

In discussing PARK(ing) Day, people search for a term that signals its scope,
its geographic and temporal breadth, and the passion it inspires among
participants. In many cases, participants refer to PARK(ing) Day as a movement, and this is repeated in much of the commentary on the event. Yet
"movement" is a poor descriptor for PARK(ing) Day.

While the boundaries of the term remain unsettled, social movements
are generally understood as "networks of informal interaction between a
plurality of individuals, groups and/or organisations, engaged in a political
and/or cultural conflict, on the basis of a shared collective identity."[1] It is
difficult to apply this to PARK(ing) Day. PARK(ing) Day is looser than social
movements; the aims, aspirations, and approaches of participants are more
diverse and more dynamic.

Participants in PARK(ing) Day may have little interaction and even little
interest in engaging with other participants; many are unaware of others
involved, at the time or before. The organizer of the park at North Sydney
Girls High School in 2013, for example, was unaware of any other parks in
Australia and set out to be the "first."

Some participants do value connection, and follow Rebar's suggestions closely: identifying their planned location on the parkingday.org map and printing and displaying Rebar's materials on the day.

> We wouldn't have done it if there wasn't that website and there hadn't been this movement. I think we needed the kind of confidence; if we were the first ones . . . I don't think we would have done it. (Jonathon Carle, Sydney)

Several participants express a desire for stronger coordination and leadership to give the event greater strength and visibility. Others, in contrast, don't bother identifying their park on the parkingday.org map, and make no effort to seek out other parks in their own city or elsewhere.

Even among those who do value the connection with others in PARK(ing) Day, it is difficult to identify the kind of unifying political or cultural conflict that characterizes social movements. Certainly there is no collective identity, and participants do not see themselves as activists in line with other social movements. Some were explicit about this:

> Well I really just like the idea of using the parking space for another purpose. I mean I'm not a total greenie but I'm not a total capitalist [laughs] either, you know. (Karen Profilio, Sydney)

> I'm not a green leftist. I don't really follow, I'm sorry I don't really follow the political movements around that area. (Suzanne Cohen, Sydney)

Most participants valued the existence of parks in other cities. When the term "movement" is used, it tends to signify the broader reach of PARK(ing) Day, rather than to define its goals or its effects. After initially describing the event as a social movement, one participant shifted when I asked him to clarify this. Deciding that "movement" is not the right term to describe PARK(ing) Day, he explained:

> It's probably overclaiming it a bit in some ways [to call PARK(ing) Day a movement]. I guess I just hope . . . I think I was just trying to find a label for it, you know. What would you call it, um, I don't know, a social initiative? Maybe, maybe some sort of social initiative might be a better term. (James Patterson, Sydney)

The existence of parks in other places is valued for the support it provides for participants' own activities. Participants like being able to look to other cities for ideas and inspiration, and describe being part of something bigger as exciting.

I read it was international, so I was more interested to participate. . . . It's bigger and I thought that it's cool to make something at the same time as the whole planet. (Elyse Benoit, Montréal)

I think that's the value in PARK(ing) Day, is actually you have this international discussion and then people talk to people and cities talk to cities, particularly when there is so much interest in things like placemaking and walkable communities and streets for people. (Bonnie Parfit, Sydney)

I think that the bigger the better. And I think that because the message is universal, . . . regardless of where you are and how different our relationship is to the public realm, in these different places it's still . . . something that everybody can relate to, so I think that is exciting. (Anais Mathez, Montréal)

Perhaps most importantly, the international reach of PARK(ing) Day provides credibility and legitimacy. The fact that PARK(ing) Day takes place in other cities is generally valued as a means of strengthening local agendas. Far from an overarching collective goal, those agendas turn out to be quite varied.

2.3   PARK(ing) as a vehicular idea

Gregor McLennan and Thomas Osborne coined the term "vehicular idea" to explain the way ideas circulate in contemporary society, and the way in which certain ideas "travel." Beginning with Zygmunt Bauman's claim that the role of the intellectual has shifted from "legislator" (authoritative, presenting definitive ideas based on theoretical insight and political commitment) to "interpreter" (more modest, relativistic, and conversational, working to advance understanding by translating "texts"),[2] McLennan and Osborne highlight the growing salience of intellectuals as "mediators": brokers of ideas.[3]

In place of hierarchical and linear models of knowledge, the production of ideas has become democratized so that almost everyone is involved in some form of knowledge work. The result has been a shift in emphasis away from individual "gurus" as the source of policy ideas.[4] With political culture emphasizing deliberation and participation, and with society increasingly networked and media-focused, this shift entails a move away from relatively stable, normative ideals to more mobile, provisional ideas: constructs like joined-up government,[5] the Third Way,[6] antisocial behavior,[7] sustainability,[8] or creative cities.[9]

Vehicular ideas can be understood as problem-solving devices, tools to move things along. They are open-ended, inclusive, and available for appropriation and, in this process of appropriation, for modification. Fluidity is an essential and productive feature. Comparable to the incompletely theorized agreements that Cass Sunstein argues are pervasive in and central to judge-made law,[10] vehicular ideas provide discursive rather than doctrinal unity, a "virtual" theoretical space in which contrary emphases and even a degree of dissent can be accommodated. They must be robust enough to provoke opposition, but of the sort that can be folded into the mix. As vehicular ideas evolve, the changes must appear immanent within the original concept, rather than new manifest claims.

The central claim in PARK(ing) Day, that paying a parking meter legitimates use of the space for purposes other than parking a car, fits well with this definition. Deployed as shorthand for ideas about authority and accessibility, the lease provided a way to claim legitimacy for the activity, and to establish its everyday, uncontroversial nature. The idea that a lease is created by paying a meter sits well with lay understandings, with a "logic" apparent in its earlier use: the potential for parking meters to create a lease was considered in some detail during the development and deployment of the new technology in the 1930s, and was the subject of litigation shortly after the introduction of the first parking meter in 1935.[11] Similarly, commentators on newly introduced parking meters in cities across America made reference to the "rental" of parking spaces during the 1940s, and more recent historians have since described parking meters in comparable terms.[12] Rebar's invocation of legality through the lease was thus one that could be easily understood and explained.

The purported lease also provided vast scope for variation by individual users: the space could be used for anything at all, just not the parking of a car. The idea was very much available for development, emphasized in Rebar's Creative Commons license and how-to guide, and its potential constituency was wide open. As the many participants in the event have demonstrated, the idea has harbored a wide range of perspectives, from statements about gay rights to challenging the dominance of big oil, from providing services for vulnerable communities to raising awareness about local environmental issues. PARK(ing) Day has proved both robust and malleable.

While vehicular ideas evoke elements of principled theory or committed ideology, they are largely resistant to more rigorous theorization.[13] A vehicular idea can be measured less by its truth or wisdom, and more by its availability, ubiquity, and quality of speaking in the moment. Vehicular ideas have multiple interpretations and succeed because of their propensity to travel, their ability "to move swiftly and smoothly between policymaking sites, and to lubricate new (or rebadged) initiatives in distant locales."[14] They are readily "mediatized." This, Osborne explains, means not just capable of being taken up by the media, but being "performative, capable of arousing attention and making a communicative difference."[15] Vehicular ideas are conceived not for longevity but mobility: they make things happen at a particular time, and may have a limited shelf life.[16]

PARK(ing) Day was very much a problem-solving device, a tool used by Rebar to catalyze reflection and propel debate about the allocation of public space and about processes of urban planning. Like other vehicular ideas, PARK(ing) Day took inspiration from principled, committed ideals: concerns about climate change, car dependence, and environmental sustainability; debates about property, ownership, and belonging; efforts to enhance democratic participation in the making of the city. Yet, conceived in a bar and deployed on the street after just a few weeks of planning, it was not an end point but a step toward one. PARK(ing) was not the product of rigorous theoretical development. The legal analysis on which the event was based was thin: Rebar made no effort to investigate the legal technicalities, factors like possession that determine whether the payment could in fact constitute a lease.[17] With diminishing participation in both San Francisco and Sydney, PARK(ing) Day may well be coming to an end.

Vehicular ideas are products of their time. The first years of the twenty-first century witnessed a marked increase in the sharing of ideas and information, with the internet and social media facilitating the immediate, low-cost and large-scale sharing of images, film, and text. Rebar's first PARK(ing) installation was held shortly after Osborne and McLennan published their work on vehicular ideas. Similarly, the number of comparable events—parking meter parties, parking meter squats, road witching, outdoor living rooms, sidewalk landscaping, (P)LOT—increased dramatically in the early 2000s (or at least the documentation and discussion of these practices increased). The coincidence of PARK(ing) Day with the explosion of social media is significant in understanding the rapid expansion of the event.

It coincided neatly with the burgeoning open source movement—reconceiving the metered parking space as a kind of platform or API that you could plug any sort of "app" into. And, of course, it took early advantage of nascent social media tools to spread way beyond San Francisco, to go viral and infect other cities, inspiring other activists and artists like us in New York City. I just think it was a really great project. Not all that different from the one in Oxford in '03, but the technology and the activists weren't really ready for it yet in '03, I think. (Aaron Naparstek, New York)

The idea of vehicularity resonates too with contemporary scholarship on policy transfer in political science.[18] Here too, mobility and mutation, transit and transaction are increasingly emphasized. PARK(ing) Day is one of many concepts to benefit from technologies facilitating the rapid sharing of ideas. Rather than a market in which the "best" policy is selected for transfer to other jurisdictions, there is an increasing understanding that policies move when they successfully combine bundles of ideas and practices and that, in the process of movement, policies are reshaped and themselves reshape the policy environment.

With respect to ideas shared digitally, W. Lance Bennett and Alexandra Segerberg emphasize the importance of this reshaping in the process of movement.[19] Ideas are well suited for digital travels when they are easy to imitate, adapt personally, and share broadly with others. Against a backdrop of structural fragmentation and individualization in postindustrial democracies, Bennett and Segeberg describe a shift from collective action—political parties and broad reform movements organized on the basis of social group identity, membership, or ideology—to what they term "connective action," in which engagement with politics is an expression of personal hopes, lifestyles, and grievances.[20] Bennett and Segeberg highlight two key elements in connective action: inclusive and easily personalized action frames (like the PARK(ing) Day lease), and digital communication technologies enabling further personalization (like the blogs, webpages, and social media accounts through which images of PARK(ing) Day are shared). Coproduction and codistribution characterize this connective logic, such that "taking public action or contributing to a common good becomes an act of personal expression and recognition or self-validation."[21]

In understanding the success of PARK(ing) Day as a vehicular idea, it is important to consider its relationship to broader trends. For vehicular ideas as for other ideas, the market is not free: the success of particular vehicular ideas is connected to politics.[22] As noted in the literature on policy transfer, the ideas that are most mobile are those that align with the interests of already powerful groups and political blocs.[23]

The coincidence between PARK(ing) Day and other trends in planning and urban policy is thus significant. PARK(ing) Day worked in part because of its alignment with the questioning of the place of cars in cities, the move toward pedestrian-oriented urban design, the deliberative or participatory turn in the planning profession, and the widespread adoption of creative city policies. In turn, the mobility of PARK(ing) Day was predicated on the wide range of supportive conditions and enabling networks on which those debates relied, including those bound up with the "viral spread of creative city policies," characterized by Jamie Peck and Nik Theodore as

> stylized, but ground-truthed claims about the underlying causes of innovation-rich growth in cities like Austin, TX and San Francisco; Richard Florida's brand of guru performativity; the easy manualization of creative-city policy techniques by consultants and other policy intermediaries; and, not least, the competitive anxieties and fiscal constraints of cities around the world, which effectively constitute a ready market for low-cost, feel good makeovers of business-as-usual forms of urban entrepreneurialism.[24]

PARK(ing) Day, many participants explained, can be understood as part of broader developments and discourse in contemporary cities. Participants described the event as indicative of a zeitgeist or a change in thinking, suggesting that PARK(ing) Day was just one of many ways in which ideas about urban development are shifting.

> I don't know how much of that is PARK(ing) Day that has contributed to that but I think it's part of a general movement towards rethinking and revalorizing urban space. (David Alfaro Clark, Montréal)

Reflection on PARK(ing) Day and these shifts is highly temporal, with many references to a particular "moment." Participants emphasize the currency, the pace, and even the mobility of the ideas at stake in PARK(ing) Day.

> I would say PARK(ing) Day . . . [is] really reflective of where we're at right now in the planning and development and design of our cities (John O'Callaghan, Sydney)

The fact that PARK(ing) Day originated in San Francisco is an important part of its influence. San Francisco is one of those "innovation-rich" places that other cities look to for policy guidance, one of the key centers singled out by Peck and Theodore: the city is regularly placed at or near the top in rankings of global standing and influence.[25] For Richard Florida, San Francisco is one of the cities "where the streets are paved with ideas," far outpacing any other US city in attracting venture capital.[26] For Richard Barbrook and Andy Cameron, the "cultural bohemianism of San Francisco" was a key component of the Californian ideology, "the heterodox orthodoxy for the information age," which they argue was rapidly copied in Europe and elsewhere ("as usual").[27] The enormous influence of California on contemporary design was the subject of an exhibition at the London Museum of Design in 2017, "California: Designing Freedom," which proclaimed "Californian products have influenced contemporary life across the globe to such an extent that in some ways we are all now Californians."[28]

For participants in Sydney and Montréal, the fact that PARK(ing) Day originated in San Francisco provided it with credibility and legitimacy. For those in San Francisco, the international scope of PARK(ing) Day was less important. One commented:

> I guess, I think my concerns with like how cities are run stops not too far beyond the borders of the city I live in . . . I guess I don't really care what happens in other places. But if I was there I would, and so I definitely think . . . that's great [that PARK(ing) Day is an international event]. (Alex Gregor, San Francisco)

PARK(ing) Day emerged from the right place, at the right time, with the right connections. Through their invocation of the lease, and of legality and legitimacy more generally, Rebar took an idea and propelled it into vehicularity.

2.4 The aesthetics of PARK(ing): legality and vehicularity

> Part of the "trick" [in a vehicular idea] is that the mediator succeeds in integrating circuits and debates in the very process of facilitating some *disjunction*.[29]

Vehicular ideas do not simply describe the sentiments of the already powerful; they link, but they also disrupt. PARK(ing) Day is powerful because it connected and contributed to several existing networks. Crucially, it did so with a novel approach. PARK(ing) Day provided a new perspective from which to consider contemporary debates about the city, and a new way of drawing people in to those debates. It did so with an everyday and seemingly uncontroversial tactic, that of "renting" a parking space.

The debates on which PARK(ing) Day drew, and into which it fed, can be linked in their focus on change. DIY urbanism, participatory planning, creative city policies, new urbanism, and transit-oriented design are all directed, albeit to varying extents, toward identifying flaws in existing processes of spatial production. Much of the work in these areas has centered on identifying problems with current laws and policies (street designs based on engineering for high-speed traffic, parking requirements based on maximum visitor numbers, planning rules based on separating different land uses), and on proposing solutions to address them (creative city indexes, deliberative design workshops, placemaking, traffic calming, mixed-use and transit-oriented developments).

Even those initiatives most like PARK(ing) Day were presented as proposals for change, as extraordinary events intended to highlight problems with the status quo. Sherk and Rakowitz's installations were exhibited as experimental projects that challenged existing systems. Sherk's 2012 *Portable Park IV* involved considerable resources and institutional support (a kickstarter campaign, collaboration with a curator and a college, support from the Getty Foundation and the shopping center where it was installed), as did Rakowitz's *(P)LOT* (hosted by art galleries in Austria and Italy). These were ideas developed by artists to get people talking, provocative installations rather than everyday activities.

The New York parking squats, Ontario parking meter parties, and Oxford road witching lacked the institutional support and artistic expertise of Sherk and Rakowitz's projects, but they were comparable in that each was led by identifiable groups or individuals, and each was conducted in a form of challenge or protest. Advertising for parking meter parties included calls to "Contact your city councillor and demand bike lanes";[30] activities included environmental protests. Like road witching and the Brooklyn gathering, the organizers of parking meter parties invited members of the public to join their party, rather than take over their own parking spaces.

In its openness, PARK(ing) Day can be distinguished too from related efforts in planning and urban design to rethink urban development. Influential texts like Donald Shoup's *The High Price of Free Parking* or Peter Newman and Jeffrey Kenworthy's *Sustainability in Cities: Overcoming Automobile Dependence* are typical of these efforts, and of many of the activities described above, in that they identify problems in current planning practices (cars are given too much space, at the expense of walking and cycling and with negative consequences for health and happiness; urban sprawl is damaging the environment and the economy, the public realm is being privatized and downgraded, community and social capital are being eroded).[31] The identification of those problems is followed by calls for change (more participatory planning, more green spaces, better infrastructure for pedestrians and cyclists, upgrades to public transport, more mixing of land uses, and greater densities in strategic locations). While the particular problems identified and the particular solutions proposed may vary (density and participatory planning, for example, do not always work together), calls for some form of change are consistent.

PARK(ing) Day does not complain about the order of things, and it does not call for reform to that order. PARK(ing) Day can be understood as a matter of aesthetics, a reworking of what philosopher Jacques Rancière describes as the "distribution of the sensible."[32] The sensible is that which is capable of being sensed, and there are multiple ways of making sense of things. The distribution of the sensible is the way in which certain orders or ways of seeing and making sense of the world are taken for granted or prioritized over others, in which "abstract and arbitrary forms of symbolization of hierarchy are embodied as perceptive givens, in which a social destination is anticipated by the evidence of a perceptive universe, of a way of being, saying and seeing."[33]

As Rancière explains, the relationships between things and the way they are sensed are explicitly connected to power.[34] The configuration of the sphere of aesthetics is strongly connected to the political distribution of the perceptible, "that system of places . . . that allots to each his or her proper role and function."[35] Politics is not a matter of laws and constitutions, Rancière argues, but of configuring the distribution of the sensible such that those laws and constitutions make sense.[36] Politics then is an effort to restage or reshape social issues, to question the boundary between the social or public and the domestic: "before all else, [politics] is an intervention in the visible and the sayable. . . . *The essential work of politics is the configuration of its own space. It is to make the world of its subjects and its operations seen.*"[37]

A disruption or repositioning of the relationship between ways of sensing constitutes "dissensus": a "perturbation of the normal relationship between sense and sense . . . that brings about a more radical way of seeing the conflict."[38] By destabilizing existing relationships, dissensus creates an opportunity to revise one's role or function, a new space of equality, "the equality of a common language and the common capacity to invent objects, stories and arguments."[39]

Rancière illustrates this with an example from a workers' newspaper during the 1848 French revolution. Here a joiner describes a day at work, and in doing so reveals the connection between ways of sensing and one's place in the world: an artisan who knows that work does not wait, and whose senses are geared to this lack of time. When the joiner stops to enjoy a view of the palace through the window, he steps outside his place in the world, and "acts as if he possessed the perspective."[40] To focus on aesthetics requires the worker to ignore certain facts (to whom the palace actually belongs, the vanity of the nobles, the labor of the workers embodied in its construction), and it is this ignorance, Rancière explains, that provides the basis for a new sensible world: "the aesthetic rupture breaks [the existing] order by constructing another as if."[41]

As a vehicular idea facilitating disjunction, PARK(ing) Day can be read as a staging of dissensus, a disruption of the established forms of perception to create a new way of seeing. As PARK(ing) Day progressed, Rebar themselves were particularly interested in the potential to unsettle perceptions of public space, inspired by Pierre Bourdieu's notions of *doxa* (beliefs that explain the way the world works and are reproduced and reinforced by the physical environment) and *habitus* (our ways of operating within it) and Michel de Certeau's notion of tactics (actions which exploit gaps within wider systems to disrupt them and to generate novel solutions).[42] Rebar saw PARK(ing) Day as operating within an undervalued niche space, exploiting a loophole, "a tactic at once radical but superficially unthreatening to the system of spatial commodification it critiqued. Although the space we collectively allocate to parking—how much, where, for whom and at what cost—is usually hotly contested, Park(ing) Day operated within a discrete unit of that contested terrain, neutralizing potential backlash with a sense of humor."[43]

PARK(ing) Day takes the parking meter, an everyday technology, and approaches it with a degree of disregard for the circumstances in which it operates. Like Rancière's joiner, Rebar ignores certain facts in framing PARK(ing) Day (how the meter was built, the ends it serves, the legal doctrines to which it connects). In doing so, Rebar escapes conventional understandings (interpretations of the parking meter as the achievement of an efficient system for managing car parking, for example, or as a tool

of money-hungry local authorities). PARK(ing) Day sidesteps these interpretations, and in turn the social order in which they are embedded, and
thereby serves to construct "another as if."[44] As Merker describes it, "With
Rebar providing others with 'permission' to act, new users rushed into this
niche, challenging the existing value system encoded within this humble,
everyday space. The parking space became a zone of potential, a surface
onto which the intentions of any number of political, social or cultural
agendas could be projected."[45]

Instead of affirming existing relationships and calling for change,
PARK(ing) Day creates new connections between things and the thoughts
attached to them. In PARK(ing) Day, as in Rancière's politics of aesthetics,
the point is not to reverse existing hierarchies (for example, by elevating
pedestrian-focused planning over the more dominant work of car-focused
traffic engineering), but to reveal a new way of looking at the world outside
those hierarchies.

In its invocation of the lease, PARK(ing) Day both challenges and confirms the order of the street. PARK(ing) Day disrupts the logic of parking
spaces as places to be used for the storage of cars, but conforms to—perhaps
entrenches—the order in which the proper use of those spaces is legitimated
through purchases via the meter. Again, the tension in Rebar's use of property is apparent, and consistent with Rancière's claim that politics is always
bound up with the police, in a relationship that is always unfolding.[46]

> It's slightly naughty and it just sort of you know, in a very middleclass safe kind
> of way of corrupting the system [laughs], and it's only for one day and you're kind
> of playing in the rules but you're not. (Kerryn Wilmot, Sydney)

Unlike its precursors, PARK(ing) Day was not presented as an activity
requiring leadership or expertise. On the contrary, PARK(ing) Day was
expressly presented as an uncontroversial activity that could be undertaken
by anyone, in any place. For Rebar, "the essence of the tactic was to legally
claim a parking space using materials that were symbolically associated
with parks—trees, lawn, and a bench. Rebar treated the idea itself as open
source and applied a Creative Commons license: as long as it was not used
for profit, we allowed it to be replicated by anyone, anywhere."[47]

Significantly, PARK(ing) Day was not conceived as a protest or a plea for
reform. Rebar did set out to prompt reflection and debate about the city
and the way spaces within it are allocated, but they placed considerable

emphasis on the legality and legitimacy of the method by which they did this. Rebar's how-to guide recommends "appealing to law enforcement's civic sense of pride rather than antagonizing them" and includes a caution: "Remember, **you are not protesting**."[48]

For participants, this distinction is important.

> I liked that it was a really different spirit to a protest. . . . We're renting that space so we can use it for what we want. So it had a really nice happy vibe to it, you know we're going to have balloons and trees and there aren't going to be police horses coming to kick us off. . . . PARK(ing) Day's just a really simple idea to take over one space, in a legal way and just use it for something else. (Eytan Rocheta, Sydney)

Paying the parking meter, Rebar argued, meant that the space could legitimately be used for activities other than the parking of cars. This claim to legality, and its explanation through the trope of the lease, exploits and perturbs the very conservatism and formalism of the law. Law itself becomes the instrument of its perversion—law becomes the vehicular idea.

> Well if you're renting space to private people, why can't we put anything there? That leverage of existing legislation that allows for the private use of public space, that's the foot in the door for PARK(ing) Day and then everything else. (Andrew Dunbar, San Francisco)

Rebar's argument about law propelled PARK(ing) Day into vehicularity: integrating networks and debates while at the same time facilitating a disjunction, staging a dissensus that creates a new space for intervention in the city.

Part Two   Property and the Performance of Legality

Figure 3.1
Ticket inspector smiles as she looks onto the curbside library (filled with books on public space) created on Market Street near Duboce Avenue, San Francisco, by Lawrence Cuevas and Dina Dobkin (pictured). Image: Lawrence Cuevas.

3 PARK(ing) Law: Pluralism and Performance

Law is central to PARK(ing) Day. The precise forms of law at play, however, are not readily apparent. In many cases, the event takes place with very little reflection on its legal aspects: Rebar's claim that a lease is created by the parking meter is simply accepted. In other cases, participants and officials look more closely at the laws at issue, and in doing so reveal a regulatory framework that is more complex, and more contingent.

Among many possible interpretations of the law at stake, the successful assertion of legality on PARK(ing) Day depends on participants believing in their right to reclaim the parking space in this way, and on the lack or inability of people with differing views to challenge those installations. In giving form to these beliefs, parks themselves help to bring purported legalities into being. By enrolling a wide range of human and nonhuman actors—parking meters, passing pedestrians, turf, potted plants, music, food, games, pets, and performers—many participants succeed (at least temporarily) in giving effect to their preferred legal interpretations.

PARK(ing) Day succeeds in its invocation of legality not because payment of a meter creates a lease, nor because there is a gap in the rules regulating parking. PARK(ing) Day is effective because of the multiplicity of interpretive possibilities and the crucial role of social practice in choosing among these. PARK(ing) Day dramatizes, and depends upon, the ongoing interplay between law and society.

3.1 PARK(ing) in a niche

Rebar's claim that PARK(ing) Day is legal draws on a reading of the San Francisco Transportation Code, which provides that it is a violation "To

Park a vehicle . . . in any Parking Space controlled by a Parking Meter without immediately making advance payment for Parking."[1]

Matthew Passmore, the member of Rebar trained (and then still working by day) as a lawyer, reasoned that this created a loophole or "niche" that could be exploited to legitimize use of the space for other purposes—like building parks.

> I was a lawyer at the time and I had looked into the law, and because of sort of sloppy legislative drafting in San Francisco, it's not expressly against the law to put something else in a parking space other than a car as long as you're paying the meter.

When Passmore mentioned this idea to Bela and Merker, the two were excited about its potential. As Merker explains:

> We read the zoning code and we read the parking code . . . I remember that being a pretty major order of business when we were planning it. We spent a lot of time, we printed out the code and we spent time together reading it at the Latin American and really had discussions about like, is this legal? . . . It is legal and so actually it's a loophole, which is really interesting and also kind of transgressive in a different way. So we're transgressing, you know, a social code, but not a legal one. And so it really clearly, when we kind of realized that that was the case, it really felt like a sweet spot.

Yet while paying a parking meter avoids incurring the penalty that would otherwise be attracted by parking a car, its significance for people wishing to undertake other activities in a parking space is less clear. Recognizing this, Passmore acknowledged that Rebar's legal argument was "flimsy." When I asked how strong he thought the argument was, Passmore replied:

> At its best, it relies on a very technical reading, "You didn't say cars and only cars," do you know what I mean? Or "Cars to the exclusion of all other uses. You didn't say that, you just said cars. So you're not expressly making other things against the law the way they do in, say, New York." So not very strong.

The argument was not tested, however, as there was no interaction at all between police or parking inspectors when Rebar installed their first park in 2005. In 2006, curious about how officials would interpret the legality of the installation, Passmore asked a passing ticket inspector:

> "So, what do you think? How would you ticket this?" And he's like, "Well, I don't think I would. Like I see you're paying the meter, and there's no license plate to write a ticket to, I would leave this for the police." And he was very cool, he was

very friendly [laughs]. We had a funny conversation, he was like "Yeah, that's interesting. Cool."

Rebar's experience is not unusual. The small scale, short duration, and largely public character of PARK(ing) Day's parks means that the legal status of the event is rarely questioned. Across all three of the cities I studied, parks are in many cases installed and removed without any interaction with police or other officials.

In both Sydney and Montréal, the rules regulating parking are expressed in terms similar to San Francisco's. Payment of a parking meter allows penalties for parking in the relevant space to be avoided, but its significance for other uses is not explained. In Montréal, the By-Law Concerning Traffic and Parking provides: "No road vehicle may be parked in a parking space controlled by a parking meter unless the parking time for that space has been paid."[2] The Road Rules applicable in Sydney provide: "A driver must not park in a ticket parking area unless a current parking ticket is displayed."[3]

While most participants in PARK(ing) Day do not attract official attention, a small number of police, rangers, and parking inspectors have engaged with some parks in all three cities. In some cases, officials have followed Rebar's analysis and applied parking restrictions to PARK(ing) Day installations. One San Francisco park was asked by a parking inspector to move at the end of the two-hour period, so as to comply with the maximum time prescribed for parking in the space.[4]

In Sydney, a park installed by a group of urban designers from the design studio SJB was challenged by a ranger in 2012. SJB had installed the park—an organic sculpture created with succulents planted in recycled coffee cups—in a parking space directly outside the building in which their office is located. There was no parking meter, so SJB had not purchased a ticket, but they planned to comply with the time limit for parking in that space. The parking inspector accepted the participants' claim that purchasing a ticket could enable use of a parking space for purposes other than parking a car. However, the parking inspector did not accept that the group could occupy a space in which parking was free. This was resolved fairly simply, following the logic of the "lease": at the parking inspector's request, the group moved their park one block along the street, to a section where meters had been installed (figures 3.2 and 3.3). They then purchased a ticket and continued without challenge.

Figures 3.2, 3.3
Staff from SJB carrying materials and then setting up for a second time in a new location with a meter, Crown Street, Surry Hills, Sydney, 2012. Images: Jonathan Knapp, SJB.

Other parking officials have suggested that participants need not even pay the parking meter, noting that parking rules don't apply to anything but cars.

> They came by and we were feeding the meter, because I think that's what it says on Rebar's instruction that you should feed the meter all day. The meter reader just said "Where am I going to chalk your tires? Don't worry." (Alex Gregor, San Francisco)

These four different responses by parking officials—enforcing the installation of parks according to the same rules as the parking of cars; treating the installation of parks as permissible only in metered parking spaces; leaving the regulation of parks to police, provided a ticket is purchased; or suggesting that parking rules do not apply to parks at all—reveal a range of official efforts to apply the laws regulating parking to a novel activity. In these divergent responses, the law looks less like a gap or niche, and more like a matter requiring careful, comprehensive, and perhaps also creative interpretation.

Application of the law always requires some degree of interpretation, as Lon Fuller explains. Refuting H. L. A. Hart's claim that the law can be applied without interpretation in "core" cases, Fuller argues that even in those cases interpretation *is* required—it is simply that in "core" or "easy" cases one can see clearly enough what the rule "is aiming at in general" that the interpretation can be conducted with little thought.[5] In *all* cases, Fuller argues, we interpret the law by asking ourselves, "What can this rule be for? What evil does it seek to avert? What good is it intended to promote? . . . We must, in other words, be sufficiently capable of putting ourselves in the position of those who drafted the rule to know what they thought 'ought to be.' It is in the light of this 'ought' that we must decide what the rule 'is.'"[6]

Highlighting the significance of parking for understandings of legality, both Hart and Fuller use an example involving parks and vehicles. For Fuller, a hypothetical rule excluding vehicles from a park is easy to apply to a noisy automobile not because "noisy automobile" is a "standard instance" of "vehicle," as Hart would have it. Instead, it is because on almost any interpretation of the purpose of the prohibition we know, "without thinking," that a noisy automobile must be excluded.[7] To determine whether a tricycle or whether a World War II vehicle mounted on a pedestal should also be excluded requires reference not to the meaning of "vehicle" but to the intent of the statute. Legal claims always require reference to the background social purpose of the law. For Fuller, there is no black-letter law: the kind of neutral, technical interpretation proposed by Hart, and by Rebar, is not possible.

Application of the rules regulating parking to PARK(ing) Day requires reference to provisions beyond the particular phrase identified by Rebar. Determining whether the installation of a park is amongst the evils to be averted or the goods to be promoted by parking regulations necessitates inquiry into the purpose of those regulations. This is not simple, as indicated by the divergence in official responses to PARK(ing) Day. One might argue that the passage of parking restrictions—when parking meters were introduced in the 1930s the streets were being clogged by the haphazard parking of cars[8]—was intended to preserve the use of the street for a wide range of uses, from commerce to protest to parades to play, to which streets had been put for many centuries.[9] On a narrower approach, parking rules might be read as intended to maximize the availability of parking spaces, particularly for potential shoppers visiting nearby businesses. A reading informed by contemporary urban policy might see the purpose of current versions of parking rules as encouraging people to walk, cycle, or take public transport rather than driving into the city, especially to congested inner-city areas. The purpose might vary between jurisdictions; within them it might even vary depending on the nature of the street. If the legality of a park under parking regulations were to be put before a judge for determination, it is difficult to predict what would be decided. PARK(ing) Day might fall within the scope of parking regulations; more likely it would not.

3.2 PARK(ing) in a larger legal landscape

Since the Middle Ages, the common law has protected public roads from obstruction by unreasonable uses. Efforts to challenge the introduction of parking meters in the 1930s failed in the face of this protection, which confirmed that the parking of cars in public streets is a privilege, not a right, and one limited by a requirement for reasonableness. The primary authority for that proposition was *R v Cross*, a case from 1812 in which the proprietor of a stage line in London was found guilty of public nuisance.[10] Deciding that 45 minutes was too long for the coach to remain in the street, Lord Ellenborough noted: "A stage-coach may set down or take up passengers in the street, this being necessary for public convenience; but it must be done in a reasonable time; and private premises must be procured for the coach to stop in during the interval between the end of one journey and the commencement of another. No one can make a stableyard of the king's highway."[11]

The bar against obstruction arises from the historical origins of public roads as easements over private land.[12] Instead of a physical boundary, highways were constituted by a right for the king and his subjects to "pass and repass." This meant that private landowners could not obstruct travelers passing over their land, and also that public authorities could neither license nor conduct any obstructions in their own right. Any unreasonable obstruction of the roadway constituted a nuisance, even if the obstructing activity occurred near and not actually on the roadway, and regardless of whether any travelers were in fact obstructed.[13] Initially enforced under common law, the right to passage and concomitant prohibition on obstructions is now codified in various transport and traffic laws applicable in Sydney, Montréal, and San Francisco.

What constitutes a reasonable use and a reasonable obstruction has shifted over time. With respect to protests and public gatherings, Rachel Vorspan documents a highly politicized approach to the determination of what was and was not reasonable during the nineteenth and twentieth centuries.[14] Focusing on the sidewalk rather than the roadway, Nicholas Blomley similarly emphasizes restrictions on public access to the street, describing a "logic of pedestrianism" operating to prioritize circulation over other activities.[15] Yet the courts have not always decided against the nontraveling public. In *DPP v Jones*, the House of Lords found that a peaceful protest on the highway near Stonehenge did not constitute a nuisance.[16] Delivering an encouraging decision for PARK(ing) Day, Lord Irvine explained that the law should not make unlawful "activities such as making a sketch, taking a photograph, handing out leaflets, collecting money for charity, singing carols, playing in a Salvation Army band, children playing a game on the pavement, having a picnic, or reading a book."[17]

In a decision with which Lords Clyde and Hutton agreed, Lord Irvine concluded, "the public highway is a public place which the public may enjoy for any reasonable purpose, provided the activity in question does not amount to a public or private nuisance and does not obstruct the highway by unreasonably impeding the primary right of the public to pass and repass: within these qualifications there is a public right of peaceful assembly on the highway."[18]

The legality of PARK(ing) Day is complicated further by the existence of other laws that could also be applied to the installation of parks. Officials have looked beyond parking regulations to assess the legality of the event in several cases. Most commonly, when police and other officials intervene on PARK(ing) Day they justify their actions with concerns about risk and safety. An instruction to close down the park installed on King Street, Newtown, in Sydney was explained by one of the police officers involved on the basis of public safety:

> The police have attended just to make sure that everything was in order and that there was no danger to any of the participants or any members of the public. . . . I'd say the reason why they were asked to move is just because of the danger they place on themselves by being on the road. But not having the appropriate safety equipment in place, you've also got to take into consideration, we look at occupational health and safety risks that the organizers of these groups have also got to take into consideration the safety and well-being of the people involved in the public assembly.[19]

Beyond the laws regulating parking, there are many other laws that are potentially relevant to PARK(ing) Day. As the police officer's comment above suggests, there are numerous laws covering public safety, occupational health and safety, public assemblies, and other matters that could be applied to PARK(ing) Day. In Sydney, an official wishing to challenge the installation of a park has a wide range of rules on which to draw. For example:

- The Roads Act 1993 (NSW) provides that "a roads authority may direct . . . any person who causes an obstruction or encroachment on a public road . . . to remove the obstruction or encroachment."[20]
- The Local Government Act 1993 (NSW) provides that "A council employee who is authorised in writing by the Commissioner of Police for the purposes of this section ('enforcement officer') may give a direction to a person in a public place if the enforcement officer believes, on reasonable grounds, that the person's behaviour or presence in the place is obstructing another person or persons or traffic."[21]
- The Local Government Act 1993 (NSW) further provides that "A council may abate a public nuisance or order a person responsible for a public nuisance to abate it" and "Nuisance consists of interference with the

enjoyment of public or private rights in a variety of ways. A nuisance is 'public' if it materially affects the reasonable comfort and convenience of a sufficient class of people to constitute the public or a section of the public. For example, any wrongful or negligent act or omission in a public road that interferes with the full, safe and convenient use by the public of their right of passage is a public nuisance."[22]

- The Law Enforcement (Powers and Responsibilities) Act 2002 (NSW) provides that "A police officer may give a direction to a person in a public place if the police officer believes on reasonable grounds that the person's behaviour or presence in the place . . . is obstructing another person or persons or traffic."[23]

Other laws are also potentially relevant, depending on the nature of activities undertaken by PARK(ing) Day participants. For parks that include activities such as serving food, serving alcohol, displaying signage, holding a performance, or painting or marking the street, many other rules and regulations might be applied.

None of these laws expressly prohibit the use of parking spaces for activities other than parking cars; each merely provides discretion to authorities that could potentially be used to question or sanction people building parks. The discretionary nature of these laws is amplified by their wording: many of the terms are not clearly defined—such as "work," "structure," "nuisance," and "assembly"—and are the subject of extensive case law. Again, much interpretive work (drawing on the social purpose of the law, not merely the text of the regulation) would be required to determine their applicability to PARK(ing) Day.

In San Francisco and Montréal, the legal context is similar. The Canadian Criminal Code, for example, includes provisions criminalizing public nuisance, loitering, or obstructing others in a public place;[24] city bylaws prohibit assemblies and gatherings that disturb the peace, public order, or safety on public thoroughfares.[25] In San Francisco, the Police Code prohibits obstructing any street, sidewalk, or passageway,[26] and the California Penal Code prohibits public nuisances.[27] There is a very broad range of rules and regulations that could be applied to challenge the installation of a park.

Rarely, however, are any of these laws raised in response to PARK(ing) Day. The vast majority of parks are installed, operated, and removed without any interactions with police, rangers, or parking inspectors. Most people undertake PARK(ing) Day in line with Rebar's approach—turning up on the day, paying the meter and building a park, then packing up and returning the space to its former condition—and most are successful in doing so without challenge from police or other officials.

For some participants, particularly those working in larger institutions such as schools and universities, greater legal certainty is required. A few participants have approached local authorities to seek permission before the event. Like the responses to physical parks installed on PARK(ing) Day, responses to prospective inquiries about the legalities of proposed parks and procedures for compliance with these vary considerably. This is because there is no readily applicable framework for the assessment or approval of PARK(ing) Day.

In San Francisco, the Transportation Code provides for the approval of events temporarily using or occupying public streets (although this is a fairly involved process targeted to major events such as film production, street fairs, and athletic events) and for the temporary exclusive use of parking meters (limited to construction, use of skip bins ["debris boxes"], and related purposes, not to more creative uses such as installing parks).[28] The Public Works Code enables the granting of permits for sidewalk landscaping and for sidewalk improvements, though these are more permanent interventions than parks (and until 2016 provided the legal basis for parklets).[29] That code provides also for the granting of permits for tables and chairs on the footpath or roadway, though such permits must be issued to businesses and must relate to chairs and tables installed adjacent to those businesses.[30]

This lack of a suitable legislative basis led to the passing of a new ordinance in 2016, providing a clearer legal basis for interventions such as parklets in the city.[31] The new ordinance amended the Administrative Code, Public Works Code, and Police Codes to establish a new "Places for People Program." This enables the City to grant approval for the creation of a "people place" by occupying the location with temporary, reversible physical treatments or improvements and/or activating the location with programming. The process is rather involved, however, and more suited to longer-lasting parklets than the fleeting parks constructed on PARK(ing) Day.

Similarly in Montréal, most boroughs have a range of bylaws for such activities, but none that are readily applicable to PARK(ing) Day. There have also been recent efforts to introduce more flexible regulatory processes.

Significantly, many boroughs have introduced permits for *placottoirs* (defined as places for meeting and relaxation, open to all and without sales or commercial service).[32] In Le Plateau-Mont-Royal, for example, the Règlement sur l'Occupation du Domaine Public provides for the approval of terraces and outdoor seating associated with cafés, and also for *placottoirs* that are not connected with cafés or restaurants.[33] Again, however, the fees, taxes, documentation, insurance, and other requirements necessary to obtain approval are poorly matched to the brief and low-budget nature of PARK(ing) Day.

In Sydney, there has been less effort to accommodate temporary events within regulatory frameworks. The Roads Act provides for the permitting of various activities in the street, such as footway restaurants, street vending, and road events, but PARK(ing) Day does not fit easily within these frameworks.[34] PARK(ing) Day takes place on the road, not the footway (defined in the Roads Act as "that part of a road as is set aside or formed as a path or way for pedestrian traffic"), and even those parks that serve food would not fall within the definition of a restaurant (defined as "premises in which food is regularly supplied on sale to the public for consumption on the premises").[35] Permits relating to street vending apply to structures erected and used "for the purpose of selling any article or service."[36] The definition of a road event is similarly unhelpful, centering on "a speed contest."[37]

The Roads Act makes provision also for the granting of consent for the erection of structures or the carrying out of works on public roads, though many PARK(ing) Day participants' activities would not constitute a "work" or "structure" (setting out a carpet with folding chairs and potted plants, for example).[38] The point at which a park might be understood as a "work" or "structure" is unclear, as neither term is defined in the Act. Under the Environmental Planning and Assessment Act 1979 and the Local Government Act 1993, in which these terms are also used but not defined, both have been the subject of considerable litigation.[39] Where a park does fit within the definition of a "work" or "structure," it would then be subject to a requirement to obtain development consent under the Environmental Planning and Assessment Act. This may be avoided in some cases, because temporary structures may be treated as exempt or complying development when certain standards are met.[40] However, even these exceed the resources accessible to participants: the requirements include obtaining written consent from the council, compliance with building standards, setbacks, and height limits, taking out public liability insurance, and, where a platform is constructed, conspicuously displaying a notice "indicating the actual distributed and concentrated load for which the stage or platform has been designed."[41]

This lack of congruence with existing permitting schemes means that there is considerable uncertainty within local authorities regarding the legal status of the event. In some cases, local authorities have used permitting processes established for other events to facilitate PARK(ing) Day. For North Sydney Girls High School, the local council used its road closure provisions to facilitate the event by closing off the whole street.[42] More often, local authorities have taken a more informal approach.

In San Francisco, the City has been careful not to provide too much assistance for PARK(ing) Day. As noted in chapter 1, staff in the mayor's office contacted Rebar to express their support for the event, and particularly for its character as an unsanctioned activity. Rather than confirming the legality of using parking spaces in this way, the City provided informal direction to police not to challenge people participating in the event. The City has also provided informal agreement to accommodate requests not to interfere with parks planned in specific places. This is generally enough, but not always. For example, San Francisco State University has had design students participate in PARK(ing) Day every year since 2007, and most years has done so without challenge. University staff advise the city parking department each year of their plans, and this, with the City's broader support for the event, has generally been enough to avoid official intervention. This is not always the case, however, and there have been a couple of encounters with police over the years. As Professor Ricardo Gomes explains:

> There was one year that somehow the parking officials were not informed that we were going to be commandeering a number of street parking spaces, and we ended up having this standoff with the parking meter officials, and then eventually the campus police. . . . Eventually, just as the police were about to break us down and move us, the parking meter person who we initially had a confrontation with came back, you know, waving a paper saying "I've got the permit, they're all clear." It was just a total miscommunication on that, and it was resolved.

In Montréal, there is high-level support for PARK(ing) Day, including from the mayor of the City of Montréal and elected officials in several boroughs. Wanting to encourage participants but having no ready legal process to follow, the CRE went to politicians in the City and individual boroughs for letters of support.[43] With that support, they then approached directors of transportation responsible for the management of parking in each borough for additional letters. These were not permits, since there was no process under which a permit could be requested. Instead they were letters stating that participants in PARK(ing) Day who pay the parking meter will not be given a ticket.

While this was effective for most of the parks installed in Montréal, it did not ensure the acceptance of PARK(ing) Day in all locations. In 2015, traffic staff remained insistent that three parks pack up on safety grounds, even when shown the letters of support from the borough.[44] This is not a problem unique to PARK(ing) Day; the complicated system of boroughs means that communication between various parts of government is an ongoing issue in Montréal.[45] In 2016, support for the event was enhanced with formal recognition in the Parking Strategy for Montréal, which includes a commitment to continue to encourage initiatives such as PARK(ing) Day.[46]

The experience in Sydney has been particularly challenging. There are supportive councils, but even with staff and policies that favor this kind of activity, the process can be difficult. In Leichhardt, the full council passed a resolution confirming its support for a park planned for PARK(ing) Day in 2013, but this was conditional on participants meeting detailed conditions, and on further proposals being assessed by both the Local Traffic Committee and the full council.[47] In nearby Marrickville, council did not provide any support for the park on Australia Street in 2013, despite strong support from the relevant staff. After the success of that event, in 2014 Marrickville council's sustainability team contacted the relevant manager and obtained verbal confirmation that rangers would not interfere with the event that year.[48]

With no clearly applicable permitting process to follow, officials often struggle to provide advice on the legality of PARK(ing) Day. In several cases, officials have told people to go ahead with their parks without pursuing formal approval, and even to pretend they had not contacted the government at all. In other cases (some within the same authority), local authorities asked participants to obtain liability insurance, to employ engineering consultants to prepare traffic management plans, and/or to direct traffic around the park during the day. Such requirements invariably required resources well beyond those available to participants, and resulted in participants either making significant (and what they saw as detrimental) modifications to their plans for PARK(ing) Day (for example, constructing parks on private land rather than on the street) or abandoning the event altogether.[49]

This is evident in the City of Sydney. The council has been discussing PARK(ing) Day for several years, but has not yet been able to agree on its position.[50] While the event involves no apparent illegality, the lack of a clear source to establish the legality of PARK(ing) Day can be problematic, as one would-be participant explains:

> In terms of the law we have received verbal advice from the City that there's nothing in the Road Rules or other traffic legislation which they administer that would make PARK(ing) Day activity unlawful provided PARKers don't sell anything, perform theatre, amplify music or swing goods on a hoist.
>
> We also received a very positive response from within the City of Sydney council when presenting the PARK(ing) Day concept and our intention to facilitate activity. That said, without official approval from your City Council there's no guarantee you won't run into trouble with the Rangers, police or other law-enforcement.[51]

There is also scope for authorities other than local councils to provide permits for PARK(ing) Day. After failing to obtain approval from the local council, the organizers of PARK(ing) Day on Australia Street, Newtown submitted a notice of intention to hold a public assembly to the local police station. This is a form setting out the name of the organizers and the plans for the "assembly," including the proposed date, time, location, size, and duration, as well as an agreement to take responsibility for organizing and conducting the proposed assembly, provided for under the Summary Offences Act 1988 (NSW).[52] The police officer at the desk made no comment when the form was handed in, and the organizers didn't receive any follow-up, so that the park became an authorized assembly under the Act.[53] Yet participating in an authorized public assembly means only that a person is not guilty of offenses relating to participating in an unlawful assembly or the obstruction of the street[54]—there are many other laws that might still apply.

3.3 Parks and positivism

Instead of a niche or loophole, a gap ripe for filling as Rebar suggested, the laws regulating PARK(ing) Day are better understood as open to interpretations that are multiple and competing. A gap implies that there is a legal norm supported by a shared understanding that that law is indeed the law, and ought to be obeyed.[55] Yet the law is not so neatly bounded.

In thinking about the way in which the law plays out in PARK(ing) Day, Hendrik Hartog's analysis of a much older conflict over the use of city streets is helpful.[56] In the early nineteenth century, Hartog explains, the keeping of pigs in the streets of New York was contested. Some residents wished to continue allowing their pigs to roam the streets, providing a cheap source of food while also removing waste from the public domain. Others wished to see an end to the practice, driven by concerns about unsightliness and danger (including, occasionally, the pigs killing children). The contest between these two positions was protracted. Despite a judicial finding of illegality in 1819, pigs continued to roam the streets until at least the 1840s. In examining this disjunction, Hartog argues that the ongoing keeping of pigs was not a practice in defiance of the law, nor evidence of a failure of enforcement. Rather, it reveals the multiplicity of legal meaning: both pig owners and the city council believed the practice to be lawful long after its judicial prohibition.

The legal right to create parks in parking spaces, like the right to keep pigs in the streets of New York, depends on its performance. What made pig keeping a right, despite a judicial decision to the contrary, was the fact that a politically active and insistent group of people believed that they did indeed possess such a right, and that those holding different views were unwilling or unable to prevent the pig keepers from making use of their purported right. In much the same way, PARK(ing) Day is constituted as legal through the success of its participants in exercising their claimed right, and through the relative passivity of their opponents.

Hartog's analysis follows from his identification of a mismatch between understandings of law as singular and coherent, and of social practices and normative identities as plural. To analyze law as hegemonic—the subject of a shared consciousness, giving rise to clearly identifiable, enforceable norms—entails a blindness to the social meanings of legal rules. A more accurate understanding of political life recognizes the existence of coexisting, conflicting and often competing visions of legal order. As Hartog explains: "Most rights, even the most conventional of property rights, are held with an awareness of partiality and of our subjection to other claims in particular circumstances. How we hold what we regard as ours changes with time and context."[57]

This socially constituted form of legality is not peculiar to pigs or to PARK(ing) Day. Consistent with Fuller's claims about the necessity for reference to the purpose behind any rule, law must always be understood in its social context. Hartog extends Fuller's claims by highlighting the breadth of social context that contributes to the shaping of legality, a point made strongly by scholars of legal pluralism.

Connecting to the work of social scientists from the early twentieth century examining the coexistence of colonial and Indigenous legal orders, legal pluralism reveals that the coincidence of multiple legal orders is not exceptional but intrinsic to social life.[58] Much more than a product of colonialism, legal pluralism results from the pervasive mixing of multiple sources of legality. In Western liberal democracies such as those of which Sydney, Montréal, and San Francisco form part, these can include the normative orders of trade unions and industry groups, corporations, religious and ethnic groups, community organizations, and informal social networks, to name just a few.

Legality emerges through the interactions between these normative orders, and this is a dynamic and ongoing process. Boaventura de Sousa Santos uses the term "interlegality" to express the way in which multiple legal orders are entwined.[59] In examples from revolutionary 1970s Portugal to the squatter settlements of Rio de Janiero, Santos shows that legal conflicts are not simply between official state law and unofficial law. Rather, conflicts arise in the intersections between multiple forms of legality: between different scales (place-based, transnational), different interpretive standpoints or references (contractual, proprietary), different formulations of interests (economic, familial, political), different privileging of interests (personal or particularistic, objective or generalizable), or different sign systems (Homeric, biblical). Social life is constituted by an intersection of different legal orders that are mixed in uneven and unstable ways as we engage with them in our minds and our actions.

This last point is significant: the constitution of, competition between, and commingling of different legal orders takes place in the imagination of law's subjects. Law is not a concrete object; it does not *do* or *say* anything itself.[60] Law is inseparable from the people who obey, enforce, draft, redraft, ignore, disobey, or otherwise engage with it. Accordingly, Martha-Marie Kleinhans and Roderick Macdonald argue that legal subjects should be understood as "law inventing," not merely law-abiding.[61] In turn, law can be understood as a mode of giving particular sense to particular things in particular places.[62]

Scholars of legal consciousness provide similar insights.[63] Drawing on detailed sociological examination of everyday interactions with a wide range of laws (from traffic laws to discrimination and employment laws), Patricia Ewick and Susan Silbey show that the understandings and meanings of law circulating in social relations are crucial for comprehending the workings of law.[64] As individuals make sense of their world, they participate in a reciprocal process through which meanings are stabilized and institutionalized. Those meanings then become part of the discursive systems that structure future meaning-making. Law is thus constrained and constituted by understandings of legality, which can in turn be understood as a feature of social interaction in which legal concepts and terminology are invoked.[65]

There are multiple ways in which people give sense to things, even the same particular things in the same particular places.[66] Also using Hart's example about the indeterminacy of rules regulating vehicles in parks, Robert Cover describes this as the problem of "too much law."[67] For Cover, there is a radical dichotomy between the social organization of law as power, and law as meaning. As he explains, "the uncontrolled character of meaning exercises a destabilizing influence upon power. Precepts must 'have meaning,' but they necessarily borrow it from materials created by social activity that is not subject to the strictures of provenance that characterize what we call formal lawmaking."[68]

Law is sustained by its social meaning, but meaning is inherently unstable, with new interpretations always being produced. Cover argues for an understanding of law as "jurisgenic," recognizing that "never only one but always many worlds are created by the too fertile forces of jurisgenesis."[69] The result of this intrinsic heterogeneity of meaning is that law is essentially contested. Legal conflicts arise not from gaps but from overlaps and clashes, from excess rather than absence.

Law cannot simply be created to suit any normative ideal, however; it must be grounded in some kind of interpretation. Rebar's story about the legality of creating parks on the street was based partly on normative ideals about public space, the place of cars in cities, and the nature of democratic participation—but it was also grounded in a reading of a particular piece of legislation, as well as broader narratives about property rights.

Even then, not all interpretations can be understood as carrying legal meaning. For Cover, the decisive factor is committed action: when the subject of that commitment is objectified, and when someone (or, more persuasively, some group) accepts the legal meaning and affirms their position through action. With examples from the First Amendment to property and corporations law, Cover demonstrates the potential for alternative stories to remake legal meaning. The ability of alternative interpretations to succeed depends on the strength of commitment (and this is relative; what is important is how commitment to the new compares to commitment to the old), and the degree to which stories resonate (again, both within the interpretive community and beyond). Ewick and Silbey make a similar point. Legal consciousness, they argue, is not merely a state of mind, and it is not entirely individual or subjective. Rather, it is "produced and revealed in what people *do* as well as what they *say*. . . . Legal consciousness is always a collective construction that simultaneously expresses, uses and creates publicly exchanged understandings."[70]

Despite quite different approaches—for Cover (and Fuller), a textual, interpretive approach; for Hartog, a sociological study—both converge on this point. Law is a vehicle for normative claims and the expression of social values, and cannot be separated from these. For PARK(ing) Day as for roaming pigs or vehicles in parks, there are no neutral, technical answers. Legal claims always refer to the background social purpose of law.

PARK(ing) Day has been the subject of multiple and divergent legal interpretations. These interpretations draw on a range of formal and informal sources, and the strength of interpretive commitments to various legal meanings depends on political, social, and normative positions. Often these are more important than the legal source from which they derive.

The idea of a niche or legal loophole was central to the commencement of PARK(ing) Day, but this was not the analysis that captured the public imagination. While appealing in many respects—particularly to a group excited by the idea of niches and everyday tactics—the loophole idea is technical and invites many questions. The right that participants in PARK(ing) Day believe they hold, and on which they justify their engagement, is often quite different. A lease is far more powerful than a loophole.

A lease can be expressed more simply, it makes sense to many people, and the idea that property rights encompass broad use rights is enticing. It is a story about law that resonates both within and beyond the interpretive communities involved in PARK(ing) Day. The Sydney PARK(ing) Day Facebook page, for example, invites people to "convert a parking space into a people park . . . by paying the meter and 'owning' the space" (figure 3.4).

Yet the lease idea is problematic. For payment of a parking meter to establish a lease, it would need to be shown that the owner of the space granted possession of the land to the purchaser of the ticket, rather than mere permission to use it for a specified purpose. A lease gives exclusive use or occupation of the land for all purposes not prohibited by the terms of the lease (or by other laws); it is an interest that can be asserted against third parties. A license is a much more modest permission, not a proprietary right but a personal right to occupy. A license allows the land to be used only for specified purposes, creating mere personal rights enforceable in contract or tort (but not the tort of trespass to land).[71]

Figure 3.4
Sydney PARK(ing) Day Facebook page inviting people to "own" a parking space. The top image shows a park built by Habitat for Humanity in which people were invited to take potted plants and to hang wishes on strings. The lower image is of a park built in the beachside suburb of Manly, for which large seats were constructed and covered in blackboard paint. Chalk was set out and people encouraged to write and draw as well as sit in the sunshine. Image: John O'Callaghan.

It is difficult to imagine how payment of a parking meter could result in possession. In determining whether there is possession to establish a lease, courts look to factors such as the nature of the premises, any restrictions on the permitted use, and the terms used by the parties to describe their agreement.[72] In all three cities, regulations refer to parking meters in negative terms.[73] There is no mention of positive rights, merely the avoidance of penalties for a particular action. In Sydney, a finding of a license rather than a lease is emphasized by the Roads Act, which prohibits the granting of a lease of the roadway outside of specified circumstances.[74] Rather than positive rights to the space, paying a parking meter merely makes lawful an action that would otherwise be unlawful: it creates a license, not a lease. Since payment of the meter just avoids incurring the penalty that would otherwise be attracted by parking a car, it offers little assistance to people wishing to undertake other activities in a parking space.

Even if a lease could be established, the idea that such a right then entitles the leaseholder to undertake any activity of their choosing does not follow. Property law has long been limited by various regulatory systems. Accordingly, the activities that owners and lessees can undertake on their land are almost always constrained. Beyond the laws regulating parking, there are many other laws that could potentially be applied to PARK(ing) Day, as Mariana Valverde's detailed examination of the plethora of laws regulating one street corner in Toronto makes clear.[75] This is particularly relevant for the many parks that include activities such as serving food, serving alcohol, displaying signage, holding a performance, or painting or marking the street.

As PARK(ing) Day grew, Rebar expanded on its legal aspects. Subsequent guides noted that different jurisdictions may have different rules, and encouraged people to investigate local laws. The "Frequently Asked Questions" on the PARK(ing) Day website instruct participants to make their own inquiries into the legality of the event: "The specifics depend on your local legal codes and it is your responsibility to check the law. In San Francisco it *appears* to be legal to do other things in a parking spot besides park a vehicle, but in some municipalities (New York City, for example) alternative activities are expressly prohibited. It's up to you to be informed and flexible when it comes to obeying your local law."[76]

Where PARK(ing) Day appears to be illegal, Rebar encourage creative approaches to the law: "It's your call, but we do encourage you to look for creative ways to work with/within the law. . . . See what you can do with what you've got."[77]

Some participants follow Rebar's advice to check their own laws, and as a result some come up with alternative interpretations about the legality of the event. For Ming Thompson, a participant in San Francisco, her main concern was that the park she built was compliant with the regulations for accessibility under the Americans with Disabilities Act 1990. This concern reflects her previous experience: Thompson is an architect used to complying with that legislation. In Sydney, urban designer Sam George explained that there are many discretionary rules and considerable scope for councils to block the construction of parks. But these rules, he argued, were relatively new, arising only with the popularity of cars in the past 50 years, and might change as attitudes to cars are again shifting. What George saw as more significant were the much older and longer-running customs regulating streets as public spaces, in which streets were places for social and economic exchange and expression—something he believes PARK(ing) Day tries to recover. Another participant based in the US, Mike Lydon, went even further along these lines, questioning how current street designs could be legal when they are so unsafe (particularly for pedestrians), and suggesting that in calming traffic and promoting alternatives to cars PARK(ing) Day is in fact *more* in line with the duties of the state to promote public safety.

One particularly technical reading was provided by Mikael St-Pierre, who checked the bylaws in Montréal and found nothing preventing use of the space for activities other than parking. He went on to explain that he never even pays the meter, since the relevant bylaw relates only to cars:

> Whenever I do it or people talk to me about it I say don't pay for it. Because how are you going to receive a ticket if you don't have a license plate? And I've never had anyone tell me afterwards that they got a ticket and no one pays for PARK(ing) Day. No one pays.

This is not a common understanding, as St-Pierre acknowledged: "I think I'm the only one in Montréal who knows that, who's actually aware of that." It is also an understanding expressed with some doubt:

> Then again, if you do something what's the worst that could happen? . . . [Parking officials] have no authority besides giving tickets. So if they ask you to move,

they can't specially move you, they can't give you a ticket because you don't have a license plate. So what are they going to do? They're going to call the police and then the police are going to come and they're going to say can you please move, you're not supposed to be there, and then you're going to move, but—and that's the worst that's going to happen and you're not a priority.

Most participants do not examine the law in this depth. Rebar's initial explanation is widely accepted, and typically without question. In interviews, when asked about the relevant laws, many participants simply explained Rebar's proposition about renting or leasing the space. Despite Rebar's mention of possible variations in local laws and encouragement to participants to consider these, few participants make any further legal investigations. Some shrugged or even laughed when asked about relevant laws, suggesting a very ready acceptance of Rebar's analysis. When asked whether he knew which laws are relevant to PARK(ing) Day, one participant replied:

Do I know which laws? No. In fact, I don't want to know. . . . There probably still are laws that govern what you can put in a space and how long you can be in a space. And those are things that I don't want to know about because . . . just the knowledge of them I think kills some of the magic about these things that just pop up into space (Noah Christman, San Francisco)

Others were more cautious, but still relied on Rebar's legal claims:

I was under the impression that you could use a car space for something else if you were paying for the meter. So I don't know if that's just an American thing . . . [seeking legal advice] would cost me more money and time and resources than makes it worthwhile. (Kylie Legge, Sydney)

PARK(ing) Day is an activity presented as lawful, and supported by action in the streets. The interpretations on which understandings of legality are based vary—for many, a lease created by paying a parking meter, for some, more technical analyses, for others, a simple acceptance that the event is legal in some unknown way. When PARK(ing) Day succeeds in its invocation of legality, what is crucial is that participants affirm their belief in the legality of the event through action. In doing so, they attempt to constitute their interpretations as legal. In many cases, they succeed. Like the politically active and insistent group of pig keepers who believed that they possessed a right to keep pigs in the streets of New York, participants in PARK(ing) Day remake legal meaning through their successful appropriations of parking spaces, and through the relative passivity of their opponents.

3.4 Performing PARK(ing) law

The claims about law in PARK(ing) Day can be understood as performative, in that they help to constitute the things that they describe.[78] While the power of a park to bring about certain realities may be less than in the more widely cited examples of performative acts—utterances such as "I do" during a marriage ceremony, the naming of a ship, the announcement of a rate rise by the Reserve Bank, the pronouncement of a judgment by a court—the claims about law in PARK(ing) Day do not simply describe an objective or preexisting reality. As Judith Butler argues, even apparently stable categories like gender, the state, or the market have no a priori existence, but are instead culturally constructed: there is no reality awaiting description.[79]

The performances of law in PARK(ing) Day do not always succeed in constituting their purported legality. A park is accepted as legal in some instances, but not all. In arguing that speech does not merely represent the world but can be constitutive of the things that it describes, John Austin noted the importance of supportive conditions in enabling speech acts to bring about that which they pronounce.[80] Performances are successful only when circumstances are "felicitous." Participants in a wedding, for example, must comply with certain conditions (notice, witnesses) and fit into socially constructed roles (bride, groom) for those utterances to have effect. Saying "I do" at an engagement party will not bring about a marriage. Others have since emphasized the conditional nature of performative acts. For Butler, breakdown is constitutive of performativity: "performativity never fully achieves its effect, and so in this sense 'fails' all the time; its failure is what necessitates its *re*iterative temporality, and we cannot think iterability without failure."[81]

This contingency means that performances should be understood not in terms of particular acts but as part of an ongoing process. Social constructions are performatively produced, again and again, through repetition, convergence, and rearticulation. With each failure or breakdown, performativity must be renewed and restarted. As Butler argues, "performativity must be understood not as a singular or deliberate 'act,' but, rather, as the reiterative and citational practice by which discourse produces the effects that it names."[82]

Claims about law in PARK(ing) Day build upon earlier claims and their successful enactment in parks in other cities. The legality of PARK(ing) Day is presented in relation to earlier performances, repeating and rearticulating the legal claims made in earlier installations. Rebar's complaint about lazy journalists putting too much emphasis on numbers misses this point. The citational force of PARK(ing) Day comes from its multiple iterations. For many participants, being able to see examples of parks built in previous years is inspiring and empowering.

> The fact that there was this movement, you know, when you Google it there's like thousands of PARK(ing) Days, it just makes it a lot easier . . . just the confidence to know that people can do it, and it won't get shut down and people don't freak out. (Jonathon Carle, Sydney)

In interviews, many participants asked about my findings from other times and places. In Sydney, where PARK(ing) Day is small, participants were delighted to hear how big the event is in Montréal.

> If you have 200 groups of people taking action in a city, like holy moly! That's powerful! . . . In terms of citizen empowerment . . . it seems wildly successful. If there's 200 groups in Montréal, say there's five or ten people involved in each group, that's a couple of thousand people who are taking action in a way that requires a lot of energy and a lot of input from them. And then how many people might see each park? Maybe 100 people or 200 people see each park, suddenly that's 40,000 people or something. . . . That's phenomenal. (James Patterson, Sydney)

In all three cities, participants who had engaged in earlier years were happy to hear that the event has continued. The repeated enactments of PARK(ing) Day—on the street, in a guide, a license, and a website with many thousands of successful examples—are important to their force. Copies of Rebar's materials and explanations of the history and international character of the event are often prominent features in parks (figure 3.5). Participants emphasize the importance of earlier and parallel iterations:

> It gives people who want to try it credibility. Like if they go to their bosses or whatever and say I want to do this, oh it's an international thing. And I think certainly going into that first one, we're like oh no this is happening all over the world today. You just don't know about it, go and check it out and you know it's online. So it does give you a little bit of status, I guess, than if it was just me doing it on my own. (Kylie Legge, Sydney)

> It's helpful that PARK(ing) Day is an international thing . . . when we try to validate or justify our efforts, we're able to point and say . . . [that] it happens in all cities. (Steve Charters, Montréal)

Figure 3.5
Materials explaining PARK(ing) Day and its history in the window of a participating
business, Plaza Saint-Hubert, Montréal, 2015. Image: Amelia Thorpe.

PARK(ing) Day is constituted through more than discourse, and the
enactment of legal claims in the street is significant. As Butler argues, bodily
and linguistic forms of performativity overlap, but are not identical. Movement or stillness, for example, "is neither my act or yours, but something
that happens by virtue of the relation between us."[83] This, Butler contends,
is why there are separate protections for freedom of speech and for freedom
of assembly: "forms of assembly already signify prior to, and apart from,
any particular demands they make. . . . The gathering signifies in excess
of what is said, and that mode of signification is a concerted bodily enactment, a plural form of performativity."[84]

Butler's argument is framed around larger, explicitly political assemblies like the Occupy movement and the Arab Spring, yet her claims can
be applied also to PARK(ing) Day. When people take to the streets together,

Butler explains, "they form something of a body politic, and even if that body politic does not speak in a single voice—even when it does not speak at all—it still forms, asserting its presence as a plural and obdurate bodily life."[85] The significance of the parks created on PARK(ing) Day extends beyond the claims made by participants (who may not make any claims at all), and the significance of the event is far greater than Rebar's original intent. The coming together of bodies on PARK(ing) Day exerts a performative force, even when they do not express a clear or unified message.

From the diverse and disparate narratives displayed in various parks, a collective demand emerges. In taking space on the street, PARK(ing) Day makes claims about it: the kinds of activities for which the street should be used, and the kinds of processes through which these should be decided.

As in Occupy and the more confrontational activities examined by Butler, the precarious way in which participants gather in PARK(ing) Day matters to the performative force of the event. For all of its playfulness, PARK(ing) Day does involve an element of danger:

> It's a little bit scary, because you're kind of going on to the street, which is usually occupied by cars, and they're fast and they're bigger than you, and they can kill you. (Safiah Moore, Sydney)

The objects and images to which participants refer when recalling other instances of the event are themselves significant parts of the process through which legality is constructed in PARK(ing) Day. Discursive claims about law take place alongside and amongst a range of performances that take other forms. As Butler explains, "it is not simply that a subject performs a speech act; rather, a set of relations and practices are constantly renewed, and agency traverses human and non-human domains."[86]

Others are more emphatic about this dispersal of agency. Working within actor network theory (ANT), Michel Callon describes a successful performance as a sociotechnical *agencement* or assemblage of human and nonhuman actors.[87] In line with Butler's emphasis on failure, ANT presents the process of assemblage as always incomplete. The fluidity of power means that any mode of ordering is inherently unstable, and in turn that constant work is required to maintain connections between elements in a network (stressing this point, Bruno Latour suggests networks might be better labeled "worknets").[88] As Callon contends, "misfires are the rules of the game."[89]

The crucial process in ANT is one of enrollment, through which human and nonhuman actors are assembled into the networks that make things happen.[90] A judicial decision, for example, is not simply handed down, but is the result of a long and complex process involving an interplay of actors—lawyers, litigants, experts and witnesses; but also stamps, folders, paper clips, and elastic bands; laws, treaties, orders, and regulations; technicians, bailiffs, clerks, and secretaries; cupboards, offices, corridors, libraries, cellars, armchairs, and desks—that produces and gives effect to the final judgment.[91]

Alongside discursive claims, legality is performed in PARK(ing) Day through the enrollment of a range of human and nonhuman actors. Parks can be understood as assemblages—of participants, legal texts, images, blog posts, roadways, footpaths, and objects like turf, potted plants, and pallet seating. The claims about law in PARK(ing) Day, like other legal claims, are made through physical bodies, objects, and spaces.

The parking meter is crucial in assembling parks as legal interventions. Rebar's first PARK(ing) installation responded to the particular opportunity created by the technology of the parking meter. Passmore came up with the idea by watching the operation of a parking meter in a space below his office. This is not the first time parking meters have been productive of new activities. As noted in chapter 1, alternative uses of the parking space came immediately after the installation of the very first parking meter in 1935. After paying the meter, residents of Oklahoma City used the spaces to play bridge and to tether horses. The meter itself was productive of new ways of seeing and using curbside space.

The parking meter remains central to the assemblages in PARK(ing) Day. Where parking meters provide printed tickets, participants will often display these prominently. In recording the event, participants frequently include the parking meter in their photos, asserting the legality of their intervention by demonstrating "compliance" with the rules for the space.

The importance of the parking meter was demonstrated vividly in 2012, in the example described earlier in which SJB were asked to move their park from a space outside their office, where parking was free, to another space one block to the north, where they could purchase a ticket. The parking inspector accepted the participants' claim that they could purchase a ticket and use the space for a purpose other than parking a car. But the purchasing of the ticket was crucial. The group could not use the space in the same way that a vehicle could. Simply occupying the space in compliance with the time limit was not enough, on the ticket inspector's reasoning, to justify the installation of the park. The presence of the parking meter created a very different condition, enabling the payment of money and thus the creation of a "lease" that could in turn justify a much wider range of uses. Just as in 1935, when the first parking meter prompted ranchers and bridge players to make alternative uses of the newly monetized space, the presence of a parking meter in Surry Hills changed the nature of the curbside space for participants and observers of PARK(ing) Day.

While parking meters are crucial, they must be assembled alongside other actors to be effective. The normative capacity of things depends on context. Noortje Marres argues that things—like carpets, taps, and brushes—are effective in engaging visitors in environmental living. But this "captivating power of things" depends on their setting.[92] In Marres's example of eco show-homes, it is through the assemblage of these objects by empirical devices (such as diary notes, blog posts, and photography) that their normativity is brought into effect. In PARK(ing) Day too, parking meters work only when they are successfully combined with other (human and nonhuman) actors (figure 3.6).

In explaining how legal meaning was once played out in New York, Hartog emphasized the people and the pigs that enacted and contested various legal interpretations. For Cover, too, the physical performance of claims about law is central to the distinction between law and storytelling: "The normative worldbuilding which constitutes 'Law' is never just a mental or spiritual act. A legal world is built only to the extent that there are commitments that place bodies on the line."[93]

The ability to enact legal interpretations on the street—to put one's body on the line—is significant to the construction of legality through PARK(ing) Day.

> It feels strange to be sitting on bitumen, because bitumen's not something that you normally physically come in contact with. . . . When you cross the road you're removed from it in a way, whereas when you're actually sitting on the bitumen and your hands are touching the tar, you really sense that you're using the space in a different way. You do feel quite subversive actually putting your hands on the tar. (Seb Crawford, Sydney)

Participants describe feeling unsure about what they were doing in the lead-up to the event. This changes when they physically occupy the street,

Figure 3.6
PARK(ing) Day installation by BAR Architects, Battery Street, San Francisco, 2016. Staff in the office collected water bottles in the month leading up to the event (and reported being shocked at the scale of the collection), then used these to construct a "pier," making reference to their location close to the port. Scraps of blue carpet and potted plants were used to suggest water and sea life alongside the pier. Image: Amelia Thorpe.

when they engage materially and viscerally with the space: alongside and against the bitumen, the parking meter, the passing traffic. Reflecting on her engagement in PARK(ing) Day over many years, one participant described this shift:

> Once we've set up, I feel quite at home that we've been able to have access to the space and do what we want in the space. But initially when we're setting up and we're putting out the cones and things, it's very much, "Oh, is this allowed? We're moving in to territory we're not usually in." (Safiah Moore, Sydney)

When I asked how that shift to feeling "at home" came about, she explained:

I think it's having our idea come into fruition, seeing everything physically there. And then having more, I think it's more familiar people, so a lot of people from the office come in and then they inhabit the space. More people around you in that foreign space makes it more acceptable.

PARK(ing) Day is effective because of its physical enactment, the way in which parks are able to draw in objects and spaces to support participants' discursive claims. As well as turf, trees, and temporary seating, parks are sustained and succeed in reshaping legal meaning by assembling a wide range of other actors: the street surface and the parking meter, alongside milk crates and potted plants, board games and barbecues, neighbors, colleagues and passing police. Participants emphasized the importance of people seeing and engaging with parks physically. Simply viewing photos or videos of the event is not enough:

I don't think there's any replacement for actually physically going to a PARK(ing) Day parklet. Because I think it's hard to imagine being in this, potentially let's say 10 by 20 foot space that's right next to potentially a very busy street, and experiencing how that feels, you know, having a bus zoom by. (Noah Christman, San Francisco)

If you see a photograph or you hear about something it's like, Oh, that's cool. . . . But if you experience it in real time, there's something about that that just makes it seem much more tangible. And you're like, Oh, it really is possible. (Liz Ogbu, San Francisco)

You can't possibly understand, you can't see how crazy it is having a barbecue, having people get their blood pressure taken and having a fruit stand on a big highway with a giant bus there. There are videos that show it a little bit, but they still minimize the impact of that right up against that. . . . Like the surrealists, you know how they said there's a spark that is intangible when you combine unexpected things and that it has a magical impact on us. I think that that's got to be done in person. It has a bigger impact by far. (Daniel Sherman, San Francisco)

Again and again, participants emphasized the importance of drawing other people in materially. Participants want people to look at their parks, to take time to stop and enter the park, to engage in conversation about PARK(ing) Day, the street, and the city. Most importantly, participants seek to engage others physically, to participate by sitting on a chair or stretching out on lawn or carpet, playing a game of pinball or corn bag, watching a performance, adding to a chalk drawing, repairing their bike, joining a yoga class, petting an animal, reading a poster, sharing a drink or a barbecue—or

Figure 3.7
PARK(ing) Day, Green Square, Sydney, 2012. Image: John O'Callaghan.

one of many other activities (figure 3.7). When car share company Zipcar set up a park outside their office in downtown San Francisco, they provided chocolate chip cookies, candy, and a range of games, including a giant Jenga set to encourage people to join them (figure 3.8).

> To scroll through a bunch of images internationally, I mean, you can get inspiration but, you know, to be embedded in it is crucial. To get an understanding of actually taking over that space, and that engagement with people. (Lydia Ho, Sydney)

By physically remaking the street, PARK(ing) Day succeeds in drawing people to think not just about how the city *could* or *should* be, but how

Figure 3.8
PARK(ing) Day installation by Zipcar featuring giant Jenga and other games, 2nd Street, San Francisco, 2016. The sign on the table reads: Come join PARK(ing) Day! Image: Amelia Thorpe.

it already *is*. In this way, PARK(ing) Day enacts or performs an alternative understanding of legality. While parking is often a highly contentious issue, particularly in the inner-city areas that are popular sites for parks, explanations of PARK(ing) Day as a legal event are mostly accepted. Participants emphasize how well their parks have been received; many report receiving no negative feedback at all. The vast majority of passersby accept the legality of the parks, often in very positive ways.

Figure 4.1
Park created by CC Puede on Cesar Chavez Street, 2009, featuring an upgraded health clinic with privacy screens. Image: Steve Rhodes.

4   Properties of PARK(ing)

Property is central to PARK(ing) Day. Beyond the technical (and tenuous) explanations about rights created by paying the parking meter, to understand PARK(ing) Day requires attention to a number of related concepts: there is the lease, and connected to this the wider range of legally enforceable property rights. There is also the more commonplace concept of ownership. Perhaps most significantly, PARK(ing) Day draws on a "sense of ownership," a concept that is explicitly not legal, yet intimately connected to property and to legality.

I begin by setting out definitions for property, ownership, and a sense of ownership, highlighting both the distinctions and the slippages between them. Slippages lie at the heart of property, and should be read as revealing not a lack of care or linguistic precision, but a deep conceptual contingency.

In the second half of this chapter I consider the role played in PARK(ing) Day by the first of these concepts, property. By claiming a lease, Rebar invoked legality and legitimacy, and in doing so propelled the event into vehicularity. Perhaps most importantly, the lease engaged the wider category of property. Inspired by the work of conceptual artist Gordon Matta-Clark, property was used as a device through which to rethink links between power, voice, and agency in shaping the city. Connecting what might seem a frivolous activity with deeply felt human needs, and with heated contemporary debates about cities and the place of people within them, property has remained an enduring concern for subsequent participants.

4.1   Proper language

Property cannot be understood merely as a legal concept, or a set of cultural meanings, or in the context of philosophical theories. Like many other culturally loaded terms, property is at once a very dense idea, full of resonance in many fields, as well as one which is extraordinarily slippery.[1]

In discussions of property, "slippery" is a descriptor that comes up frequently. Property is a term that is notoriously difficult to define with precision, and it is one that slips often into related terms. Four are particularly relevant here: property rights, property, ownership, and a sense of ownership.

A lease is one example of a property right, an entitlement we might also call "formal property" or "legal title." Rebar's purported lease is problematic because there are well-recognized legal tests with which the existence of a lease can be established. A lease entails the grant of exclusive use or occupation of the land for all purposes not prohibited by its terms (subject, however, to restrictions imposed by other laws); it is an interest that can be asserted against third parties. While the precise boundaries of a particular lease may give rise to disputes, those disputes can be resolved in court.

Alongside leases, many other rights are also recognized as property rights: covenants, easements, mortgages, and copyright, to name just a few. As for leases, disputes regarding the scope of such rights can be resolved in court. Disputes regarding the features unifying the range of property rights, however, are much harder to resolve. As Kevin and Susan Francis Gray contend: "Few concepts are quite so fragile, so elusive and so often misused as the idea of property."[2]

As an overarching category, property in common law theory is generally understood not as a right to a thing, but rather as a separable bundle of rights between persons that shift according to the context and the object in question.[3] The rights or "sticks" comprising the property bundle have proved extremely variable, including a wide range of rights and responsibilities tailored to particular contexts.[4] Developments in gene technology and online currencies, for example, reveal and reshape the limits of the property concept,[5] while even "core" instances of property (the right to exclude visitors from one's home, for example) are rife with contingencies and limitations.

This variability has been a cause of concern, prompting efforts to bring greater clarity and coherence to property as a concept. Such efforts are often framed around the right to exclude as the definitive core or essence or property,[6] perhaps tempered by a recognition that exclusion will occasionally be supplemented by governance strategies,[7] or by a conception of exclusion as a matter of an exclusive right to "set the agenda" for the thing in question.[8]

Accounts of property centered on exclusion remain contested, however, with critics highlighting examples where the right to exclude is inferior to other rights or even lacking altogether.[9] Recognizing and accepting plurality but still focused on a unifying theory, others have suggested alternative theories to explain property as a concept, drawing on concepts like personhood,[10] dignity and human flourishing,[11] or personal autonomy.[12] Yet these theories are also open to question, with issues like systemic inequality or legacies of indigenous dispossession making it difficult to argue that property can be understood as an institution centered on human flourishing, dignity, or autonomy.

Efforts to explain and justify property reflect the power of the concept among theorists, but also its deep resonance well beyond such debates. Many scholars begin with claims about colloquial understandings of property, noting perhaps a propensity among children to claim "it's mine" from a young age, or the endurance of Blackstonian conceptions of property as "sole and despotic dominion," despite their near-universally accepted inaccuracy.[13] Assertions about lay conceptions are also varied. Property is associated with despotism and dispossession, but also with respect and responsibility, stewardship and care.[14]

Increasingly, and more convincingly, scholars are conceptualizing property as more fundamentally plural, making no attempt to provide such theoretical coherence. Property on these accounts is primarily a social practice, one structured and sustained by "the multiple ways in which it is imagined, discussed, inhabited, and fought over."[15] Scholars such as Jennifer Nedelsky, Davina Cooper, and Nicholas Blomley emphasize the work that property does in society, the role that it plays in shaping social relations.[16]

Property is closely linked with propriety. A claim to property can be read as a claim to what is proper, and an effort to persuade others of the propriety of that claim.[17] For Gray and Gray, the deep indeterminacy spanning property reflects its socially constituted character: "the notion of a 'property right' may ultimately have more to do with perceptions of 'rightness' than with any understanding of enforceable exclusory title. . . . To have 'property' in land is not merely to allege some casual physical affinity with a particular piece of land, but rather to stake out some sort of claim to the legitimacy of one's personal space in this land."[18] Property, then, can be understood as a legal concept, but one that derives both form and force from its social context.

4.2 Ownership

Closely connected to and often overlapping with property is a second term, ownership. For many, ownership is synonymous with property, denoting rights to people, places, and things. In thinking about property concepts and the relationships between them with respect to PARK(ing) Day, ownership might best be understood as an in-between idea: at times comparable to property, at others to the more affective and colloquial sense of ownership. Like property, ownership is a term with powerful resonance.

Ownership can be understood as more than property, but also less. While property is a legal construct, ownership is a term without legal force.[19] This distinction, however, is also slippery. In many cases, ownership is synonymous with property, indicative not of different ideas but of the different sources of the English language.[20] Ownership does arise in legal discussions, in terms like "land ownership," "traditional owner," "property owner," "owner-occupier," and "owners' corporation." Ownership is not a legal concept in itself, but one that is often closely linked with legal concepts.

The indeterminacy of ownership was clearly apparent in interviews. When asked, many participants said that the city owns the street; some named the roads department or some other public authority instead of or as well as the city. Rarely, though, did people finish their answers at this point. One participant answered initially that "streets are public spaces; however, technically, council and government own the streets." After a few moments she came back to this, explaining:

> Maybe there's two types of ownership. Maybe one is owning by using and the other is owning by controlling. So the government and council control what happens on it, pretty much, and then the people who use it kind of temporarily own it. Yeah, just had a think about it. (Elise O'Ryan, Sydney)

Who owns the street was not one of my initial questions; it was something I asked as a follow-up to one interviewee's answer to another question. His response was rich, prompting me to ask this again in the next interview, and then to make it a standard question in subsequent interviews. Like Elise, above, many others spoke about different forms of ownership, distinguishing normative and technical understandings.

> Technically it's the city, but the users of the street are the citizens. (Jean-Philippe Di Marco)

My heart, yeah, my heart says the people own the street. And, you know, politically the city owns the street. The city though is also made of people. (Anaïs Mathez, Montréal)

Ah! Oh geez. That's a deep one isn't it? I think the community owns the street. But I think perceptions . . . vary. And that's part of our problem. So at the moment in our community most car drivers think they own the street. Or at best, RMS [Roads and Maritime Services] or you know the local roads authority owns the street. But I don't think that's the right answer. I think it's a people thing. (Kerryn Wilmot, Sydney)

RMS owns the street. But they shouldn't. They don't technically own the street but they do. . . . There's a few other stakeholders involved, but if RMS has a dislike for something they will get their way I think generally. (Eytan Rocheta, Sydney)

Many described ownership as multiple and overlapping, noting the coexistence of different owners, and the potential for ownership to shift.

I would say that it's the residents who own the street because you know they, they vote with their dollars when they shop, they decide which streets to work on, which streets to live on, which streets to walk on! Um, the police might feel differently because they police the streets. The city might feel differently because they own, at least, a certain part of the sidewalk and lots of the trees. There's obviously a lot of actors who own the street. (Anonymous participant, Montréal)

The regulars and the locals own the street. . . . Some places are better at articulating who the locals are than others. . . . I often see business owners on the street, you know, sweeping out the front of their store or cleaning their windows or something like this, so I think that those moments of, of ownership suggest that they probably own it more than anyone else. (John O'Callaghan, Sydney)

It is public space. Technically I would say we all own the streets . . . [but] in a very real sense cars occupy the street and kind of dominate the street but it's, it's sort of an occupation that has to be won back. (Maclean, Montréal)

Use, control, and responsibility were often mentioned to explain who owns the street. Some participants noted that property owners are responsible for the maintenance of the adjoining sidewalk, and that through this they owned the sidewalk. Others spoke about the ability for agencies responsible for infrastructure to close off or open up the street as constituting ownership. Still others described citizens "taking back" ownership by taking over maintenance of the street:

Who owns the street? More and more citizens, used to be just the city. . . . There was this limit, the grass was the limit, but nowadays, we have a lot of movements in Montréal, where people, they are actually taking off some concrete in the middle of the sidewalk . . . for example and they put flowers in the middle of the sidewalk . . . it's owned by citizens and the maintenance is by citizens . . . so citizens are taking their place back in the city. (Marc-André Carignan, Montréal)

Many spoke about ownership as negotiated and enacted. Emphasizing the importance of normative conceptions as *constitutive* and not merely descriptive, people spoke about ownership as something decided collectively.

The person who owns the street is the person we will let own the street. (Jeanne Dagenais-Lespérance, Montréal)

I would say that ownership of the street is, in practice and in reality, it is a kind of volatile and dynamic mixture of government governance and private interests. (Robin Abad Ocubillo, San Francisco)

If you have the right intentions, you can own the street. (Kris Spann, Sydney)

The boundaries of ownership are far from clear. Ownership might be understood as entailing control, and this might come from formal property rights. But an ability to control a space can also come from social context, from a recognition by others that the kind of use to which the object of ownership should be put is appropriate. A claim to use the street to repair its infrastructure or to create some benefit for the wider community might be recognized if others see this as justified, regardless of who holds the formal legal title to the site in question. As anthropologists Mark Busse and Veronica Strang contend, "ownership is a culturally and historically specific system of symbolic communication through which people act and through which they negotiate social and political relations."[21]

Ownership is a slippery and shifting idea, one with a powerful cultural resonance. Ownership overlaps and often coincides with property, a term with which it is often treated as synonymous. Ownership overlaps and is used interchangeably also with another concept: a sense of ownership.

4.3   A sense of ownership: belonging

A sense of ownership can be understood as further removed from legality. A property right, like a lease, can be conceptualized and clearly defined as a legal right. Property as a more general category becomes harder to pin down, yet still retains a strong connection with law. Ownership follows as a more colloquial concept, one connected to legal rights and often used synonymously with property, yet also used to refer to intuitive, normative ideas less amenable to judicial determination: a prime example of the slipperiness of proprietary concepts.

With the prefix "sense of," this final concept makes no claim to legal status. A sense of ownership is defined not according to legal standards, but feelings and informal understandings. A sense of ownership may take many forms. It might be a feeling of ownership for the street, or part of the street, where the participants in PARK(ing) Day installed their park, or it might be a feeling of ownership on a much larger scale, for the neighborhood or even the city as a whole. In explaining the concept, some participants describe a sense of ownership as being able to "recognize yourself" in a particular place. Others suggested a sense of ownership could be understood as having "skin in the game," feeling invested in the street, the neighborhood, or the city.

Within psychology, it is recognized that people can feel ownership for things to which they have no formal property rights. Following Pierce, Kostova, and Dirks, psychological ownership is defined as "the state in which individuals feel as though the target of ownership or a piece of that target is 'theirs'."[22] Psychological ownership encompasses a sense of possession, a relationship of close connection (where the object becomes a part of the extended self), and an affective sensation (feelings of pleasure, efficacy, and competence).

Psychological ownership is important because it allows people to fulfil basic human motives: efficacy and effectance, self-identity (self-definition, for expressing one's self-identity and for maintaining the continuity of the self over time), and having a place to dwell.[23] Connecting to a long and diverse set of scholarship, from William James to Margaret Mead, Jean-Paul Sartre to Karl Polanyi, Martin Heidegger to Simone Weil, feelings of ownership are understood to be "part of the human condition."[24] Consistent with the right to the city and with the deeply felt desire to contribute described by participants in PARK(ing) Day, the literature on psychological ownership links a desire for ownership with innate human needs.[25]

Psychological ownership often coincides with legal title, yet the two may exist independently.[26] A person can feel ownership for a place without it being property—a favorite park, a table in a café, a seat on a train. People can also have proprietary rights but not feel any ownership for the thing or place in question—as apparent in buildings taken over by squatters, or in vacant land overgrown by weeds or filled with rubbish. Claiming something as one's own requires that the "owner" finds personal meaning in the object's symbolic properties.[27]

> This place belongs to me and I belong to it. . . . I identify with this place and I want this place identified with me ('Deep Jawa, San Francisco)

One term that came up often in descriptions of a sense of ownership is belonging, or, in Montréal, *appartenance*. Belonging is a term with a rich literature, appearing often in the context of citizenship, ethnicity, and identity politics, used to invoke ideas of attachment, identity, connection to place and to community. Like ownership, it is a term that is often taken as self-explanatory, its meaning a matter of intuition and common sense.[28] Where some effort is made to define it, belonging is often described as having two dimensions.[29] The first is a personal, intimate feeling of being "at home," a relationship between subject and object. The second is more political, a discursive resource that constructs, claims, or justifies (or resists) inclusion or exclusion in relation to the wider community.

Belonging is widely understood as intimately connected to identity and one's sense of self, and as such is something for which people yearn or long.[30] The crucial importance of belonging is reflected in a vast literature on the ways people belong to various groups, and the social, economic, and political effects of moments when belongings are displaced (for example, through industrialization or migration).[31] As bell hooks observes, belonging is something people may spend their lives searching for.[32] Belonging is linked in many examples with higher levels of engagement and political voice,[33] and claims about belonging have been interpreted as claims to secure participatory space in planning debates.[34] The French *appartenance* makes this link especially clear: coming from the verb *appartenir*, "to hold a part in," the term makes a direct connection between owning and contributing to something bigger.

Like belonging, a sense of ownership is connected to empowerment, but it is not defined simply by a personal sense of identity or agency. Empowerment, which can be understood as "a mechanism by which people, organizations, and communities gain mastery over their affairs," focuses on relationships between individuals and communities.[35] A sense of ownership, in contrast, involves not just relationships between and within groups of people, but relationships that are spatially grounded. A sense of ownership concerns a feeling of belonging to a particular place—this is *my* street, *my* neighborhood, *my* city—and with this a feeling of being able to speak for that place. A sense of ownership might in turn lead to broader empowerment, particularly (but not necessarily) in view of the long history of political power and franchise being connected to property. The connection and the agency that come with a sense of ownership are grounded in a particular physical location, and may not extend beyond that place.

In interviews, there was some debate about terminology. Not all participants describe the feelings at issue as a sense of ownership. Some suggested that belonging, community, or connection might be more appropriate terms for the relationships and aspirations at issue. However, further discussion typically moved back to ownership. Belonging, community, and connection are narrower concepts that miss important aspects. A sense of ownership emerged as a stronger priority across interviews because of the link to property, and the power that property ownership bestows. Beyond the feelings of attachment at stake in belonging, a sense of ownership invokes power and voice. A sense of ownership gives participants the ability to shape their city. As one participant explains:

> I guess [a sense of ownership] would be that somehow I feel like my fate or my well-being or quality of life is tied to something, and that I can actually influence what happens with that thing based on my participation. So it's like a kind of mutually reinforcing relationship, I'm getting something from it, but I'm also able to contribute something to it. (Liz Ogbu, San Francisco)

A sense of ownership encompasses feelings of attachment, identity, connection, and community, but also some degree of specificity and power. A sense of ownership starts with a feeling, but goes beyond this to end up with a claim about rights that can be asserted over others.

The sense of ownership involved in PARK(ing) Day can be compared to the claims made by participants in another activity through which city streets are appropriated: the digging out of parking spaces during snowy winters in North America. In cities such as Chicago, Pittsburgh, and Boston, there is a well-established tradition in which people who clear snow from a parking space claim ongoing rights to use that space. When the digger drives away, the continuing nature of those rights is expressed by placing objects (most commonly chairs) into the space as a sign to others not to park there. Those objects are generally recognized and respected. Drivers who disregard the placeholders will often return to their car to find an angry note or, in extreme cases, scratched paintwork or slashed tires. In many cases, diggers will claim rights to the space for a lengthy period, often for as long as the surrounding snow remains in place.

The appropriation of parking spaces in this way has generated significant interest among legal scholars. The practice is not sanctioned by formal legal rules, and is expressly prohibited in some cities (New York and Washington, for example). Yet the scholarship generated by the practice focuses on its legality, not its illegality. Those digging out and claiming ongoing rights to control use of the parking spots are understood as making a property claim, which others in turn recognize as a (generally, though not always) valid property right. For Carol Rose, the practice highlights the importance of communication to possession, and the way in which law (and society) rewards clear acts of demarcation.[36] For Richard Epstein, it demonstrates the way in which property regimes shift over time, and particularly the way in which top-down (regulatory) regimes interact with bottom-up systems in specific contexts.[37]

For Susan Silbey, the allocation of dug-out parking spaces is significant in demonstrating the way in which understandings of property are invoked (often tacitly) in everyday life, and how a shared legal culture is necessary to understand such actions.[38] For both the diggers of snow who make claims on parking spaces and the drivers of other cars who respect them, understandings of law are important in making sense of the practice. On Silbey's analysis, understandings of property are central in enabling people to choose between alternative interpretations of the issues in question, and to shape their behavior accordingly. Legal narratives provide grounding for the claims made by snow diggers, and these are reinforced through their resonance with normative ideals about labor, desert, and fairness.

In much the same way that Rose, Epstein, and Silbey argue that claims to snow-cleared parking spaces are claims about property, the claims about ownership discussed by participants in PARK(ing) Day can also be understood as proprietary. While claims to snow-cleared parking spaces recall private property with their emphasis on exclusive use, the claims about ownership involved in PARK(ing) Day (and in participatory planning more generally) are more akin to common property, with their claim to voice and influence rather than exclusive control.[39] Yet they can be likened to property in important respects: claims about ownership address questions of the allocation of rights and responsibilities in regard to land, and draw on conceptions of law and legality to do so.

Davina Cooper's analysis of property practices is helpful in thinking about the way in which a sense of ownership relates to property.[40] Cooper argues that conventional accounts of property are too rigid in their definitions of what does and does not constitute property. In focusing only on a narrowly defined set of entitlements, such accounts miss the fine-grained and overlapping character of the rights, duties, and norms through which property contributes to social life.[41] A more productive alternative, Cooper suggests, is one that centers on belonging.

Property is not a focus of the literature on belonging, other than in more general references to the links between socioeconomic status and patterns of inclusion and exclusion. In her exploration of belonging as central to property, Cooper thus focuses not on the literature on belonging, but on empirical research into the way in which belonging and property operate in practice. Cooper's analysis derives primarily from field work at Summerhill School, an alternative residential school in the UK in which rules are made and disputes settled by the students and staff together.[42]

Conventional accounts of property focus on what Cooper calls "subject-object belonging": an instrumental, hierarchical form of belonging concerned with the ownership and use of belongings. This enables property to be understood as a bundle of severable and discrete rights, a matter of what belongs to the owner in question. It can be fungible, measurable, and accessible through a simple transaction: much like the property that Rebar suggests is attainable by paying a parking meter.

Cooper argues that subject-object belonging is just one dimension of belonging, and that "part-whole belonging" and "proper attachment" must also be considered for an accurate understanding of property and the roles that it plays in social life.[43] Part-whole belonging is the more personal dimension, describing a relationship between two (or more) bodies that is mutually formative. While the relationship will often be asymmetrical (house and garden, child and family, citizen and nation), the formation of each part depends on the other. Constitutive and also empowering, part-whole belonging can be understood as the attributes, qualities, or characteristics of the thing—its properties—that enable that thing to extend or imprint itself in the world (including intangible property, such as whiteness, in line with Cheryl Harris's analysis).[44]

Proper attachment, Cooper's third dimension, is a more political form of belonging. This is a relationship of proximity, attachment, or connection, as in "I belong here," "he belongs to me," or "he belongs with his mother." Belonging in this sense is shaped by who else belongs, and might entail expectations of propriety among other members of the community to which one belongs.

Belonging is central to property for Cooper. However, as she explains, "not all forms of belonging count."[45] So while belonging is at the heart of property relations, it is the coupling of belonging with authoritative practices that produces relationships of property. At Summerhill, Cooper finds that these practices include: recognition, clarification, simplification, definition, and power. Recognition confirms and creates property, giving effect to some relations of belonging but not others. Clarification, simplification, and definition establish the contours and boundaries of property, solidifying belonging such that it becomes intelligible as proprietary. The power at stake may be within or beyond the relationship of belonging, but is crucial: whether belonging becomes intelligible as property depends on the capacity of that codification to make a difference.

Cooper's analysis resonates with the sense of ownership described by participants in PARK(ing) Day. Belonging is important in understanding a sense of ownership, but it is not sufficient to describe the relationships at issue. A sense of ownership involves personal connections but, crucially, connections that incorporate claims about rights. As with the chairs placed in snow-cleared parking spaces, a sense of ownership provides the basis for claims that can be asserted over others. A sense of ownership might be understood as something in between: more than belonging, but not (yet) property. Over time, and through authoritative practices, a sense of ownership might develop further into property.

This connection to power and rights means that ownership is not simply a personal or psychological matter; one cannot influence or contribute to something without acknowledgment from others. Just as property rights rely on a general acceptance of the rights flowing from legal title, recognition is important also to a sense of ownership. A sense of ownership is relational, involving entitlement that is recognized by others.

The degree of separation between property, ownership, and a sense of ownership is debatable: another instance of slipperiness. The idea that leases and other property rights can be placed at one end of a spectrum, with legality and specificity decreasing toward a sense of ownership at the other end, is helpful in understanding various forms of property and the relationships between them. It is also misleading. The slippage between property and ownership reflects the degree to which these concepts are entangled, and mutually constitutive.

Just as property and ownership are often treated as synonymous, ownership and a sense of ownership overlap to a significant extent. In interviews, participants used the terms interchangeably. Many spoke simply of ownership, without the "sense of," and I have often found myself tempted to do the same. Neither term is clearly bounded; both imply a normative decision about values and voice, about relationships between and among the subjects and objects of property.

4.4   Renting space

A metered parking spot is an inexpensive short-term lease for a 10′ x 20′ plot of land. . . . Just as it is completely within the rights of individuals to buy up shares of a publicly-traded company, Park(ing) Day participants paid meters and exercised their option to do something other than park cars in real estate that they, for the moment, owned.[46]

The lease provided powerful language with which to explain the legal status of PARK(ing) Day. While a niche or loophole is a rather complicated justification, a lease is enticingly simple. A lease is one of the best-known legal concepts, and the idea that a lease is created when money is paid into a parking meter makes sense in lay terms.

Significantly, the lease coincided with Rebar's interest in pushing the boundaries of property. Inspired by the work of conceptual artist Gordon Matta-Clark, property was an explicit focus of the initial PARK(ing) installation. Matta-Clark challenged ideas of property in a series of projects in the 1970s, most dramatically and directly by making large-scale incisions into buildings.[47] These were buildings scheduled for demolition, and the cuts were made with the permission of the relevant owners. The cuts were often spectacular: a two-story house sliced right through the middle; a multistory building with large ellipse-shaped holes cut through several floors.

For Rebar, Matta-Clark's *Reality Properties: Fake Estates* was particularly exciting. Fascinated by the idea of untenable but ownable space, Matta-Clark purchased small parcels of land in New York: slivers of curbsides, alleyways and other tiny lots.[48] Sold at auction for $25 each, these were pieces of land that were affordable because they were seen by most to have little value. In *Reality Properties*, Matta-Clark combined the title deeds for these properties with maps and montaged images of each site, effectively highlighting and critiquing the arbitrariness of property demarcation.[49]

The allocation of property is an issue of widespread and longstanding concern. Property is widely recognized as a human right and a fundamental need.[50] A person cannot perform essential tasks without some access to property: the ability of owners to exclude nonowners means that property is intimately connected to the performance of basic human activities like sleeping, bathing, or cooking. For those without private property, restrictions on the use of public property can make it very difficult to "be" in any place.[51]

Access to property is a concern at the heart of one of PARK(ing) Day's precursors, *Bosom Buddies*, the sitcom in which the opening credits include a scene of the show's two stars paying a meter then using the space to sun themselves on folding chairs. The premise of *Bosom Buddies* is that Kip Wilson and Henry Desmond (played by Tom Hanks and Peter Scolari) cannot afford to rent a home in New York; the first episode begins with the pair being woken by a wrecking ball swinging through their apartment. Kip and Henry disguise themselves as women so that they can live in a female-only hotel, the only place they can afford. Alongside the meter rental, the opening credits include more familiar efforts to "be" in New York without property, such as bathing in a park fountain.

Like Matta-Clark's piecemeal purchases, the parking meter for Rebar was an affordable path to property and, through this, a way to provoke reflection on the commodification of land. The stakes of that commodification have escalated in the decades since Matta-Clark's interventions: almost daily the media features reports of a housing crisis, rapidly rising intergenerational inequality, and young people being locked out of property forever.[52] With growing numbers of people unable to access housing in urban centers, the workings of the contemporary property market are increasingly being questioned by scholars, and by activists pursuing more equitable allocations of property through campaigns like Occupy.[53] This is particularly apparent in global cities like San Francisco and Sydney, but increasingly evident elsewhere, including in Montréal.

By presenting an inexpensive means to obtain a piece of property— albeit a small and temporary piece—Rebar provided a glimmer of hope in an increasingly dark debate. The heat of these debates helps to explain the interest in PARK(ing) Day. By invoking property and its price, PARK(ing) Day resonates with deeply felt concerns and campaigns about access to the city. The trick with which Rebar did this, presenting a short-term, affordable and accessible rental opportunity, is important in understanding the power of PARK(ing) Day as a vehicular idea.

PARK(ing) Day resonates with campaigns like Occupy, yet it can also be distinguished from them. In contrast to the Occupy movement, to squatting or to other radical forms of activism around housing and space in the city, PARK(ing) Day does not challenge the current regimes of property allocation. As one participant explains:

> It was important to me that it was allowed. I don't know, I wasn't trying to break the system. I was working with the system. I didn't want to get in trouble and I didn't want it to be antagonistic. I didn't want it to be antagonistic. I wouldn't have done it if I felt it was antagonistic. (Daniel Sherman, San Francisco)

This is significant in understanding the kinds of people who participate in PARK(ing) Day. In their discussion of the evolution of property law, Eduardo Peñalver and Sonia Katyal argue that litigation and lobbying for law reform are tools of the haves, while illegal activities like squatting are the tools of the have nots.[54] Both, they argue, are important to property as an institution. While the tools of the haves have traditionally been privileged, illegal activities should also be appreciated for their role in enabling property to remain broadly faithful to shifting norms, values, and social realities. In making this point, Peñalver and Katyal at times struggle to define what is legal and what is not (a problem they note in relation to intellectual property, prompting a focus on property "altlaws" rather than "outlaws").[55] PARK(ing) Day complicates this further, showing clearly the limits of the legal/illegal binary, and in doing so revealing the fertility of the interstitial space.

> PARK(ing) Day is the kind of transgression, you know, your mom would feel comfortable doing. (Blaine Merker, San Francisco)

PARK(ing) Day sits in between the legal and the illegal, and its constituency is similarly mixed. Participants in PARK(ing) Day are generally renters; if they own property, it is typically an apartment or a small home (and likely heavily mortgaged, in need of renovation, or both). Participants are rarely in possession of the resources necessary for the litigation or significant lobbying activities undertaken by the haves. Yet they do bring other forms of capital. While the informal nature of PARK(ing) Day means there are no official records, my research suggests that privilege is at play: class, race, and gender are important in understanding who gets involved. Participants in PARK(ing) Day are often young professionals—junior designers, engineers, public servants, business owners, even lawyers. They are often white, and frequently male.

Participants in PARK(ing) Day are typically people with more to lose from activities like squatting than the have nots, perhaps even the potential to become haves in the future. PARK(ing) Day might be understood as a technique in between the legal and illegal binary described by Peñalver and Katyal: a means for law reform suitable to the "could haves."

Rebar's purported lease is important to this. The event is presented as legal, yet the resources required for engagement are fairly small. There is no need to be a well-resourced property owner to participate in the event, but there is also no need to put any property one does possess on the line. Rebar's claim to legality makes PARK(ing) Day safe and accessible; one need not abandon property or hopes of its attainment.

4.5   Rights to the city: property and participation in the planning process

Property is a particularly empowering legal right. In contrast to another form of permissibility (say, a license to use the space in a particular way), a property right brings with it a vast range of possibilities. By arguing that payment of the meter created a lease, Rebar claimed the parking space itself, and with this a concomitant right to engage in decision-making about the future of the city around it.

Debates about property are about access to housing, but they are also about access to the city itself. Beyond providing a base for the completion of basic tasks, property is intimately and intuitively connected to feelings of self-affirmation, autonomy, and control over the way we constitute ourselves in the world.[56] Property ownership has long been associated with wealth and power, and understood as fundamental to the privileges of democracy, citizenship, and political participation.[57] While formal links between property and suffrage have been removed in most places, connections between property and political rights continue to resonate in contemporary debates.[58]

Property is closely connected to participation in the shaping of the city. There is a voluminous literature suggesting that property owners are more likely to engage in planning processes, and more likely to be heard when they do.[59] Much of this focuses on the NIMBY (Not In My Back Yard) objector,[60] the homeowner who may acknowledge the benefits of a proposed development but advocate its location further away (places of worship for minority religions, for example, in industrial rather than residential areas).[61] At the other extreme, the connection between property and capital under neoliberalism means that large property developers are often able to dominate the planning process, whether adjusting and avoiding planning controls or persuading governments to prioritize nearby infrastructure and services so as to increase the profitability of their developments.[62] The power of property is apparent also when planning matters go to court, where the rights of nonowners to participate are limited and frequently questioned.[63] Property brings with it voice and a right to engage.

Conversely, a lack of property can entail a lack of voice. Discussing the operation of provisions enabling existing landowners to comment on proposals for new development, Alan Evans describes an "insider–outsider problem": property owners are given an additional forum to influence planning not available to the unidentified people who would live in housing if development went ahead,[64] much less to those marginalized in more fundamental ways. As Evans argues, this is one of the ways in which the planning system is geared to preserving the status quo.

Beyond planning processes, the influence of property plays out in informal negotiations through which property owners are able to influence the uses of areas beyond their formal control. In the context of the interactions between street vendors and owners of adjacent buildings in New York, Ryan Devlin describes an informal sense of ownership over spaces beyond the property boundary.[65] In Devlin's examples, property owners rely on techniques of surveillance, intimidation, and physical interventions—all unsanctioned—to control adjoining public spaces for which they feel a sense of ownership or entitlement, yet to which they have no formal property rights. Also in New York, Amnon Lehavi highlights the way in which people without formal property rights may effectively manage and control public parks, at times advancing their own interests while working against the interests of other users.[66]

Common in the literature on contemporary shifts in urban governance are references to enclosure: gated residential communities; securitized shopping malls that control, exclude, and segregate undesirable populations.[67]

Globalization and neoliberal economic restructuring have vastly increased the separation between rich and poor, as Edward Soja explains:

> Not only are residences becoming increasingly gated, guarded, and wrapped in advanced security, surveillance, and alarm systems, so too are many other activities, land uses, and everyday objects in the urban environment, from shopping malls and libraries to razor-wire protected refuse bins and spiked park benches designed to stave off incursions of the homeless and hungry. Microtechnologies of social and spatial control infest everyday life and pile up to produce a tightly meshed and prisonlike geography punctuated by protective enclosures and overseen by ubiquitous watchful eyes.[68]

Concerns are also raised about exclusion and displacement that take place conceptually, with a shift toward urban spaces produced by and for a much smaller group of people.[69] New forms of governance are displacing elected decision-making bodies: public-private partnerships, private and quasi-private development corporations, and expert-based consent authorities are increasingly prominent.[70] Instead of democratic decision-making, the integration of state and corporate interests means that city-making is increasingly directed by private interests, with little scope for public involvement.

Reflecting the connection between property, citizenship, and participation in planning and urban development, many of the campaigns around property in urban centers like San Francisco and Sydney assert a right to the city. First proposed by Henri Lefebvre in 1968, the right to the city is a call for an end to the displacement of low-income and marginalized urban communities, but it is a call for more than a right to remain. The US-based Right to the City Alliance, for example, explains: "The idea of a right to the city frames and activates a new kind of urban politic that asserts that everyone, particularly the disenfranchised, not only have a right to the city, but as inhabitants, have a right to shape it, design it."[71]

Based on use value rather than exchange value, the right to the city is a claim to inhabit in a full sense. It is a right to access and occupy urban space, but also to participate in the creation of space that meets the needs of the inhabitants of the city. The right to the city is based on Lefebvre's understanding of the city as *oeuvre*, an unintentional and collective work of art, embedded in everyday life.[72] In contrast to the frameworks for public consultation that were then being formalized in law (frameworks Lefebvre dismissed as "acquiescence at a small price"),[73] the right to the city entails not consultation but genuine participation (accessing and influencing decisions that produce urban space) and appropriation (accessing, occupying, and using urban space, including creating new space that meets the needs of the inhabitants of the city). Those who live in a city, Lefebvre argued, must be able to participate in the creative, daily activity through which the *oeuvre* of that city is produced.[74]

The right to the city has generated a vast literature, as well as considerable interest in activist and policy circles.[75] Central to the attraction of the right to the city is its emphasis on active and engaged urban citizenship. In contrast to private property and the capitalist system of accumulation with which it is so deeply entangled, the right to the city is based on inhabitance: use rather than exchange. The right to the city brings to the fore questions about who and what gets to determine the value and use of the things and spaces of the city. For Lefebvre, the right to the city was particularly important for the working class, "rejected from the centres towards the peripheries, dispossessed of the city, expropriated thus from the best outcomes of its activity."[76] More recent scholars have emphasized its applicability to other dispossessed groups: women, migrants, racial and ethnic minorities, people with disabilities.[77]

The right to the city suggests that the city and urban life are very much stakes in the struggles against neoliberalism that often take place there.[78] It has been taken up enthusiastically as a right that is accessible to those without formal property, and also as a right that captures and expresses a basic human desire to participate in shaping urban space. As David Harvey explains:

> The question of what kind of city we want cannot be divorced from the question of what kind of people we want to be, what kinds of social relations we seek, what relations to nature we cherish, what style of life we desire, what aesthetic values we hold. The right to the city is, therefore, far more than a right of individual or group access to the resources that the city embodies: it is a right to change and reinvent the city more after our hearts' desire. . . . The freedom to make and remake ourselves and our cities is . . . one of the most precious yet most neglected of our human rights.[79]

By asserting a right to use and to shape urban space, (re)inserting noncommercial spaces into increasingly privatized cities where people can feel unwelcome—even barred—if they are not purchasing something, PARK(ing) Day can be read as claiming the right to the city. The link between PARK(ing)

Day and the right to the city is one that is often made in commentary on the event,[80] and on other examples of DIY urbanism.[81] Lusi Morhayim, for example, argues: "PARK(ing) Day provides an open canvas to the residents of the city to share their urban needs and temporarily recreate part of a public street to respond to their needs. Appropriation of space creates a public forum and fosters discussion in the public sphere. . . . The park(ing) spots foster spatial communication of the right to the city."[82]

Descriptions of PARK(ing) Day as satisfying a human need or expressing the right to the city recur among participants. Many emphasize the importance of claiming the space and making it theirs, at least temporarily.

> It's a reflection on, it's my city, it's my street and I want to be a human that has his space and I am asking one day in the year just to use the space differently. (Félix Gravel, Montréal)

The interventions made on PARK(ing) Day are small in scale and short in duration. Their potential to achieve longer-lasting and wider-reaching change is similarly limited, and participants are aware of this. Many of the issues of concern to participants—issues like homelessness and the housing crisis, white privilege and colonial dispossession, climate change and the rampant ecological destruction being wrought by current models of development—are far beyond the scope of such tiny, temporary interventions. In considering the significance of these limits, it is important to note that the other opportunities for public participation in decision-making about the built environment are far from perfect. PARK(ing) Day might seem far removed from Lefebvre's call for the right to the city, or from the concerns animating contemporary elaborations of the concept. Yet, for at least some people, the limited scope for meaningful participation in other planning processes means that PARK(ing) Day is valuable as an opportunity to express, or to work toward, a right to the city.

Since the "communicative" or "collaborative" turn of the 1990s, public participation has been prominent in both the policy and practice of planning.[83] Exhibitions, submissions, and hearings are legally required for many planning processes in Sydney, San Francisco, and Montréal, as in many other cities. A search on the noticeboard or website of any planning authority will invariably reveal at least one call for submissions on proposals for development, perhaps also an opportunity to speak at a public hearing.

Despite these opportunities and the participatory rhetoric surrounding them, the consultation and tokenism highlighted so vividly in Sherry Arnstein's 1969 Ladder of Citizen Participation remain prevalent today.[84] As many critics have noted, there are few legislative requirements for participatory processes to actually influence decision-making, with the result that there is often a disconnect between the preferences elicited through participatory processes and the decisions that eventuate. Others go further, drawing on ideas of the "postpolitical" to argue that participatory processes are carefully managed to provide the appearance of engagement and legitimacy, while minimizing the potential for those with conflicting views to be heard.[85] In this context, it is not surprising that these opportunities for participation generate little energy or enthusiasm.

PARK(ing) Day presents a very different format for participation. While writing a submission is typically an abstract and isolating process (submissions are written in private, sent to an unknown reader, their contents rarely even acknowledged), PARK(ing) Day generates tangible change with immediate feedback. Similarly, while speaking at a hearing can be intimidating for people not used to making formal presentations, with the format and number of speakers often tightly controlled (and neighboring property owners given priority), PARK(ing) Day is open to anyone, in any format they wish. PARK(ing) Day provides opportunities to work collaboratively with others on developing ideas for the future, physically testing those, and doing so in public. Far from the scripted, carefully controlled processes offered by state planning authorities, PARK(ing) Day invites and encourages creativity and experimentation. For participants, the ability to express oneself in the city, to develop visions for the future and to do so collaboratively, is highly valued.

In Montréal, many interviewees noted the very low rates of homeownership across the city as an important factor in the desire to "own" public parts of the city (I was told several times that around 70 percent of residents do not own their home).[86] A lack of homeownership was noted as a driver for participation in other cities also. For PARK(ing) Day participants, the creation of parks is valued as a rare opportunity to take ownership and express oneself in a small part of the city.

> You know if you have your own little piece of world, whether that's you own your apartment or you own a plot of land or you own a house or whatever, you've got something, right. If you don't own something, what you do have is the city. So

you go into the city and you try to take some ownership somewhere, I think to satisfy some sort of human need around being able to shape your environment. You can shape your backyard, you can shape your front yard, you can paint your condo on the inside, you can do whatever you want to your apartment when you own these things. It's a little bit more difficult when you don't. So it's kind of a release valve for that. (Mike Lydon, New York)

Andres Toro, a community organizer in Montréal, suggested that the popularity of PARK(ing) Day can be explained by the weather and the demographics of the city. Montréal, he explained, is full of students, and for much of the year it is extremely expensive to do anything—the heavy snowfall means you need to be indoors, or to engage in organized activities. For both, "you always have to pay." PARK(ing) Day, in contrast, presents an affordable opportunity to shape the city. This, Toro claims, is why it has been taken up with such enthusiasm.

For the student-run McGill Spaces Project, PARK(ing) Day provided an exciting opportunity to contribute to the form of the university and the spaces around it. Many of the members of the McGill Spaces Project are not from Montréal (director Alan Chen, for example, is originally from Vancouver), and valued PARK(ing) Day as a way to engage with and embed the group into the local community. The McGill Spaces Project used PARK(ing) Day as a launch event in 2014, and participated again the next year (figure 4.2). In both years, they created a temporary space and within that space invited people to join them in building and decorating furniture and artworks that would be used after the event:

It wasn't just a display for us to show off, we wanted the community to be able to contribute and to see their contributions afterwards. (Alan Chen, Montréal)

Beyond having a home of one's own, participants in all three cities emphasized the importance of property in more public places. PARK(ing) Day offers a way to contribute, at least temporarily, to the *oeuvre* of the city. Participants linked access to property directly to self-expression in the public realm:

This idea . . . is something that I feel is very valuable, because I can feel like we can buy into the real estate on our main street, and have our culture and our community represented in actual property on the street. (Kris Spann, Sydney)

The opportunity to access property and, importantly, the cultural and political agency that comes with it is a key part of the value and appeal

Figure 4.2
PARK(ing) Day installation by students from McGill University, Rue University, Montréal, 2015. The group provided paints and a range of things for people to paint on: furniture (made from recycled materials, later donated to a local community center) and small boards for paintings. Image: Amelia Thorpe.

of PARK(ing) Day. It is helpful in explaining why people participate in PARK(ing) Day, and why so many people are inspired to get involved as soon as they hear about the event. The link to property, and particularly to the ability to express oneself through it, helps to explain also why people go to such lengths to do so. In discussing why he and his staff contributed many hours over many years building parks in San Francisco, Andrew Dunbar explains:

> I think it sustains us . . . it's sustaining, you know, to spend a little more on organic. So that's what PARK(ing) Day is . . . it's more expensive to do it, but it makes you healthier.

PARK(ing) Day is about much more than the purported lease created by paying the meter. By invoking property, PARK(ing) Day highlights the slipperiness of ownership, the ways in which the lines between particular proprietary rights (the lease), broader legal categories (property), everyday concepts (ownership), and deeply felt emotions (sense of ownership) are fluid and overlapping. Rebar's claim to property is a claim to legitimacy but, more fundamentally, it is a claim to power, voice, and agency. PARK(ing) Day is significant as a political claim beyond the appropriation of a space in which to be: participants seek a right to the city in a full sense, to participation and appropriation, a meaningful role in shaping the future of their cities.

Figure 5.1
PARK(ing) Day installation—complete with host in costume and in character—by Société de Transport de Montréal, Rue Saint-Catherine, Montréal, 2015. Passersby enthusiastically took up the STM's invitation to play a game. Image: Amelia Thorpe.

5 Building Ownership

While Rebar's claim to property in PARK(ing) Day is wrong on technicalities—no lease is created by paying a parking meter—it is not wrong at a deeper level. Property is indeed central to the performance of legality in PARK(ing) Day. The scope and significance of property is far more complex, however, than Rebar suggest.

Building on the exploration of the concept of property in the previous chapter, in this chapter I argue that the claims to property made in PARK(ing) Day are deeper social claims about ownership, and that property not only connects to ownership but depends upon it. A focus on the conceptions underpinning such claims reveals that understandings of ownership and ideas about property theory are mutually constitutive.

Rebar's purported lease works alongside, and in many cases because of, an informal sense of ownership. A sense of ownership provides the grounding for a lease. While the lease builds on a sense of ownership, it adds to it too. More than a game or gimmick, acquisition of a "lease" does operate in some ways like the acquisition of formal title in providing a base for the development of ownership. Consistent with the literature on psychological ownership and on belonging, such feelings are easier to develop when they coincide with legal title (or, at least, when the "owner" believes they coincide with legal title). The idea of a lease provides an additional layer of authority on which a more informal sense of ownership can be advanced.

> It sparks a sense of ownership because you're told by these Rebar guys you have the right to do this, and so against your doubts, you do it. . . . I think it's very powerful then to be like, what else can you do? (Amy Seek, San Francisco)

A belief that they have acquired a lease empowers participants to go beyond their usual ways of expressing feelings of belonging and connection, enabling the appropriation and transformation of the street. In facilitating these activities, the lease also adds to a sense of ownership at a deeper level. Through the process of building a park, participants say that their sense of ownership is strengthened: the performance of legality in PARK(ing) Day is itself productive.

These interactions reveal the intimate and mutually constitutive relationships between formal and informal conceptions of property. In explaining how PARK(ing) Day builds a sense of ownership, participants draw—often indirectly, but sometimes explicitly—on concepts that are well known in property scholarship. What is interesting is that these claims are made by people without knowledge of property theory. This resonance between popular understandings and scholarly theories of property suggests that the latter are themselves to some degree intuitive, emerging out of everyday life. Property theory, like the technical and institutional structures it sustains, is revealed through participants' claims to be deeply entangled with values and feelings, drawing on and sustained by normative ideas and folk understandings.

Perhaps unsurprisingly, many interviews revealed echoes of that most influential property story, the claim that proprietary rights can be derived from work or labor. Yet labor is far from sufficient to establish ownership. Participants also explained the development of ownership in ways that resonate with other approaches to property, particularly personhood and relational understandings. In contrast to the imagined histories of labor-based appropriation, examination of the ways in which people construct ownership in PARK(ing) Day provides a thicker, richer, and more temporally nuanced story. In line with Davina Cooper's analysis, property is developed and sustained through multiple practices. For participants in PARK(ing) Day, various descriptive and justificatory approaches do not compete but work together to produce a sense of ownership.

Participants highlighted other factors too. The spatial and material qualities of the streets and objects with which people engage in PARK(ing) Day, for example, are significant in explaining how a sense of ownership is strengthened through the event. Another factor that was important for many, but emphasized much less in accounts of more mainstream property forms, is joy. Ownership is something that people choose to take, and play, pleasure, delight, and even love are key drivers of that choice. The fun and frivolous aspects of PARK(ing) Day are not simply enjoyable, but productive.

This invocation of additional paths to ownership echoes Robert Cover's claims about the fertile forces of jurisgenesis. PARK(ing) Day provides a strong example of the open-ended nature of legal interpretation. Consistent with the claims made by Cover and by Hartog, the line between what is legal and what is not is gray and always open to extension.

5.1   Labor

In discussing ways in which a sense of ownership might be developed, participants often mention labor. People describe making very significant investments of time and effort in preparing for PARK(ing) Day, encompassing many hours over weeks or even months before the event, and they often referred to this effort in discussing their feelings of ownership for the street and the neighborhood. Participants describe feelings of achievement and pride following PARK(ing) Day; many note that successfully hosting a park was very satisfying, producing lasting feelings of connection to and ownership of the street, the community, or even the city.

> I think it was a lot more work than we thought it was going to be [laughs]. Yes, yeah, but I thought it was really successful and I loved it. (Jonathan Knapp, Sydney)

Participants discuss exhaustion and effort, but also a sense of achievement flowing from this: the fact that PARK(ing) Day requires work is part of its appeal, and its value. Participants take pleasure and pride in creating something, and in telling their stories they emphasize the craft involved. The giant pinball machine built by the San Francisco office of Bohlin Cywinski Jackson (figure 5.2), for example, involved several weeks of work by four architects, building up to very late nights in the office by a much larger team.

Participants point out things they have made, particularly clever and thrifty uses of scraps to produce something out of nothing. Several described collecting waste materials in the lead-up to the event—water bottles, coffee cups, scraps of timber, used cardboard, carpet, and other discarded objects—then working to turn these into things of value such as seats, sculptures, and sites for play.

> Together we built a public space with no money and for one day it was the best public space in Montréal. (Jérôme Glad, Montréal)

Figure 5.2
PARK(ing) Day installation by Bohlin Cywinski Jackson featuring plywood pinball machine and seating, Grant Avenue, San Francisco, 2016. The pinball was popular with people passing by, attracting quite a crowd. Architects from BCJ were on hand with various tools to keep it working throughout the day, having (not quite) finished the project in the early hours of that morning. Image: Amelia Thorpe.

The idea of ownership deriving from physical work or effort is consistent with one of the best-known property theories, that of labor as the justification for original appropriation. This is typically traced to John Locke, who argued that private property was produced by mixing one's labor with the things of the external world.[1] Locke began with the premise that God gave the world to all (men) in common, and also "reason to make use of it to the best advantage of life, and convenience."[2] Accordingly, there must be a means to appropriate the fruits of nature so that they can be of use and benefit to particular men. The solution, he argued, derives from the property that every man has in his own person and the work of his body (something Locke took to be self-evident and did not explain).[3] By picking up acorns from under an oak or gathering apples from trees in the wood, Locke claimed, "that labour put a distinction between them and common: that added something to them more than nature, the common mother of all, had done, and so they became his private right."[4] This was a "law of reason," necessary to enable the fruits of the commons to be of use.[5]

Locke's theory has been subject to intense critique, for issues ranging from problems of reasoning to Locke's implication in histories of dispossession and inequality.[6] Questions have been raised about the amount of labor required for appropriation (as Robert Nozick asks, would tipping a can of soup into the ocean be enough to claim it?) and the justification for rights of infinite duration (well beyond the time necessary to derive benefit from the commons). Yet the labor story remains powerful, and numerous scholars have made efforts to resolve these issues in various alternative labor-based theories.[7]

The idea of labor justifying ownership appears also well beyond this literature. Perhaps because rewarding effort "seems intuitively just,"[8] the labor story can be found in many places. Anders Corr notes use of the labor theory by squatters to justify proprietary rights in places from New York to the Brazilian Amazon.[9] In claims by long-term tenants for rights to remain resident in the gentrifying Downtown Eastside of Vancouver, Nicholas Blomley notes, "Perhaps implicit here is not only the claim of dignified rest, following an active life, but that of Lockean entitlement. By mixing his labor with the land, he has made the province 'ours'; it is only appropriate that we respect his modest claim to his home."[10]

At Summerhill School, Cooper describes a striking resonance with Locke's labor-based theory in a student's claims for possession of part of the school grounds. This was based on the work he had done in removing nettles from the space:

> He was brought up [Summerhill term for the process where one person brings a case against another] at a school meeting on the basis that the space he had recoded as "settled" was too large, its boundaries too expansive (see also Locke 1988, 288–291). However, after discussion, the school meeting recognized his rights of possession: the boy's labor conjoined with his property assertion transformed and redefined the space—what had previously been "vacant" was now of value thanks to the labor he had vested in it.[11]

Perhaps most famously for property scholars, labor is an important part of the literature discussing the proprietary nature of claims to parking spaces dug out from snow. Richard Epstein and Susan Silbey each note strong echoes of Lockean theory in discussions about rights to park in those spaces.[12] Silbey is particularly explicit about this connection, with her title "J. Locke, Op. Cit," and in doing so has attracted considerable interest.[13] Silbey explains: "The person who places the object in the shovelled out spot, references, knowingly or not, Locke's labour theory of property . . . the snow shoveler performed the labour of removing the snow and publicly announces her claim to the use value produced."[14]

Yet property is about more than labor. For Robert Munzer, labor plays a significant but incomplete role in justifying property.[15] Capturing factors that people commonly value, such as effort, ability, persistence, industriousness, time spent, achievement, responsibility, leadership, and motivating capacity, labor provides an anchor for other principles.

With respect to the claiming of parking spaces dug out from snow, labor does not tell the whole story. In their analyses of the practice, Epstein, Silbey, and Carol Rose all find that other issues are also at play. Silbey argues that the practice is intelligible only as an expression of legal culture. The placeholders can be understood as communicative transactions that invoke general legal concepts, but also specific understandings about who can use the particular space in question, for what and for how long.[16]

The act of digging is generally accepted as sufficient for the appropriation of the parking space in front of one's own home. Such claims are more tenuous, however, for acts of digging in other locations—outside another person's home, for example. While this point is not emphasized by Epstein, Silbey, or Rose, it is apparent in the material they cite.[17] Epstein is most explicit about this, commenting: "it appears, at least in some neighborhoods, that some home owners are able to shoo away other individuals who try to dig out the snow near their front door. They seem to be able to reserve the first right to dig it out for themselves."[18]

Epstein notes also that the practice can be seen only in certain areas.[19] On denser streets lacking a one-to-one correspondence between a parking space and residence—streets on which, as explained below, a sense of ownership may be harder to establish—it appears less likely that people will either dig out or lay claim to parking spaces.

The labor involved in building a park can be compared to the labor involved in clearing snow from a parking space. While perhaps less physically demanding than shoveling snow, the work required to build a park is often more involved.

Participants in PARK(ing) Day, like the diggers of snow cited by Silbey and Epstein, saw labor as significant to feelings of ownership. But many were skeptical about the extent of this impact. Consistently, participants suggested that labor is important, but that other factors carry more weight—factors such as time, social networks, responsibility, self-expression, and identity.

In an interesting example of the interplay between folk and scholarly conceptions, these additional factors can be understood not as weakening or challenging labor-based theories but as strengthening them. Many of the shortcomings of labor-based theories might be addressed through these factors: self-expression and identity help to answer Nozick's soup can hypothetical, matters of time help address the duration of rights, and relational and community concerns help to determine the extent of ownership and its relation to other claims.

5.2 Personhood

Beyond the effort involved in building a park, participants emphasize the degree of control they had over the work involved when describing the feelings of ownership that followed from PARK(ing) Day. Much more than labor as work or "sweat equity," people connect ownership to the creative and expressive aspects of their contributions. Consistent with references to ownership as "recognizing oneself," participants emphasize the transformative nature of the efforts through which ownership is produced.

> We feel that intimacy. It's like, at the end of the day, like you poured a piece of your soul in that . . . it's a piece of you in there. (Carlo Tadeo, Montréal)

For many participants, the creation of parks is valuable as a rare opportunity to shape a small part of the city. By participating in PARK(ing) Day, people are able to take control of the space and express themselves in it, and this is significant in developing their feelings of ownership.

> When I come by, every time, when I'm with my girlfriend or something, I tell her there was something there. It was done the way we want. (Jean-Philippe Di Marco, Montréal)

I pass by it a lot and it still has its role that it's always had of being the street, but I do remember, you know. And when I go, I smile. It's nice. (Daniel Sherman, San Francisco)

While less ubiquitous than labor, the connection between ownership and identity has generated a rich literature within property scholarship. Theories of property based on identity are typically traced to the work of Georg Hegel.[20] Hegel's starting point is a conception of individuals as abstract units of free will with no concrete existence. From there, property is necessary for the development of identity: "Not until he has property does the person exist as reason."[21] By enabling individuals to act in and to shape the external, objective world, property facilitates the embodiment of the will in objective form.[22] Taking possession of oneself, Hegel explains, consists "in translating into *actuality* what one is in terms of one's concept (as *possibility*, capacity [*Vermögen*], or predisposition). By this means, what one is in concept is posited for the first time as one's own, and also as an object [*Gegenstand*] distinct from simple self-consciousness."[23]

The necessity for private property follows from this: "Since I give my will existence [*Dasein*] through property, property must also have the determination of being this specific entity, of being mine."[24] Superficially, Hegel's theory appears similar to that of Locke. Yet where property for Locke was necessary to enable men to benefit from the fruits of the commons, Hegel sees property in less instrumental terms: "property, as the first *existence* [*Dasein*] of freedom, is an essential end for itself."[25] The starting point and the means for acquisition vary also. Locke begins with property as owned by all (men) in common. Hegel, however, begins with all things as unowned, available for appropriation because of their lack of subjectivity.[26] When it comes to acquisition, Locke's owner puts himself into the object through the process of labor, with appropriation derived from the mixing of the propertied self and the object. There is no such mixing in Hegel's theory. Rather, property emerges as part of the process of making the will objective and externalized.[27]

In modern property scholarship, personhood theory is often referred to through the work of Margaret Radin. Radin draws partly from Hegel, and partly from an "intuitive" understanding that certain objects people possess are closely bound up with their identity.[28] Such items—a wedding ring, a family heirloom, a person's home—are part of the way we constitute ourselves as continuing personal entities in the world, relating to both the external environment and other people. This, for Radin, is the moral basis of property. Distinguishing between what she calls "personhood property" and other "fungible property," Radin argues that claims for personhood property are morally superior to claims for other forms of property.[29] The importance of this distinction, she argues, is apparent in its reflection in legal doctrines from privacy to residential tenancy to takings law.

Ownership as something developed through self-expression and as connected to identity were strong themes for participants. Beyond labor as effort, which could be understood as mastery or subject-object belonging in Cooper's terms, self-directed and expressive labor encompasses the *constitutive* relationships of part-whole belonging (as when a child "belongs" to a family or a garden "belongs" to a dwelling) and proper attachment (as in "I belong here").

Personhood is important in understanding the nature of ownership as well as its production. A sense of ownership matters because it allows people to fulfill basic human motives, and it is through the satisfaction of these needs that ownership is constituted.

This is consistent with the literature on the right to the city, with its emphasis on a human need to contribute to the *oeuvre* of the city, to participate in shaping the environment to meet one's needs and desires. It is consistent also with the literature on psychological ownership, which makes similar connections between the reasons for which such feelings are significant and the means by which they can be developed. Scholars of psychological ownership argue that the desire to "own" things comes from basic and deeply felt human needs: for feelings of efficacy and competence; for self-definition, for expressing one's self-identity and maintaining the continuity of the self over time; and for a place of one's own in which to dwell.[30] Three main paths or routes to psychological ownership are recognized, flowing from these needs: controlling the ownership target, coming to know the target intimately, and investing the self in the target.[31] These are related—investing oneself in the target produces intimacy and requires at least some degree of control—and typically work together.

While participants often emphasized the importance of the control allowed through PARK(ing) Day, a tension emerged in respect to the extent of such control. In many interviews, participants suggested that they would like Rebar, or someone else, to take more leadership in PARK(ing) Day. This came up particularly in discussions about participants' aspirations for the future of the event. Many said they would like PARK(ing) Day to grow much larger in scale, to become more visible and longer-lasting, perhaps taking over whole streets or neighborhoods, continuing for days or weeks, and involving many more people.

With further discussion, participants often revised these suggestions. One participant suggested that PARK(ing) Day could have more impact if everyone built parks in the same place. Later he reconsidered, reflecting on the importance of participation in the event connecting to feelings of ownership.

> Going back on my earlier comment about saying "This is the street where PARK(ing) Day happens," I suppose where that would fail is it's not our street. (Jonathan Knapp, Sydney)

Several participants noted the value in PARK(ing) Day being citizen-led, and recognized that too much guidance or direction would be damaging to the event, and to the ability of participants to express or develop a sense of ownership. There is a delicate balance to be struck between allowing control and facilitating engagement.

> You lose that idea of ownership or belonging because you're asking people to read the recipe. . . . You need to create this kind of in-between space of giving materials for people to create, yet not totally saying what they should be doing. (Jeanne Dagenais-Lespérance, Montréal)

Personhood is helpful in understanding the nature of ownership as well as its sources. While Locke's theory was intended to endow property rights with permanent validity, most other theories recognize that property rights may wax and wane. The doctrine of adverse possession is perhaps the clearest example of the way even formal property rights can be extinguished over the passage of time. As Rose explains, a failure to *"keep on* speaking" can result in the loss of property rights.[32] For Hegel, ongoing occupancy—expression of the will—is necessary to maintain a property relationship.[33] For Radin, categories can shift: the wedding ring, for example, may become fungible property over the passage of time.[34] A right to property based on personhood requires active, self-conscious social membership and enfranchisement.[35]

> I think it can be a way to develop a sense of ownership . . . of deepening a connection to a community . . . to observe activities that perhaps you're normally not aware [of]. . . . PARK(ing) Day can be like that . . . if you're there as of 8 in the

morning and you're there until the afternoon. You can see the different patterns of when people are on the street and what kind of people are on the street and where they're going and all that. That you necessarily wouldn't see, if you're just kind of running out of the metro to your office. (David Alfaro Clark, Montréal)

I think owning the street is about being present in it, either through being physically present, or through purposely placing an object that you want to be in the street. . . . It could be very ephemeral; if kids draw on the street, they can own their little sidewalk square for a moment. (Jeanne Dagenais-Lespérance, Montréal)

A temporally contingent conception of ownership is consistent also with the scholarship on psychological ownership. Developing psychological ownership is understood as taking time; psychological ownership emerges through an iterative process, with potential to dissipate if not maintained.[36] While control and self-expression are emphasized as the two main paths to ownership, intimacy is important—and requires more extended engagement.[37] In line with this literature, participants in PARK(ing) Day also emphasized the connections between time, ownership, and intimacy: walking around the neighborhood, taking pets to the park, greeting or chatting with neighbors over the fence, spending afternoons sitting on the veranda, working in the school or community garden, playing as (and later with) children in the street or the laneway over months, years, and even decades. In thinking about the ways in which a sense of ownership can be developed, participants stress the importance of knowledge and familiarity, and the importance of time in establishing these.

Feelings of ownership take time to develop, and their duration is not indefinite. Just as formal property rights can be lost over time, ownership requires active and ongoing performance to be sustained.

5.3 Relational theories of property

There was so much spirit when the community came together to make it their own, that the space now has so much resonance in the community. . . . It's become so much more than what it used to be, I think because of the fact that people came together to dedicate their time and energy to making it their own and did it in the company of others. (Alan Chen, Montréal)

In discussing the importance of creative labor to the development of ownership, participants note the particular importance of creating something with, and in the presence of, other people. A sense of ownership is not simply a matter of expressing or developing oneself, but must also involve relationships with the wider community. Participants seek to engage others on PARK(ing) Day—physically, through games, performances, and other activities, and also discursively, in conversation about PARK(ing) Day, the street, and the city—and they seek to sustain that engagement for long as possible.

> You want to be heard, you want to be seen, you want the reflection. (Marc-André Carignan, Montréal)

This conception of ownership as produced in relation to others resonates with an increasing interest among property scholars in property as socially constructed, contingent and contextual. Rather than focusing on the rights associated with ownership, there is a growing literature that understands property in relational terms.[38]

Jennifer Nedelsky has been particularly influential in conceptualizing property as relational.[39] Nedelsky begins with feminist theory, and its critique of the boundary as a metaphor for selfhood, holding that the model of the rational, self-determining individual is inadequate and politically problematic because relationships are crucial to the formation of identity. She then argues that such critiques are equally applicable to property, that the boundary metaphor fails to capture the complex interconnection between individuals and society and the entanglement of property within this. With respect to property as well as to people, an emphasis on separation and opposition is misplaced. A focus on boundary and exclusion, Nedelsky explains, "turns our attention away from relationship and thus away from the true source and consequences of the patterns of power that property constitutes."[40] Since identity is formed through relationships, and since property both contributes and responds to relationships, she argues, a focus on relationships is necessary to understand property, its sources and its consequences.[41]

Others make similar claims. Drawing on Nedelsky, progressive property scholars argue that property models focusing on rights held by owners are inadequate to explain the workings of property, and that property must be understood as a social institution that serves, shapes, and reflects human values.[42] For Margaret Davies, developments in heritage, environmental, and planning law, including the incorporation of stewardship in several Australian laws, reveal "a heightened concern for the relationships within which property is situated."[43] With respect to property rights in water, Eric Freyfogle argues that the courts are willing to recognize that an individual water user is linked to a complex array of people who are affected by her use and whose uses affect her, with the result that property rights must be understood not as autonomous and objectively definable but as context-specific, interconnected, and relative.[44]

Narrative and performative understandings point also to the importance of relationships in understanding property. In claiming that property is at heart a matter of persuasive communication, of "yelling loudly enough to all who may be interested" in a way that others understand and, significantly, accept, Rose depicts property as fundamentally intersubjective.[45] For Blomley, property must be understood as a social construction, one that is iteratively produced in specific social contexts.[46]

> The sites for such performances are diverse: real property, for example, is produced through humble acts of fence-building, mortgage foreclosures, judicial pronouncements, debates around the use of force in the protection of one's home, burglary, instructions to children not to cross someone else's lawn, the installation of security systems, law review articles, the creation of a cadastre, the cutting of hedges, World Bank funding initiatives, struggles over gentrification, property registration, indigenous mobilisations and on and on.[47]

Relational explanations of the way in which ownership is produced in PARK(ing) Day build on the insights provided by other theories. A relational approach is best understood not as displacing labor or personhood theories but as supplementing them. Just as scholars in psychology have noted that there are multiple routes through which psychological ownership can be developed, and that these are additive,[48] personhood can be understood as adding to labor-based theories, highlighting the expressive and identity-forming aspects of labor; and relational understandings develop this further. Labor, and the opportunities for self-actualization that it provides, are particularly significant when undertaken in relation to others.

Relational aspects are not typically emphasized in discussions of personhood theory,[49] yet intersubjective dimensions have long been recognized within such approaches. For Hegel, property entails a relation with others: "My inner act of will which says that something is mine must also become recognizable by others."[50] The process of having one's will—one's property—recognized is critical, as a person can become fully developed only in the context of a community of others: "This relation [Beziehung] of will to will is the true distinctive ground in which freedom has its *existence*."[51] As Hegel explains, property thus "anticipates a relation to others."[52]

Hegel emphasizes the importance of property not as the product of one subjective will in isolation, but in the context of a common will, which he describes as the sphere of contract. It is through contracting, he argues, that "parties *recognize* each other as persons and owners of property."[53] That recognition in turn provides the basis for negotiated exchanges enabling the development of moral and ethical life. The relational and communal aspects of personhood theory have been emphasized and further developed by several scholars.[54] Michael Salter, for example, argues that participation in collective shaping of the environment is important to the development of personality in the full sense.[55]

This overlap between individual and relational aspects is consistent with Cooper's claim that ownership arises out of belonging. While belonging is often described as having multiple dimensions, these dimensions cannot really be separated. To be able to feel at home in a place is not just a personal matter but also a social one: across the literature, there is a recognition that belonging cannot be an isolated, individual affair.[56] Scholars of belonging argue that it is always a process of negotiation, involving both claims and grants.[57]

Cooper's conceptualization of the dimensions of belonging is similarly fluid. As she acknowledges, both part-whole belonging and proper attachment take shape in and through the other, in a dynamic and mutually formative relationship: "where you belong, or what you belong to, is shaped by who else belongs."[58] Sarah Keenan argues that the slippage is more fundamental, and that all three dimensions in fact collapse into each other.[59] Belonging is connected to identity, but neither the subject nor the object of belonging possess an identity that is independent of relationships between or beyond them, with the result that various dimensions of belonging cannot be distinguished.

Whether belonging can be separated into distinct dimensions is an ongoing debate. For present purposes, it is sufficient to recognize that aspects of belonging work together, cumulatively, to produce ownership. Difficulties in separating dimensions of belonging are significant in revealing the importance of the connections between different approaches to property, how they are each inadequate alone so that their accretion is crucial.

PARK(ing) Day is effective in developing a sense of ownership when it allows people to express themselves creatively, and to do so in relation to others. Highlighting the importance of intersubjectivity, drawing people in is a central goal for participants, and an important measure of success.

> I think [parks] should engage. The passive ones are a lot less interesting. . . . The ones that are engaging at the level of someone's imagination or about another experience that the city provides, are I think the most exciting. (Zoee Astrachan, San Francisco)

> In that first meeting a lot of things we gravitated towards were games. And I think that sort of speaks to the engagement side. (Nick Conard, San Francisco)

> It was one of the best experiences because people just come up and play miniature golf for free, that's another one of those magical, magical insertions into the day that you otherwise would not get. Since then, we've done other things, continuing that active approach . . . anything to get people engaged. (Noah Christman, San Francisco)

Consistently, participants describe putting considerable effort into involving passersby, engaging the media, attracting attention and affirmation. In determining the types of activities undertaken, participants focus on ways to engage as many people as possible. Accordingly, games or food feature prominently in many parks.

> One thing I learned long ago is if you have free food, people will come. And so that's what we did. (Daniel Sherman, San Francisco)

SPUR, the San Francisco Bay Area Planning and Urban Research Association, an organization that has participated in PARK(ing) Day every year since 2006, has found parks featuring food to be particularly successful among their many interventions. In 2011, SPUR partnered with Sergio De La Torre and Chris Treggiari to host *El Puesto*, their traveling food installation (figure 5.3). From around 9am, SPUR gave out around 200 time-stamped tickets for seatings. At lunchtime, people returned with the tickets to join seatings in groups of 10–12 for a lunch of chicken mole:

> So you'd come and you'd get like a 20-minute window where you could eat a couple of tacos and hang out with other just random people that had happened to stop by. And it was fantastic, it was great, and I loved it. (Noah Christman, San Francisco)

Finding ways to facilitate interaction is typically a key factor in the selection of locations for PARK(ing) Day.

Figure 5.3
El Puesto, PARK(ing) Day installation by SPUR with Sergio De La Torre and Chris Treggiari, Mission Street, San Francisco, 2011. Image: Noah Christman, SPUR.

> We decided that was pretty much the best location we had in terms of getting enough people to see it but also not being such a busy road that people wouldn't want to stop and have a look. (Sara Wilkinson, Sydney)

> For us it was about wanting a space that was in a thoroughfare for our own people because the students wanted to be able to engage with their mates and people they know and other students. And in both cases we tried to have it near a food outlet, a café, because it was about where people congregate. (Seb Crawford, Sydney)

Back in 2005, the site selected by Rebar for the initial PARK(ing) installation was chosen as one lacking green space, to highlight social and environmental issues in planning.[60] Among the many potential sites that could satisfy that criterion, the one chosen was selected for its photographic potential. As Merker explained:

> It's very high-visibility. JB and I . . . spent a couple days scouting different places, along Mission Street mostly, watching how the sun moved across them, and hanging out across the street and just watching people use the space, and really tried to pick the most photogenic spot.

This emphasis on visibility recurs in the selection of locations for subsequent parks.

> I think it was primarily a question of visibility. We decided to do it on the square because it's a very visible spot. (David Alfaro Clark, Montréal)

> I chose a spot that's like close to the metro, but also that's a nice little busy area. (Anonymous participant, Montréal)

> Because [of] the design and the plants and the color of everything, we were able to attract everyone. (Trevor Sell, San Francisco)

Being visible and, importantly, being *seen* are often a high priority in the design of parks. In explaining the elements used to fill their parks, participants often spoke about choosing things that would be visually arresting. Participants want parks that will contrast with their surroundings—plants, bright colors, balloons—and through this will draw people to them. Balloons have been popular as a tool to attract attention (figures 5.4 and 5.5).

Concerns with visibility extend beyond the actual events. As well as seeking to engage people physically in their park, participants often make further efforts to publicize PARK(ing) Day activities beyond and after their installation through photos, press, and social media.

> I was really passionate about it, I set up the website, Facebook . . . going back to that viral element, I wanted to spread the word, I wanted to get people interested. (John O'Callaghan, Sydney)

> Once [Rebar] started an interactive map . . . we made sure to pin ourselves and put ourselves on there so that we basically felt like we got more mileage out of the whole thing, just in terms of acknowledgment for being involved. (Zoee Astrachan, San Francisco)

> We just wanted to show it in our social media. . . . Our communication service did [updates] every hour. (Aline Berthe, Montréal)

In discussing how their parks went, many participants measure success in terms of the responses they generated: how many people saw, stopped, commented, commented favorably.

> It was the most fun thing of PARK(ing) Day, explaining the concept, interaction with people. (Jean-Philippe Di Marco, Montréal)

> It was really lovely. We got absolutely, it was wild, we almost caused a traffic jam . . . no one was beeping or anything, all the traffic was literally just stopped and watching . . . I felt so good. I thought, keep going here! (Suzanne Cohen, Sydney)

Figure 5.4
Park by Arcadia Landscape Architecture, Altis Architects, Crawford Architects, and DWP, Pyrmont Street, Sydney, 2012. Image: Crawford Architects.

> It almost became like a community engagement forum within itself . . . it snow-balled into this slow trickling of ideas and positive reinforcement. (Trevor Sell, San Francisco)

Responses after the event are important also. In evaluating their parks, participants considered whether and to what extent they were recognized in the media or other venues.

> We put on this website . . . it was in the school newsletter . . . [and] a small article in the *Mosman Daily*. I was hoping for front-page news. Must've been a big news week that week because some of the images were great. We had the photographer there for a long time. (Karen Profilio, Sydney)

Figure 5.5
"Lighter than Air" park by INTERSTICE Architects, Public Bikes and Harrington Galleries. Blue was chosen as the color of the bike shop; the long balloons were inspired by bicycle tubes. Larger inflatables created a play space inside that was popular with children. Valencia Street, San Francisco, 2012. Image: INTERSTICE Architects.

Arup responded relatively well to it . . . the planning group reported it at their yearly report . . . [as] one of the flagship things that we've done for this year. . . . The recognition of that was quite nice, and also a thing that made it successful. (Safiah Moore, Sydney)

Efforts to publicize parks after the event can be understood as attempts to extend the temporal duration of the sense of ownership produced through PARK(ing) Day. Documenting parks in photos and videos, sharing these on social media, and attracting the attention of journalists and politicians provide a way to obtain wider recognition for the event; they also provide a way to prolong the duration of the intervention and its associated claims to belonging and ownership.

A sense of ownership is more than a matter of labor or personal connection to the subject of ownership: labor is valued as a way to express oneself in relation to other people. Participants choose to own, and seek acceptance from others for that choice. Having their activities acknowledged and affirmed is important to both the existence of ownership and the personal meaning derived from it. For participants in PARK(ing) Day, a sense of ownership is dependent at least in part on the reactions of others.

> I think I do feel a sense of ownership over an ability to do something like this. . . . It's a real confidence booster to be able to say, I did this, and I got a lot of positive feedback or response. And I got people to appreciate this. . . . You don't know if at any point someone's going to say "Hey, cut that out." But it sort of reinforces itself as people give positive comments." (Alex Gregor, San Francisco)

This emphasis on recognition and relationships is helpful in understanding the nature of ownership as well as its development. While private property is often associated with social and environmental damage, ownership is more likely to be associated with stewardship, care, and community. Perhaps because of the need for affirmation, people tend to build parks that contribute to the community. Games, health clinics, massages, and giveaways are not simply ways to engage people, but to gain approval for the way in which the street has been remade. Explaining why CC Puede decided to provide a barbecue and health clinic for day laborers, one participant explained this as an acknowledgment of other groups' connections to the site:

> I think that in particular we did need to, it was helpful to get buy-in and participation from the day laborers. [The laborers] and the Day Laborer's Union there that we had worked with, they have a lot of ownership of the street. (Daniel Sherman, San Francisco)

For participation to produce feelings of ownership, it is important to be seen. Conversely, participants in PARK(ing) Day described feelings of failure, and a lack of ownership, when people did not come to their events, didn't engage with them, or didn't respond positively. A direct challenge, particularly from officials, can diminish or work against the development of a sense of ownership. But a sense of ownership can also be weakened or impeded without such challenges.

> Most important, we do the *aménagement*, the *design urbain* around the space, but they do the PARK(ing) Day. If there is no *fréquence*, the place doesn't take the importance, no? Even if we put a roller-coaster there, it doesn't matter. (Andres Toro, Montréal)

Ownership exists as part of a complex and dynamic system. Participants in PARK(ing) Day claim ownership with and from other people, and recognition of those claims is crucial for developing and maintaining a sense of ownership. The processes through which participation in PARK(ing) Day produces a sense of ownership are multiple and mutually reinforcing. Building a park is valuable for the development of a sense of ownership because it provides so many different ways in which this sense of ownership can be claimed and cemented: the work of putting the park together, the act of exercising control over the space, the ability to express oneself in creating the park, the visibility and publicity of parks, opportunities to gain recognition and affirmation from others, and the ongoing potential to display and discuss images and recollections of the event on social and other media during and after the day.

5.4 Grounding ownership in space

A sense of ownership depends not only on relationships with people, but with the physical space itself. The labor and relationships that give rise to a sense of ownership do so in specific locations with particular physical characteristics, often making use of material things, and those locations, things, and characteristics are significant in the development of a sense of ownership.

Spatial and material characteristics are important for conventional forms of property, as scholars such as Blomley, Keenan, and Emilie Cloatre and Dave Cowan have demonstrated.[61] For a sense of ownership their significance is particularly acute. While conventional forms of property can be grounded by reference to a legal document, feelings of ownership are much more reliant on their spatial and material context.

Space can be understood as a constraint on the production of a sense of ownership. Particular material conditions are necessary before labor can be undertaken, much less before it can be productive of feelings of ownership. As critics of Locke and the enclosure movement his theory supported have so forcefully noted, one cannot work to appropriate land or other resources if there is none left in common.[62] Spatial context is important too to self-expression and interactions with others, shaping how and whether participants are able to remake the space or use this as the basis for social engagement. A sense of ownership cannot be sustained without some spatial or physical grounding.

For Sarah Keenan, space is central to property.[63] Drawing on Doreen Massey's analysis of space as relational and constitutive,[64] Keenan builds on Cooper's claim that relationships of belonging are central to property by arguing that belonging must be understood in spatial terms. Following Massey, Keenan contends that identities—of both the subjects and the objects of belonging—are always situated in places that are themselves dynamic and relationally constructed. Both property and person are constructed by, and dependent upon, a whole range of contingent and often conflicting forces. For Keenan to "own" her home, networks of conceptual, social, and physical relations must first have constructed Keenan herself and the house and land in question, and further networks of relations must hold up the relations between them as one of belonging.[65]

Property happens, Keenan explains, when space accommodates the subject in a way in which the subject is embedded in a network of relations of belonging, when certain relations of belonging are "held up" as property. Accordingly, in her examination of challenges to the compulsory multiyear leases introduced on Aboriginal land by the Australian government, Keenan argues that the central issue was not the land but the space of belonging that the leases require and, over time, will reproduce.[66]

Just as Epstein notes that parking spaces are more likely to be dug out from snow and claimed in some streets than others, people are more likely to build parks for PARK(ing) Day in certain places. Parks are rarely installed on highways or major roads (places where traffic moves fast and rarely stops) or quiet suburban streets (places where there is very little activity or visibility). Most parks are located in inner-city areas where there is already a mix of uses and users in and around the space: streets lined with shops, small businesses, and medium/high-density housing, with transport and services so that there are people around. Parking spaces on these streets are more popular for participants, and participation in these spaces is more likely to be productive of a sense of ownership. Valencia Street in the Mission District of San Francisco, which has been a hub for parks on PARK(ing) Day and also for more permanent parklets, has important physical as well as social characteristics. As one resident explains:

> Guerrero, which is the next street over, is designed for cars, and it's really a traffic sewer. So Valencia was always the slower, more neighborhoody, but it got even more so when the bike lanes came in. . . . Valencia Street is loved, people throng to it and they spend lots of time here. ('Deep Jawa, San Francisco)

When participants do build parks in less sympathetic spaces, it is much harder to develop or sustain feelings of ownership. One participant, who had been directed by her employer to set up a park on a highway, explained the experience in very negative terms:

> The first year the borough decided that they would like us to . . . set up a booth over the . . . overpass. So unfortunately the employees spent about four hours sitting on top of a highway, which caused everyone to be extremely sick. It's not a good idea to sit for four hours on top of a highway . . . [and] I don't think it really had a very big impact. (Anonymous participant, Montréal)

In each of these descriptions participants mention spatial networks and identities, but also physical properties. This connection between the spatial and material is important in understanding the way in which a sense of ownership can be developed (or "held up") through PARK(ing) Day. Material objects—like the trees that Irus Braverman argues reflect, mediate, and reinforce the war between Israel and Palestine through their planting, cultivation, and uprooting,[67] the hedges that Blomley argues were crucial in remaking understandings of property underpinning the British enclosure movement,[68] or the potted plants, leaky ceilings, cigarette butts, and other everyday objects that Dave Cowan, Helen Carr, and Alison Wallace argue constitute the particular form of property known as shared ownership[69]—perform important physical, symbolic, and legal work in shaping, sustaining, or subverting spatial relationships and identities.

Other literatures offer related insights. Scholars of psychological ownership recognize that physical properties make some things more amenable to ownership than others.[70] Attention to material and physical properties is central to the scholarship on ANT and the wider "material turn," a heightened scholarly interest in objects, technologies, and ecologies.[71] As discussed in chapter 3, the material world is not simply a passive site for social activity, but composed of things that are active participants in the shaping of social, political, and legal life. The materiality of the street itself is important to the development of a sense of ownership through PARK(ing) Day.

> Sitting in the street physically is, it's a very different perspective on things. (Zvi Leve, Montréal)

Material conditions are important determinants of what can and cannot be owned, and of the ease with which feelings of ownership can be developed and maintained. Just as Noortje Marres claims that things have agency, but that this "captivating power" depends on their setting,[72] participants suggested that ownership can be developed more in some spaces than others. Streets providing opportunities to engage physically are more fertile sites for the development of ownership: those with active frontages, cafés, small shops, places to sit, things to look at, shade, and attractive landscaping. Where the physical environment is more hostile—where there are lots of large trucks, for example—it is much harder to claim or develop feelings of ownership.

The importance of creative expression is related to this. By making a park in a parking space, people not only claim ownership but render the space more able to be owned. PARK(ing) Day provides an opportunity for participants to sustain and extend relationships of belonging.

> You can't just go and sit on the concrete as it is, but if you make the concrete more comfortable then you can sit and enjoy it and then it becomes something that you can feel ownership over. . . . Having interacted more deeply with your own urban environment you feel more of an ownership over it. (James Patterson, Sydney)

Attention to the material as well as discursive properties of the spatial networks in which PARK(ing) Day is situated is important in understanding the way in which feelings of ownership can be produced through the event. The parking meter is frequently a central object around which parks are constructed; where available, printed meter receipts will often be displayed prominently. The importance of the meter as a physical object was highlighted by one participant, who asked me whether PARK(ing) Day might be under threat from technological shifts: if smart parking systems remove the need for physical meters, he asked, might the event also be rendered obsolete?

Certain objects reappear regularly not simply because of their hipster credentials or circulation through social media, but because of their effectiveness in enabling participants to express and develop a sense of ownership (figure 5.6). A key component of almost all parks is something to cover over the road surface (carpets, real or fake grass, old pallets, blankets, sand, soil, chalk), usually coupled with objects that provide a barrier between the park and passing traffic (potted plants, hay bales, and various forms of fencing, as well as less protective materials like balloons and bunting that provide more psychological enclosure). Games, giveaways, and materials

Figure 5.6
PARK(ing) Day installation by Habitat for Humanity with parking meter receipt on display, Derby Place, Glebe, Sydney, 2014. Image: Amelia Thorpe.

allowing passersby to engage or contribute are also common: food (tacos, lemonade, cookies), games (Scrabble, ping pong, Jenga), art materials (paint, pens, chalk), and specialized equipment (enabling participants to provide services like massages, health checks, and bicycle tune-ups).

Borrowed, recycled, and handcrafted objects are particularly popular, reflecting the generally low budgets available for PARK(ing) Day as well as the community and environmental motivations of many participants. Borrowed and recycled objects—coffee cups, potted plants, live chickens—can be useful in symbolizing participants' labor, creativity, and connections: the care and work that went into gathering, growing, and assembling the elements of the park.

Emphasizing the importance of objects, several participants showed me physical objects—games, furniture, and decorations—that they had made for PARK(ing) Day and still kept years later. When she saw I had brought my youngest daughter along to the interview, Kylie Legge offered her a soft rat-shaped toy. During our discussion, she explained its connection to PARK(ing) Day:

> My thing was like oh ok, well here's some money to the staff, come up with a design and duh-duh-duh and they did this big snakes and ladders board . . . it was a play space sort of thing. . . . That's what actually Ratty is from. He was one of the pieces . . . the staff brought their friends and they made these cool stencil art things and all the numbers and stuff like that.

Other participants discussed the ongoing evolution of objects used in PARK(ing) Day. These were things kept not just as mementos, but used and developed further: street furniture, small buildings, plants, and seating in the office.[73]

Participants often describe a shift taking place through the material experience of claiming and reshaping a parking space on PARK(ing) Day. To begin, many said that they felt uncomfortable or out of place. Filling the space with things, making it more pleasant to sit in, less exposed to traffic and more attractive to people passing by, makes a space more comfortable and amendable to ownership. After spending time in their park, participants recall feeling more at home and in a space that is "theirs."

> By the end of the day it felt more comfortable. Especially once we had more people there and it was completely set up and we had been hanging out there for a while, it definitely felt more comfortable. (Lindsey Flanagan, San Francisco)

> I think we all felt that it was our space. . . . When the police came around, everyone came up with a reason why we should stay. Whereas going in . . . they probably wouldn't have been able to come up with any. . . . So yeah, maybe there was enough ownership built. (Kylie Legge, Sydney)

The objects used in PARK(ing) Day can be significant not only in the production of a sense of ownership, but also in its absence. Reflecting on the success of her park in engaging people, one participant emphasized the limitations of the particular objects used:

> The mini golf was a good idea. . . . They had a green carpet and everything was, it wasn't cheap you know? Us, it was simple like a table, chairs, and a chess game. Like maybe a little bit boring. But them with their mini golf, it was very funny and very well constructed. (Elyse Benoit, Montréal)

Far from neutral or passive, the sites and objects engaged in PARK(ing) Day are active participants in the expression and development of ownership through the event.

5.5 Play, pleasure, and love

It's just so fun! (Carlo Tadeo, Montréal)

Fun is a word that comes up frequently in discussions of PARK(ing) Day. When I visited parks, there was invariably a celebratory mood among participants and passersby: making the street into a more public and sociable space is a joyful experience (figure 5.7). In all three cities across all four years, PARK(ing) Day was characterized by a palpable sense of celebration. The vast majority of parks are festive spaces, with participants clearly

Figure 5.7
PARK(ing) Day installation by TechShop, Howard Street, San Francisco, 2016. This man was passing by and stopped to enjoy the pop-up park, along with a free lemonade from WRT's nearby park. He explained to me that he knew PARK(ing) Day well, having seen parks in several previous years, but had forgotten this was the day. As you can see from his grin, he was very happy to have stumbled upon the three parks on this street. Image: Amelia Thorpe.

Figure 5.8
PARK(ing) Day installation by Rayside Labossière, featuring baby farm animals, honey-making, and a range of activities for children and the local community. Rue Ontario, Montréal, 2014. Image: Rayside Labossière.

excited to have pulled the space together, in a very public setting, and to watch others enjoying their contributions to the street.

Reflecting on the event afterward, participants refer frequently to play and pleasure, magic and surprises, to delight and even love. Engaging children is often a marker of success, and many parks are designed specifically to encourage this (figures 5.8 and 5.9). For many, the physical experience of being on the street was significant and even transformative.

> That's where it really grabs you and that's where, and part of it is that illicit feeling of "Hey, I'm sitting in a parking spot taking up this parking spot," right? That's part of the joy of the whole thing. I don't think that transmits photographically. ('Deep Jawa)

Beyond explaining how participants felt during the event, these emotions are important in understanding how PARK(ing) Day contributes to the development of a sense of ownership. Fun is part of the power of PARK(ing) Day.

Figure 5.9
PARK(ing) Day installation by Rayside Laboissière (detail). Image: Rayside Labossière.

> What was interesting about PARK(ing) Day is taking something that seems so crazy . . . and that it could be fun and dynamic and actually change the way you feel about the city. (Liz Ogbu, San Francisco)

> It resonates so much because if . . . people are having fun on the street, you have to feel something. . . . This is what struck me the most . . . it's kind of really a small thing, but impacts so much. (Philippe Letarte, Montréal)

In explaining how PARK(ing) Day builds ownership, many participants make comparisons to the spaces in which children play. Just as running,

Figure 5.10
PARK(ing) Day installation by UQAM students Philippe Letarte and Mikael St-Pierre (pictured), Rue Saint-Catherine, Montréal, 2012. Image: Thierry Sénécal.

skipping, bike riding, chalk drawing, and ball throwing lead children and families to feel that they own a street or laneway, participants suggest that the playfulness of PARK(ing) Day is important in its contribution to ownership.

> That's what drew people in, the fun of it. So I think that's the most critical thing. That sense of whimsy . . . you can't walk by an interesting parklet without smiling first. And probably wanting to be part of it. ('Deep Jawa, San Francisco)

> It's the pleasure to appropriate the street. You feel like it's a bit, it's close to occupied. (Félix Gravel, Montréal)

In 2012, the popular vote in the competition hosted by the CRE and ADUQ went to a park in which UQAM students Philippe Letarte and Mikael St-Pierre had set up a mini hockey rink (figure 5.10). Letarte explained the reasoning for this:

Figure 5.11
PARK(ing) Day installation constructed by neighboring design firms, the Office of Cheryl Barton and Quinn Landscape Architects, featuring chalk, AstroTurf, potted plants, pets, staff in costumes, and lots of laughter, 11th Street, San Francisco, 2016. Image: Amelia Thorpe.

> Because hockey appeals to everyone. I mean you want to have someone who—I don't want people to just look and just see oh that's nice flowers and that's nice stuff. Hey they're playing, can I play? Yes of course you can. And hockey is relevant for everyone. Every boy and girl plays hockey once in his life in this town.

Games, and particularly games that take people back to childhood memories of play, are popular choices for PARK(ing) Day. In describing why they went to so much effort to build a giant pinball machine, one of the young architects involved explained:

> It's a little like when you have in parks, like, large chess sets, right? We considered things like battleships or . . . ski ball or something. It was the idea that it's something kind of fun and can pull people from their daily lives and kind of have this kid moment out on the street. (Nick Conard, San Francisco)

Fun sustains labor, and it also sustains the interactions that enable recognition and affirmation (figure 5.11). In seeking to involve passersby, participants emphasize fun and frivolity, wonder and whimsy: unexpected moments of joy on the street. The aim is not simply to engage others, but to engage them in play.

> If you want people to get involved or to react you have to make them play . . . [so that] people can see that cities can be more playful, that they can interact with their city. (Philippe Letarte, Montréal)

While emotions—particularly joy and delight—are rarely discussed in property scholarship, their importance is recognized in other fields. Lisa Peattie's work on conviviality has been influential in planning, highlighting the value of small, fleeting connections that make us feel happier or part of a community.[74] Conviviality, she explained, is valuable in providing a way to "rise above [problems] by celebration."[75] For Peattie, a key source of conviviality was sociable eating, and she called for planners to provide more opportunities for sharing food in public to strengthen community bonds. With so many parks providing free food and drinks, PARK(ing) Day might be read as a response to this call. The importance of food was recognized by participants:

> The food co-op group were really important to me at the time because it was all about relationships with people and building community, sharing food together, being passionate about food together. It was just such a really positive and welcoming thing, and so I think I really was just drawn to that quite strongly, and then PARK(ing) Day was quite related really because it was that positive community, let's transform the world, let's do it together right now and do something, and create something together. All of that really fed into why I was attracted to it. (James Patterson, Sydney)

More recent examinations of conviviality, play, and delight in urban studies emphasize the value of noninstrumental uses of public space in enabling people to resolve the tensions of modern life, and in allowing for the emergence of new possibilities.[76]

Positive emotions are increasingly valued in social movements, with pleasure pursued so as to inspire and sustain engagement,[77] and play itself has been suggested as a potentially potent tool for efforts to imagine and enact more progressive forms of governance.[78] Positive emotions are important also in providing protection against burnout.[79] PARK(ing) Day, like other forms of activism, can involve significant effort, and some element of fun and pleasure is necessary to make that effort worthwhile. Fun supports the labor that in turn supports the development of a sense of ownership.

The whole thing just felt really positive which . . . stands in contrast to a lot of other [activism]. . . . I really like and value participating in actions that . . . [are] focused on challenging power but . . . it's pretty draining in some ways. . . . To me it was actually, the thing that I really took away from it was that it was really fun . . . [at the end I thought] why does this have to stop? (James Patterson, Sydney)

We worked extremely well together on it and we had a lot of fun, and we went, can we do this all the time? (Ming Thompson, San Francisco)

Mark Purcell makes this point strongly in his discussion of civic engagement.[80] Arguing that democracy is something for which we must continually strive, Purcell emphasizes the importance of a precipitating event, something that pushes people to become aware and to become active. From there, Purcell argues, people can develop a taste for further engagement. This is because in taking action, particularly with others, people can find joy, "a down-deep delight that we can discover when we take up the responsibility of managing our affairs together."[81] Participants in PARK(ing) Day frequently report this kind of joyful "discovery."

It sort of reinforces itself as people give positive comments or they say "That was fun. That was great." (Alex Gregor, San Francisco)

Fun, pleasure, and delight connect also to participants' self-expression, enhancing their ability to find meaning and identity through engagement in PARK(ing) Day.

Some participants went even further, going beyond joy, pleasure, and delight to link ownership with love.

It was an expression of love for the city. Because I do, I genuinely do love the city. . . . I don't think you want to own something that you don't love or you wouldn't want to. . . . Love like that can come from both ways, you can learn to love a place by taking ownership maybe. I'm not sure which came first. (Peter Gibson, Montréal)

To me, the currency is the love. . . . In an ideal world, that's what would grant you property, is how much you loved something. (Blaine Merker, San Francisco)

Ownership is something that people decide to take. The idea of actively choosing to "take" ownership comes up often in the literature.[82] It was also noted by participants. Accordingly, the subject of ownership must be something that people want to claim. PARK(ing) Day contributes to this.

The residents of the block decide that they really, really liked that little basketball hoop on that parklet and they want to keep it there for their kids and then they're all going to maybe chip in ten bucks or so to like build it permanently. . . . Events like PARK(ing) Day help inspire people to agree to things or at least like discover that there's a lot of things that they all like (Anais Mathez, Montréal)

PARK(ing) Day helps to make parking spaces more desirable subjects for ownership through physical and material transformations, but also through the emotional experience. Joy, delight, and playfulness are not simply a sideline of PARK(ing) Day, but an important part of the event's power in building a sense of ownership.

Figure 6.1
Amy Seek discussing PARK(ing) Day with police, San Francisco, 2006. Image: Andrew
Fort / Amy Seek.

6   Performing Property

Moving from concepts to performance, this chapter examines the practical consequences of the connections between property, ownership, and a sense of ownership. The claims to property made in PARK(ing) Day are social claims about ownership, and it is with and through such claims that property is constructed. In PARK(ing) Day, participants attempt to assemble social and material support for their claims to ownership and to property, and the success of their parks depends on their ability to do so.

PARK(ing) Day suggests that a sense of ownership and property work together to give effect to claims about legality and propriety. While legal analysis reveals Rebar's "lease" to be no more than a conceit, the assertion of this property right is important, providing a trigger or grounding for the expression of other forms of ownership. A sense of ownership is a crucial motivator for participation in PARK(ing) Day, driving people to go to the significant effort involved in installing a park, and to put their bodies on the line to sustain claims about law in doing so. A sense of ownership matters too in participants' decisions about where to locate their parks: in the vast majority of cases, people build parks in spaces that are in some sense already "theirs."

The importance of ownership is perhaps most apparent in how parks are received by others. Examination of the cases in which participants interact with officials suggests that understandings of ownership exert a powerful influence on the legality of parking spaces. The high level of discretion involved in regulating the installation of parks in parking spaces—an activity that is not expressly prohibited, but to which many laws could be applied by an unsympathetic official—means that legal actors must look beyond the text of relevant rules to determine how they should be applied. Consistent with the claims made by Robert Cover and by Hendrik Hartog, the line between what counts as property and what does not is far from clear. For officials making determinations about legality, a sense of ownership is crucial.

PARK(ing) Day also highlights the connection between ownership and privilege. While a parking meter is accessible to everyone, the sense of ownership necessary to sustain the use of a parking space for alternative purposes is not. Participants challenge current distributions of property—sometimes implicitly, sometimes directly—resonating with other forms of activism in contemporary cities. Yet in their reliance on ownership, participants highlight its dependence upon wider networks and structural conditions.

6.1   Ownership and participation

> I absolutely think that ownership's always important, otherwise why get involved, right? Like what other motivations will get people to get involved in things? I think if you don't feel part of a community or if you don't feel like you belong somewhere then there's not much motivation to get involved in something. . . . Ownership is why we did this project anyway because we wanted to give something or be part of something in our own community. (Elise O'Ryan, Sydney)

A sense of ownership is crucial in understanding the performances of property involved in PARK(ing) Day. In discussing their right to be on the street, participants rarely rely on Rebar's explanation of the property at issue. In almost all of the interviews, it was not until I asked participants directly about their knowledge of applicable laws that the subject came up. The response was typically brief: a simple story about paying the meter, a box that was ticked.

> If you pay your meter, you're going by the law, you're paying for that spot. So what issues can there be? (Dieb Khoury, Sydney)

> As long as you paid the meter you're technically entitled to use the space as you wish. (Seb Crawford, Sydney)

> We're not breaking any laws. We paid for our ticket. (Elise O'Ryan, Sydney)

Participants spent much more time explaining the importance of informal ownership to their engagement in the event. Just as Elyse, one of the proprietors of the Librairie Parenthèse, likened her motivation for engagement to wanting to help an old couple rekindle the passion of their first years together, many participants spoke of deeply felt emotional connections animating their contributions. The feelings of belonging, connection, or love involved in ownership are powerful motivators for participation in PARK(ing) Day.

> I don't know about the legal aspects but without ownership people don't choose to make much of an effort I think. (Eytan Rocheta, Sydney)

> The school community, knowing the passersby, knowing the pedestrians and the cyclists, people that would stop by, was key. If I plotted a space somewhere else, you know, even in [this area], I wouldn't have done it probably. . . . That familiarity, you just feel in your comfort zone . . . you feel empowered and powerful. (Lydia Ho, Sydney)

The importance of a sense of ownership is apparent in the places in which people site their parks. Across all three cities, most participants choose locations for PARK(ing) Day on streets with which they have an established relationship. People tend to build parks in spaces outside their office, business, home, or institution, and to emphasize the importance of being part of their local community in selecting those spaces.

> We really wanted to bring something to our own community because we live just down the road. (Elyse Benoit, Montréal)

> The reason I chose that was because it did lead straight out of our car park on to the street . . . that whole little nook felt like it was ours. (Karen Profilio, Sydney)

In some cases, participants felt that other locations might have been preferable, particularly in attracting attention. Yet such advantages were rarely enough to motivate people to move beyond the spaces for which they felt a sense of ownership.

> It's always in front of our building. . . . It's hard as a whole on PARK(ing) Day if it's all spread out so people don't really see the full impact of it, so they often ask people to sort of cluster, but we've always been against it because for us it's a part of being open to our neighborhood and our community, so we just stay . . . we don't really go away from it. (Catherine Thibault, Montréal)

Where people don't have a sense of ownership, they are less likely to get involved. INTERSTICE Architects participated in PARK(ing) Day every year between 2006 and 2013. After the 2013 event, their office moved to a different building. As newcomers to the area, INTERSTICE did not participate in PARK(ing) Day in 2014. In 2015, they joined the event once again, though on a more intermittent basis (INTERSTICE participated in PARK(ing) Day in 2015, 2017, and 2019).

This link between a sense of ownership and engagement in city-making is widely acknowledged in planning and related fields. Perhaps most famously, Jane Jacobs extolled the virtues of neighborhoods in which local residents and workers feel a sense of ownership.[1] Jacobs celebrated what she described as an "intricate ballet" of everyday rituals through which local "eyes on the street" maintain social order, peace, and safety: taking out garbage; watering plants; children of various ages walking, rollerskating, cycling, or tricycling to and from school; residents sweeping up candy wrappers dropped by those children; shopowners unlocking carts, hanging out signs, stacking crates, making and receiving deliveries; neighbors nodding briefly or chatting at length; taxis delivering and collecting passengers; office workers stopping for lunch or groceries on the way home, followed later by students and night workers.[2] Oscar Newman drew on similar ideas about the ownership of public spaces in recommending strategies to reduce crime.[3] While Jacobs focused on spaces characterized by a strong sense of ownership, Newman inverted this, comparing crime rates in New York housing projects to identify unsafe spaces. Newman argued that the higher crime rates found in high-rise apartment buildings could be attributed to the residents' lack of ownership, responsibility, and personal control.[4]

Professionals working in planning and community development regularly describe the creation of a sense of ownership as a key indicator of both good planning processes and good planning outcomes.[5] One of the key benefits claimed from a large-scale participatory planning exercise undertaken in Western Australia, for example, was that the process generated "ownership," which in turn supported implementation of the plan.[6] Organizers claimed that participation in the process "gave the community a sense of 'ownership' of the strategy—to the point where many took action to defend it against inaccurate commentaries being made about it."[7]

Outside of government, activists often describe their work in similar terms, viewing the creation of a sense of ownership within the relevant community as a central objective. For example, Emma Rees-Raaijmakers, explaining why she established the organization Archikidz! in Australia, stated that her aim was "to create a sense of ownership of the city" among young people.[8] Dave Meslin, who founded a community group working on public space in Toronto, gives an evocative description of a sense of ownership as a "gateway drug" necessary for participation, both an outcome and a motivator of engagement:

The funny thing about guerrilla gardening is that as soon as you stick that spoon through the top layer of soil, it's like putting a flag on the moon. It's like a dog peeing on a fire hydrant too perhaps. You're saying, "this is mine." And it might be the first time in your life that you've actually physically altered something outside of your private space. And it's saying, "this doesn't belong to anyone else except for me." Not more, not exclusive to other people, but it doesn't belong to anyone else more than it belongs to me. It belongs to us and we can shape it. And I think that's a kind of a gateway drug that opens up doors in your mind. That if you could change that, you could also change your transit system, your library, your parks, your pools.[9]

The link between a sense of ownership and participation in PARK(ing) Day, and in civic contributions more generally, is consistent with the literature on psychological ownership. Studies of psychological ownership focus primarily on the participatory benefits of such feelings. Efforts have been made to understand psychological ownership precisely because it is associated with better performance and "extra-role behavior" among employees (that is, engaging in tasks additional to those required in the job), and with greater loyalty among customers.[10] Building on successful efforts to improve employee performance through financial ownership (by giving them shares in the company, for example), much of the literature on psychological ownership describes and represents efforts to produce similar effects through nonfinancial means.

Implicit across these ideas that ownership is desirable in planning, is necessary for activism, and can lead to extra-role behavior in companies, is an assumption that more formal property rights entail these kinds of orientations and commitments. Property, while a legal concept, is one with a power that extends beyond its legal incidents. Despite their formal separation, the historical connections between property and political power remain potent. Property is shaped not just by courts but by social understandings; its power extends well beyond the rights and duties recognized in law.

PARK(ing) Day shows that those rights and duties are socially fixed. In their descriptions of the feelings and understandings underpinning the construction of parks, participants reveal ways in which things can be owned without being property, and that such ownership can bring with it (at least some of) the power and agency more typically attributed to holders of legal title. With this potential for more accessible forms of property there is scope to unsettle or intervene in dominant processes of city-making, a possibility celebrated by people like Jacobs, Rees-Raaijmakers, and Meslin. Like mainstream property, however, a sense of ownership is not equally accessible to all, and its emancipatory potential should not be overestimated.

6.2 Ownership and legality

> It really does have to be in your backyard or adjacent to your building . . . close enough that we can say "We're right there," and point out that this is somewhere we do activate and we're passing through constantly. (Alex Gregor, San Francisco)

Beyond motivating and enabling participation in the event, a sense of ownership is important in understanding how PARK(ing) Day and its claims about legality are received by both officials and the wider public. Folk understandings of ownership are not merely aligned with theoretical conceptions, but work directly to structure technical understandings of property as an institution. A sense of ownership is crucial in determining whether people challenge the appropriation of parking spaces, and whether officials accept the legal interpretations presented by participants.

> When you have a vested interest and the emotion is attached, the outcome is always better. . . . That's why we literally did it in the parking spot outside our front door, because that's the one we all connect with. (Jonathan Knapp, Sydney)

Most contributions to PARK(ing) Day attract very positive responses. In a small number of cases, some people have viewed parks as unwelcome additions to the street. In all three cities I found examples in which this has led to parks being shut down by police: three in Sydney, two in Montréal, two in San Francisco. In each of these cases, a sense of ownership was important. Those parks that attracted police attention provide a strong indication that a sense of ownership is not just a matter of personal feelings, but brings tangible consequences that influence the implementation of formal law. A sense of ownership shapes the making of claims to "leases" on PARK(ing) Day; it also shapes responses to those claims.

The relational and performative nature of ownership is important in understanding its role in determining how parks are received. What is at stake is not simply the ownership felt by participants but whether this is recognized by others and, particularly, whether it conflicts with other claims to the space. Reflecting on twelve years leading the Institut du Nouveau Monde (Institute for the New World), an organization established with the aim of increasing citizen participation in the democratic life of

Montréal, Michel Venne emphasized this point. Ownership, he explained, emerges out of human needs, and grows in places where people have the power and responsibility to meet those needs. The celebrated Champs des Possibles in Montréal—created without permission on unused railway land by people living in the area, and successfully defended by those people when the landowner tried to sell the land—is a place for which the local community was able to build both a community garden and a sense of ownership because

> people living in the neighborhood . . . they have to get out, to breathe and to meet . . . and there was not only physically empty space but there was a space, a public space, that was not an issue for the usual suspects.

Identifying a parking space that is not already "owned," or not "owned" in ways that conflict with the event, is crucial. Most parks are located in places for which participants have a preexisting sense of ownership, and most parks are installed and occupied without challenge. When participants lack ownership and, particularly, when the other actors they draw into their parks possess a sense of ownership at odds with the event, claims about the legality of PARK(ing) Day are less likely to stick.

The earliest of the contested parks I found was one built for the first PARK(ing) Day in 2006. Led by a young landscape architect, Amy Seek, it was called a "Do It Yourself Local Lemonade Stand." To make a statement about the environmental impacts of agriculture as well as public space, she had sourced lemons grown within 12 miles of the area. Seek provided lemons, squeezers, syrup, and water for people to assemble their own drinks (by not actually preparing the lemonade, she hoped to avoid violating food service regulations) (figures 6.2 and 6.3). The ingredients were laid out under the shade of donated citrus trees, all transported to the site with a borrowed truck.

> When we got the trees out it was really beautiful, . . . a crowd amongst the trees, and we had a couple of picnic tables and these chequered blankets. My friend had lent her grandfather's lemon squeezer, which was one of these ones that pulls down with a lever. That was very enticing for people to use, they wanted to try that . . . then a crowd just gathered and started talking about lemonade and how their grandmother made it this way. It was just a very friendly environment, people were coming and going. (Amy Seek, San Francisco)

Most people who saw the park responded positively; Seek recalls that staff from a nearby hotel were "really happy, they thought it was hilarious

Figure 6.2
PARK(ing) Day installation by Amy Seek, "Do It Yourself Local Lemonade," with potted citrus trees providing shade around picnic tables laid out ready for lemonade-making. Cyril Magnin Street, San Francisco, 2006. Image: Amy Seek.

and lovely." But one woman objected, and called the police. She waited in her car until the police arrived, then demanded that the police shut it down. According to Seek, the police were not bothered and simply laughed when they saw the installation. The objecting woman insisted that the park be closed, however, and the police did eventually require Seek to move along.

Seek had located the park in downtown San Francisco, in a busy commercial district near Union Square. This was not a site for which she felt any ownership; there was no scouting or planning involved in its selection, and no engagement or attempts to build relationships with neighbors. It was simply a busy spot with plenty of street activity, and one where a parking space was available at the time.

While Seek had no sense of ownership or connection to the site of her PARK(ing) Day installation, the woman who challenged her did. As Seek

Figure 6.3
Making lemonade with a press borrowed from a friend's grandfather. Cyril Magnin
Street, San Francisco, 2006. Image: Amy Seek.

explains, the reason the objecting woman complained, and waited to make
sure the authorities acted on her complaint, was that she "thought that was
her street."

Seek's decision to locate her park in a space with which she had no connection was deliberate, but also taken with some hesitation. Initially, she
had planned to build her park in her own neighborhood, but Rebar asked
her to choose a downtown site for greater visibility. While Seek agreed, she
"felt the weight" of appropriating a space that was not "hers":

> Knowing that there was this sense of ownership [felt by others], that's why I
> didn't want to be downtown . . . and so I definitely felt the weight of this, that I
> was doing something silly amidst serious stuff.

In Sydney, ownership was similarly problematic for the park built in
Newtown in 2008. Initially, the installation was well received. Patterson
and his friends arrived early in the morning, found an empty parking space

on King Street and set up with grass, trees, and a perimeter fence. Eytan
Rocheta, one of Patterson's collaborators, describes the installation:

> Suddenly there was a little park there on the side of the road. So we sat down and
> people came and talked to us and there was generally a very good vibe for the first
> few hours, and it was really nice. People with kids came, there were strollers. Lots
> of people were talking to us.

After a couple of hours, the pop-up park was spotted by a council ranger
who did not approve. The ranger was unpersuaded by the groups' claims
about the legality of the event, despite their explanations about its international precursors and compliance with the local road rules; he insisted
that the park was unsafe and must be removed. The ranger in turn called
the police, who were similarly dismissive of the group's claims about the
legality of the park (figure 6.4). Patterson describes the shift:

> We just laid it all out and hung out and then a few other friends came along. It
> was really good. We had maybe ten people hanging out there and then people
> were walking past and asking about stuff so that was really fun. Then, I don't
> know, we were maybe there for about an hour and a half or something and this
> parking inspector came along and got really upset . . . he was obviously just some-
> one with a bee in his bonnet . . . then he called the police and then they came. . . .
> They were like, you guys have got to go, but they weren't aggressive or anything.
> It was just like, you've got to go.

For Patterson, Rocheta, and their friends, King Street was a place they
enjoyed visiting, but to which they had little connection. The group were
studying on the other side of the city, and they all lived even further
beyond the campus. They thought Newtown was cool and that PARK(ing)
Day could make a positive contribution to it, but they did not have strong
relationships with the area. There was no particular connection to the parking space they chose; their only outreach was a brief conversation with an
adjacent shop as they were setting up:

> I can't even remember why we chose that spot, I think just because, yeah I think
> we liked Newtown because it's vibrant and also because it's weird that it's such a
> vibrant place with so many, such a cool place and so many like, so much open-
> ness and creativity and all these things going on and yet it's got one of the most
> busy and unfriendly kind of streets . . . right through the middle of it. (James
> Patterson, Sydney)

The significance of this lack of connection for the success of the park was
later acknowledged:

Figure 6.4
Police look on as participants remove the park they had installed on King Street, Newtown, Sydney, 2008. Image: Adrian Emilsen.

> It might've been different if we did it within our community, yeah. Absolutely. (Eytan Rocheta, Sydney)

The group's lack of ownership was problematic because the space was one for which other people already felt a strong sense of ownership: conditions for the performance of property through PARK(ing) Day were far from felicitous. The challenge to the park came from a ranger with a strong sense of ownership built from many years patrolling the street and its surroundings. As a council employee later explained:

> he's not in the organization [any more], and that's probably a good thing. I think he would stop lots of people doing things that they actually had a legal right to do.

The adjacent business was supportive when the group first explained the idea, but quickly shifted after the ranger arrived:

> He was funny because he was really supportive at the time. He was like, oh this is really cool! Yeah, yeah, yeah! Yeah of course you can do that, yeah no worries! And then he came out and he's just hanging out with us for a bit. But then as soon as the parking inspector and the police came then he got really, he was sort of like, oh you guys have got to go. You got to go! And he got like, he kind of flipped. I think he just got nervous, so yeah. (James Patterson, Sydney)

On PARK(ing) Day, the participants' connection to King Street (a place they liked but didn't visit regularly) and to the business next to their park (a brief conversation with the nearest shop on the morning of the event) were insufficient to displace preexisting relationships, especially the ranger's long-held views about what should (and shouldn't) be encouraged. Much more work would have been required to assemble the kind of network necessary to sustain the event.

Montréal provides another example. In 2015, the park installed by the architecture and planning firm Rayside Labossière was instructed by a police officer to pack up and leave the street. This was a surprise for the participants, who had a strong sense of ownership built up over decades of engagement in the local community, had participated in PARK(ing) Day successfully in the very same space on two previous occasions, and were armed with a letter of support from the City of Montréal.

The interactions between Rayside Labossière and the police highlight the complexity and the dynamism of ownership. Rayside Labossière built the park outside their office on Rue Ontario. While the firm is well known in the neighborhood, Rue Ontario connects to a bridge linking the Île de Montréal with the wider region, and as such is an important route for commuters. Accordingly,

> it's constant negotiation . . . between local and regional considerations around traffic. (Ron Rayside, Montréal)

The contest between local and regional interests in the street means that understandings of who and what belongs are far less settled. They are also more temporally contingent: at peak hour the contest is particularly extreme. In this case, when a driver made a complaint, it appears the police preferred the commuters' claims to the street in interpreting the regulatory framework.

The content of Rayside Labossière's park is also significant. In the two previous years, the office built parks that provided fun activities for the community: in 2013, Lego blocks, a bicycle connected to the rooftop garden that people could pedal to bring fresh herbs down to the street, chalk and balloons; in 2014, a micro farm with goats, chickens, bunnies, honey-making and honey-tasting. In 2015, however, they took a much simpler approach, moving desks and computers to set up a minioffice on the street for the day (figure 6.5). Explaining the idea before the event, one of the organizers described their rationale:

> We decided to just go with the idea that we always pushed, of an involved corporate citizen. . . . We're just going to stick everything outside and work outside for the day. . . . It's about [showing that] businesses shouldn't be stuck behind their doors. They should play a role in their community and the community should get to know them. (Catherine Thibault, Montréal)

Figure 6.5
Staff from Rayside Labossière enjoy the sunshine while working in their outdoor office, Rue Ontario, Montréal, 2015. Image: Rayside Labossière.

Figure 6.6
Staff from Place Partners at work around a table on Oxford Street, Sydney, 2014.
Image: Place Partners.

Like games and petting farms, this is an idea that has been tried elsewhere. In Sydney in 2014, Place Partners set up an office in a parking space
across the road from their building on Oxford Street (figure 6.6). Place Partners' experience was much like that of Rayside Labossière, with police asking them to shut down the park and move off the street.[11]

Like Rayside Labossière, Place Partners came to the event with a strong
history of engagement and a strong sense of ownership, and a previous
experience of participating successfully in PARK(ing) Day in the same space.
In 2011, Place Partners worked with a neighboring landscape architecture
practice to fill two parking spaces with materials with which they invited
the community to play (a giant game of Snakes and Ladders) and to rest
(grass and bean bags). Also like Rayside Labossière, Place Partners' office is
located on a contested street: Oxford Street is an important local street but
also a congested regional thoroughfare, making it much harder to establish
a sense of ownership.

For Place Partners as for Rayside Labossière, the decision to fill a parking
space with an office was intended as an expression of corporate citizenship,
a material demonstration of their engagement in and commitment to the

local community. To others, the impression created may have been quite different. One of my students visited Place Partners' park in 2014. She didn't enter the park or engage with any of the participants, however: she read the space as exclusive and closed to outsiders. Despite having traveled to the site specifically to see and understand PARK(ing) Day in practice, she remained at a distance, watched briefly, then left. Instead of giving back or creating public space like the games, petting zoos, and resting spaces of previous parks, the act of setting up offices read as a private use: not an expression of ownership developed relationally and with community recognition, but an appropriation of public space for private use. In that context, the decisions by police in both cities to require removal of the parking space offices at the request of car drivers using the street are not difficult to understand.

These examples are not typical of PARK(ing) Day; most participants build parks without challenge. They are typical, however, among the (relatively small) range of parks that attract opposition. Unlike the businesses, residents, and institutions that participated successfully in PARK(ing) Day on streets that are in some sense already theirs, parks that run into problems are located in places where participants' connections are more tenuous and where others possess a stronger sense of ownership for the space. When participants have a more developed sense of ownership, and especially when this is recognized by others in the area, participation in PARK(ing) Day tends to be received positively. In places where participants' claims conflict with established relationships, parks are more likely to be challenged. As one participant explains:

> Probably the permit that we needed, an informal permit that we needed was the buy-in from the residents. (Anonymous participant, Sydney)

The importance of ownership was recognized early in the evolution of PARK(ing) Day by the organizers of the event:

> There is this bit of guidance that popped up early on and I felt was really helpful. It involved picking your spot. We encourage people to scout out the ideal spot for their PARK(ing) Day installation, and we encourage folks that if that spot was in front of a business, . . . that they really take a moment to engage with the people who own that business and get to know them, and invite them to participate or at least be okay with PARK(ing) Day happening right in front of them. Where people didn't do that, there was conflict. Where they did, there was some great things that could happen like people bringing out water or inviting them to use the bathroom, things like that. (Matthew Shaffer, San Francisco)

The significance of ownership and prior relationships with the space are recognized also in commentary on the event. Reflecting on her own participation in PARK(ing) Day in Washington, DC, Stine Ejsing-Dunn noted that passersby were slow to engage with the installation "despite the free muffins and games."[12] Ejsing-Dunn suggests this might have been because

> we were outsiders—unknown in the neighborhood. . . . One powerful outcome of setting up the temporal park was that organizers realized what their presence meant to those who inhabit the neighborhood. The Park(ing) Day event was set up to draw attention to citizens' relationship to the urban landscape; however, what it succeeded to do was to alert participants to the fact that this temporary park constituted a performance, and perhaps even a provocation in the neighborhood—an alien encounter.[13]

Parking spaces may be very similar on paper, the relevant rules about time limits and parking rates may even be identical, but reactions to them can shift depending on informal understandings of ownership.

An absence of supportive relationships will not necessarily lead to problems. In all three cities, there have been parks built by people without prior connections to the area that have not attracted opposition. The students from UTS who built the park at Bondi Beach in 2016, for example, had little connection to the parking space they chose. The group was led by Lebanese-Australian students from parts of Sydney geographically and culturally far removed Bondi, which is in the heart of Sydney's privileged eastern suburbs, yet their park did not attract opposition.

> The police came past and gave us the thumbs up, which was great, we loved that. I remember we gave them a lemonade. (Dieb Khoury, Sydney)

Bondi Beach is one of Sydney's most popular tourist destinations and an area that has long been understood as shared, open and available to visitors from outside the area. While the activities in the park—drinking lemonade, relaxing on bean bags, and playing guitars—are not normally undertaken in parking spaces, they are familiar and readily accepted activities in the local area.

A lack of ownership among participants is most likely to be problematic when conversion of the space into a park conflicts with other relationships to the street. As in the examples above, technical explanations about leases and legality provide little help when confronted by someone with a conflicting understanding of how the space is owned.

6.3   Ownership and privilege

> The right to be here and the sense of belonging it creates are reinforced insti-
> tutionally and socially; profound personal sentiment is enabled by structural
> conditions.[14]

Ownership is not equally accessible to all. Like property, a sense of ownership connects to power and privilege as well as participation. Many of the
critiques that Marxist, race, and feminist theorists have leveled at private
property can be applied also to informal ownership. Just as property can
be subverted or unsettled but often tends to reproduce the status quo, the
relational nature of ownership means that it too is often implicated in the
maintenance of hegemonic power relations.

The crucial role of ownership in motivating and enabling participation
in PARK(ing) Day is important in understanding the demographics of participants and the places in which parks tend to be located. While the informal nature of PARK(ing) Day makes it difficult to identify all of the parks
that have been created, and in turn to determine where they were located
or who was involved, my research suggests that the patterns of PARK(ing)
Day align with other forms of DIY urbanism.[15] Participants tend to be people with the kinds of privilege that make ownership more accessible, and
because they generally participate in the places for which they feel a sense
of ownership, parks tend to be installed in the relatively affluent areas in
which they live and work.

PARK(ing) Day is most prevalent in inner-city areas, and participants
are often relatively privileged "could haves." Young designers, artists, built
environment professionals, and environmental activists are the main (or
at least the most visible) participants because of the networks through
which PARK(ing) Day has been disseminated—websites like BoingBoing
and Archinet, events like the Venice Biennale, organizations like ADUQ,
the AIA, the CRE and TPL—but also because they are more likely to have a
preexisting sense of ownership.

For those who don't belong, it is much harder to access even the informal
ownership on which claims to public parking spaces might be grounded.
Elise O'Ryan's comment above highlights not only the value of ownership,
but the significance of its absence:

> If you don't feel part of a community or if you don't feel like you belong some-
> where, then there's not much motivation to get involved.

The ability to access ownership is clearly socially situated. Informal ownership may be more attainable than private property, but it is by no means accessible to everyone. Just as scholars working on the right to the city have highlighted the significant influence of factors like race, class, gender, and (dis)ability in its attainment, informal ownership is shaped also by the presence (or absence) of various forms of privilege. This was an issue that concerned some participants:

> Obviously John and I, you know, are both imbued with an incredible amount of privilege to be able to do this, right? We're white, overeducated men, we have no fear of the police, you know, no fear of, I mean we thought we'd probably get arrested, but . . . we're not going to go to prison for this, we're not getting shot. There was never a sense this is dangerous, you know. (Matthew Passmore, San Francisco)

> I wonder if it was myself, you know, upper middle-class white dude in my own neighborhood doing this, if the police might just look at me and shrug or laugh it off or let me get off easy versus you know in our country still if you're a minority, if you tend to be poor, have fewer resources, you have literally less agency in the public ground. . . . It's a form of privilege in some ways to move out in the public realm and break the law intentionally and get away with it. (Mike Lydon, New York)

For urban anthropologist and mobility activist Adonia Lugo, the decision by police to shut down her LA park in 2009 can be explained by race:

> I spent a few minutes trying to explain to the officers that this event was taking place all over town, with other sites to be found a short distance west on Wilshire, and that it seemed discriminatory to say it could not happen in MacArthur Park. They did not budge; our brown bodies simply were not allowed to remain in the street.

> Bringing Park(ing) Day to MacArthur Park was supposed to be a symbolic statement about the inclusion of all Angelenos in the city's sustainable future. Instead, it became a reaffirmation that bodies in the street get policed differently.[16]

Race can be an important factor in shaping ownership and in turn in shaping the way people engage (or don't engage) in PARK(ing) Day, and the responses those engagements generate among the wider community. Because ownership is developed and sustained through multiple practices, however, race alone is not determinative. In my interviews I spoke to many non-white people whose parks had attracted very positive responses—people born (or with parents born) in countries including Singapore, Malaysia, India, Colombia, and Nigeria. I also spoke to white people whose parks had not.

I did not speak to any indigenous people: I found no evidence of any engaging in PARK(ing) Day at all. This absence was a concern for some participants. San Francisco, Sydney, and Montréal are all settler colonial cities, and activists pursuing more just urban spaces are increasingly cognizant of the need to address the legacies of colonial dispossession.[17] Yet bridging this divide can be very difficult, requiring engagement far beyond the scope of short-term interventions like PARK(ing) Day, as one participant explained:

> It's been so long and there was so much injustice . . . it's really hard . . . we tend to not be able to reach out with them. When we talk to other organizations as well they have the same difficulties, except the ones who are really, really specialized. . . . You know, we're white, young and hip and graduates from law school. I'm going to help you? . . . They're going to say no, you're not part of this town. (Philippe Letarte, Montréal)

Like Letarte, many participants in PARK(ing) Day are aware of their privilege, and struggle to work out what to do in this context. The parks installed in San Francisco by CC Puede are one example of participants trying to use the event to contribute to more equitable urban relations. While day laborers were not part of the group who planned the events, their needs were the focus of the event. Free health checks, a barbecue, and fresh fruit were provided in an effort to address, albeit in a very small way, the massive inequalities and injustices that the group saw in the street and the city more generally.

> Cesar Chavez Street also has a lot of the day laborers that people are hiring to work that are often illegal, that wait around to be picked up . . . so we decided we'd build a clinic . . . the idea there was that we would help and we would pull people in for real, tangible benefit. (Daniel Sherman, San Francisco)

Other groups have also tried to use PARK(ing) Day to give back to less privileged members of their communities, or to highlight and critique wider patterns of inequality. In their efforts to design parks that would benefit the local community, Rayside Labossière focused not only on local families and workers, but also visitors to the nearby needle exchange and homeless drop-in center. Further West, Notre-Dame-de-Grâce Community Council used PARK(ing) Day as part of ongoing advocacy in Westhaven, a low-income community with a high immigrant population. They installed their park in an alleyway to support calls for this to be made a permanent park, as part of a broader effort to highlight and address the lack of green space in the area, particularly safe spaces for children to play.

For others, privilege provides a reason not to act. Reflecting on her participation in PARK(ing) Day and its political significance, one participant noted the bounded nature of her ownership and ability to engage in public space.

> I mean, I've always been very, very careful, because I'm half Chinese, I'm very careful about racism and I think I'm a pretty approachable person, so I don't think those things would have impacted how we engage with people here on this side. If we were to locate this closer to the Block in Redfern [a prominent Indigenous site] then I probably wouldn't have that cultural understanding or, you know, permission to, to be there as such. (Lydia Ho, Sydney)

Another Asian woman in Sydney, Julietta Jung, was inspired by PARK(ing) Day to put together a park in the suburb where she grew up. She wanted to do this near the local shops, which were located across the railway from her home, "on the other side of the tracks." Socioeconomically, this was a very different part of the suburb, and Jung thought PARK(ing) Day might help to improve the street for the community there. She put out calls for collaborators on the Sydney PARK(ing) Day webpage and, recognizing the importance of local connections to making something like PARK(ing) Day work, she got involved with a local community center. Jung decided not to proceed with the park: through the process of volunteering with the community center, she realized how removed she was from the street and the concerns of the people there:

> I had this vision in my own mind, by myself. . . . They had different issues, they had more resourcing issues than I could imagine. It just didn't seem appropriate, this fun little activity. . . . I kind of backed down on the whole idea . . . I needed to do the engagement first, I needed to connect with the people instead of just coming out and saying I've got this great idea . . . it's a bit insensitive.

PARK(ing) Day can be a reflective activity. For at least some participants, the event can lead to greater awareness about uneven spatial politics, the potential impacts of interventions in public space, and both the extent and limits of their own privilege.

6.4   Sustaining ownership

PARK(ing) Day is significant as a space where ownership is expressed and where it is tested, and also where it can be sustained and strengthened. As more than belonging but not (yet) property, a sense of ownership requires ongoing enactment to be sustained and—potentially, with enough of the right kinds of enactments (the kinds of property practices outlined by Davina Cooper)—to solidify into rights that might approximate more formal property. PARK(ing) Day is not, however, an event through which such solidification can be completed.

A sense of ownership must be practiced time and again. While the experience of building a park for PARK(ing) Day is frequently productive of ownership, this invariably builds on social and material connections established over longer periods of time. Many participants emphasized the length of time they had known and cared about the area, their relationships with the place and the people there, and other ways in which they had contributed or hoped to do so. Participants with a strong sense of ownership had often lived in the same place for a long period.

> We've been socially involved in this neighborhood for about, I don't know, almost 30 years . . . we work like that in several neighborhoods but [here, where we built the park is] the neighborhood that probably we're the most involved [because] historically [we] just lived here for a long time. (Ron Rayside, Montréal)

> We've got a great connection to this place. Everyone knows the businesses, people live generally in the local area, either walking distance or a short drive. We know . . . every little nook and cranny. . . . And I've only been here six years, whereas other people have been here for 18 or 20 years. . . . We love it. (Jonathan Knapp, Sydney)

The performative, citational nature of ownership was apparent even in interviews: for some participants, the process of explaining what happened on PARK(ing) Day itself helped to strengthen feelings of ownership. In reflecting on the park he installed on King Street, Newtown, for example, Eytan Rocheta initially said that PARK(ing) Day had no impact. After further discussion, however, he shifted to describing his experience as "profound," explaining that PARK(ing) Day "did spark. It did really make me engaged . . . and allowed for that ownership."

Several other participants became more confident in their assertions as their interviews progressed. In a number of cases, participants made brief or tentative mentions of ownership, appropriation, or belonging early in the interview, prior to being asked any questions about it. When asked more directly about the importance of ownership later in the interview, participants expressed themselves with more certainty. With the interview providing an opportunity to claim and to celebrate their ownership, participants were increasingly emphatic and enthusiastic.

Here my role as a researcher should also be noted. Quite a few participants asked what I had learned in other interviews. As my research progressed, I was increasingly able to respond by explaining how others understood ownership and its role in the event. With confirmation that ownership was important to others, participants were more forceful—and often more animated—in making such claims themselves.

Ownership is in some sense immanent, developed through actions, including the action of speaking about it. Discussing ownership, and discussing the steps taken to develop it—including going through the extensive effort involved, giving form to their creative ideas and identities, the degree to which their actions were affirmed by passersby, and the ways in which they were materially and spatially connected to the street and the city—help to strengthen the feelings of ownership produced through PARK(ing) Day. Having that ownership affirmed through discussion in interviews provided further support, working to sustain and even extend the sense of ownership produced on the day. Conversely, without sustained performance, a sense of ownership can be weakened or even lost. Connections can be broken if they are not nurtured.

A sense of ownership can be developed through PARK(ing) Day, but the potential for this is limited by the temporary nature of the event: participants claim a lease, not a more lasting form of property like freehold tenure. Consistent with the emphasis on temporality in scholarship on belonging, psychological ownership, and theories of property based on personhood and on performance, time plays an important role in the development of a sense of ownership.

> Time, if you're comfortable in the street and if you know the street, it's yours. [Montréal] is my city because I know the streets. (Jean-Philippe Di Marco, Montréal)

Sarah Keenan is emphatic about the way in which time shapes property rights. While individual instances of property can have any duration, relationships of belonging are far less likely to be short than long-lasting. Because each occurrence of property is dependent upon the past, some level of permanence is usually required for something or someone to belong. "Subjects and objects do not randomly land in networks of belonging and become embedded there, but are funnelled into that position by the pre-existing shape of the world around."[18]

The importance of time, and the weaker connection between ownership and events of short duration, was one of the key critiques of PARK(ing) Day. In thinking about whether the event has any impact, several participants suggested that its duration was too short to contribute to feelings of ownership.

> It quickly reverts back to its original state. . . . Once it gets removed completely I think that ownership fades away . . . unless there's some small hidden reminder, the wood's a bit ajar from where the nail was in or, you know. If it's gone back to its original state then, then the ownership [claps]. I don't know, for me the ownership it will go quite quickly. (Eytan Rocheta, Sydney)

> It was a very temporary thing, so I don't know if it really had that big of an impact because we only had it set up for a couple of hours. (Annalise Riechert, San Francisco)

> If it's gone, well it's just a memory. It's like playing there, you have good memories of using that space but there's nothing left. . . . I suppose if it comes back every year, then it's not totally temporary. It's recurrent, so there's something to that space. (Philippe Marchand, Montréal)

PARK(ing) Day perhaps comes closest to producing more "solid" forms of property in cases where participants go on to make longer-lasting interventions after the event. Caffè Greco in the North Beach area of San Francisco is one of a number of businesses that followed the construction of parks on several PARK(ing) Days with the installation of parklets (figure 6.7).[19] Installed with permission from the City under permitting processes established in 2010, parklets rely on rights that are more conventional and readily comprehensible than the sense of ownership animating parks built for PARK(ing) Day.

In Montréal, Rayside Labossière were inspired by PARK(ing) Day to make a more permanent intervention on the street outside their office (notably, this was prior to their contested contribution to PARK(ing) Day in 2015). Like Caffè Greco, Rayside Labossière had participated in PARK(ing) Day multiple times and were ready to push the idea further. They developed a new kind of street furniture incorporating places to sit and stand, with an idea that they might sometimes hold office meetings there, and that others in the community, particularly the drop-in center for homeless people next door, could also use the space for gathering or resting (figure 6.8).

Figure 6.7
Parklet outside Caffè Greco, 423 Columbus Avenue, San Francisco, designed by
Rebar. Image: San Francisco Planning Department.

Rayside Labossière had secured support from the City for this, and a pilot
project was under way at the time of our interview. The intention was that
this would inform a permitting system to enable the installation of similar
interventions in other parts of the city.

In these kinds of interventions the practices of simplification, codification, and power described by Cooper are apparent. In contrast to the
parks built for PARK(ing) Day, these installations entail the preparation of
drawings, filling out of forms, payment of fees, and certification by various
officials. The rights created and the steps to obtain them are enumerated
with precision; the power that follows is accordingly much more certain.

PARK(ing) Day is not an end point, but a step along the way. Just as
scholars of democracy or social movements argue these are made by
care and attention to them,[20] property is built through performance, by

Figure 6.8
Ron Rayside and Catherine Thibault with street furniture prototype, Rue Ontario, Montréal, 2015. Image: Amelia Thorpe.

the accretion of practices of ownership. PARK(ing) Day is significant as a mechanism by which a sense of ownership can be given prominence, perhaps also greater power, and a nudge toward the kinds of practices through which it can be further strengthened.

Part Three   Politics and Possibility

Figure 7.1
Sunset Parklet, Judah Street, San Francisco. Hosted by Other Avenues Food Store
and Sea Breeze Café, designed by INTERSTICE Architects, 2014. Image: INTERSTICE
Architects.

7   Products of PARK(ing)

What do people get out of PARK(ing) Day? People are drawn to the event by the ease and legitimacy of the opportunity it presents for participation in shaping the city. For many, the idea that paying a parking meter legitimates public and very visible interventions is exciting and inspiring. Particularly enticing is the potential for those brief interventions to bring about some longer-lasting change.

Most often, participants join PARK(ing) Day with hopes of reshaping the city in some way. Policy and physical shifts are the goals people mention first; they are also the goals that people refer to in evaluating the event. Some make very bold claims about the success of PARK(ing) Day in achieving such change; others are more dismissive, suggesting that tiny, temporary interventions like PARK(ing) Day do not have any lasting impact, and that shifts in planning and policy should be attributed instead to other activities.

In reflecting on their engagement and its effects after the event, participants often raised a different set of impacts. For many, the most significant products of PARK(ing) Day turn out to be more personal and more diffuse. Building a park on PARK(ing) Day can be an affective experience, prompting a rethinking of the city and one's place within it. This is rarely pursued explicitly, often unexpected, and in some cases was not even recognized until participants reflected on the event in our discussions. Perhaps most significant among the personal impacts described by participants is the development of a sense of ownership for the site and its surroundings. Feelings of ownership are in many cases strengthened and sustained through participation in PARK(ing) Day, and can in turn lead participants to engage in the city in other, more lasting ways.

Instead of a linear path from idea to implementation, objectives to out-comes, PARK(ing) Day can be understood as a prefigurative practice: an open, experimental acting out of alternatives with unpredictable conse-quences for participants and for the cities with which they engage. The creation of a parklet policy by the City of San Francisco is perhaps the most recognizable example of this: that the 2005 PARK(ing) installation would lead to this kind of change was not even contemplated by Rebar at the time.

There is also the possibility that PARK(ing) Day might bring about less positive change, particularly when considered amongst other forms of DIY urbanism. While pop-up parks are generally seen as too transient to con-tribute to processes of gentrification, some participants were concerned that the event might distract or divert attention away from more meaning-ful advocacy. The close connection between ownership and privilege is also significant: while PARK(ing) Day opens up opportunities for participation in city-making, those opportunities are not open to everyone, at least not equally.

7.1   Changing the city

People use it as a reference. (Carlo Tadeo, Montréal)

The development most often attributed to PARK(ing) Day—both by partici-pants and in wider commentary on the event—is the emergence of parklets (figure 7.1). Particularly in San Francisco, PARK(ing) Day is generally under-stood as the event that prompted the City to develop a program to facili-tate the conversion of parking spaces into semipermanent public spaces. Participants also link the event with a range of other changes: new policies and regulations promoting and prescribing measures to increase amenity for pedestrians and cyclists; shifts in both public and official attitudes and expectations about how the city can and should be regulated.

Parklets have a direct connection to PARK(ing) Day. In 2010, Rebar pro-duced a modular system for a "walklet," a more permanent version of the kinds of parks built on PARK(ing) Day. This was conceived as an extension of the sidewalk to enable pedestrians to walk around the tables and chairs that took up space outside of cafés and restaurants. When Rebar took this to Andres Power, a planner with the City, he loved the idea but suggested a modification: pedestrians should retain the sidewalk, and the chairs and tables should instead move into the parking space. Power also suggested a catchier name for these interventions: parklets.[1]

Rebar worked with the City of San Francisco to develop a trial of the parklet concept, including developing a design manual for the City.[2] Rebar designed a prototype modular parklet for the City (later displayed on Rebar's website, available for purchase as the Walklet), as well as site-specific parks for two clients (one outside Caffè Greco in North Beach, the other the conversion of an old Citroen van into a parklet outside the Rapha bike shop in the Marina district, somewhat controversial as the permit was not obtained until after construction). The idea took off quickly: by the end of 2010, there were twelve parklets in development;[3] by the beginning of 2013, 38 parklets had been installed across the city;[4] by March 2015, that number exceeded 50.[5]

Many of the parklets built in San Francisco were on sites that had previously been used for parks on PARK(ing) Day: outside Caffè Greco, for example, and in front of the Brainwash Café on Folsom Street in the SoMa district. This link can be seen clearly on Valencia Street, once a popular location for PARK(ing) Day, as Passmore recalls:

> Just a couple of years ago I was on the phone on PARK(ing) Day with a reporter from ABC News and she said, "You know, we want to go out and find a concentration of parks. Where should we go?" And I was just getting off the BART in the Mission and I said "Oh well, I'm about to ride my bike down Valencia Street to the studio. So I'll call you, usually there's a dozen of them on Valencia." So I started riding down Valencia and I saw a parklet, parklet, parklet, parklet, no PARK(ing) Day installations, but parklets, officially sanctioned PARK(ing) Day-type installations. So that was maybe 2013 when I realized San Francisco has moved past the sort of questions that we brought up with PARK(ing) Day.

PARK(ing) Day is widely understood as giving rise to parklets around the world as well as locally, with San Francisco seen as a key influence for parklet programs in other cities.[6] San Francisco's parklet policy has been well publicized, and has provided a model for the many cities adopting parklet programs since 2010.[7] Studies examining the positive impacts of parklets on local business in San Francisco provided important support for the establishment of parklet policies in other jurisdictions.[8] In Sydney, several planners from various local authorities have traveled to San Francisco and visited various parklets across the city, and San Francisco's parklet policy has been an important resource for local authorities examining and developing their own policies.

In turn, parklets are recognized as contributing to other developments at the city level in San Francisco. The 2012 Urban Prototyping Festival and 2015 Market Street Prototyping Festival (MSPF) were often mentioned. John Bela makes a strong link between these events and PARK(ing) Day, suggesting they were directly inspired by the PARK(ing) Day-to-parklet story, and conceived with the aim of replicating this kind of trajectory from DIY beginnings to citywide adoption.[9] This is clearest in the MSPF, a partnership between the City, the Yerba Buena Center for the Arts, and the Knight Foundation from 2015. The MSPF was established with the aim of generating ideas that could in turn be developed into new permit instruments or operating procedures comparable to the parklet program. It began with an open call for proposals, from which around 50 projects were selected. Successful entrants were given $2,000 for materials and support from design professionals to develop their proposals into installations; these were then installed for three days in April, grouped in five clusters along Market Street. The Festival ran again in 2016, with hashtags allowing passersby to vote for their favorite installation and in turn inform the City's planning process for the Market Street area (figure 7.2). Several former participants in PARK(ing) Day have been involved in the Festival.

PARK(ing) Day has been connected also to policy shifts, including policies aimed at enhancing walkability, activation, and creativity in cities, and reducing the focus on cars in urban planning and design. During my time in San Francisco, many participants were excited to tell me about the preparation (and, near the end of my stay, the passing) of a new ordinance amending the San Francisco Planning Code to provide a clear legal basis for "parks" and related activities.

> The new ordinance . . . you couldn't get a more positive example of how this sort of stuff gets pulled into part of the city's process. ('Deep Jawa, San Francisco)

These connections are recognized even within the City, as one official explained:

> Generally the attitude and orientation of San Francisco's policies, our street policies, our public space policies, our transportation policies, you know, are in some way advanced and propelled by this international movement that PARK(ing) Day is. And so there are many other things, I mean I, you know, in San Francisco in particular, that have driven the development of things like our Better Streets plan and stuff like that. But it's part of that forward movement, it's part of that thrust. So I think that there have been policy impacts, certainly. I mean here in 2016,

Figure 7.2
Market Street Prototyping Festival, Market Street, San Francisco, 2016. The sign-board gives instructions on how to vote for installations in the festival, with voting intended to inform the development of the best prototypes into longer-term interventions. Image: Amelia Thorpe.

we're trying to pass an ordinance, you know, at long last that will facilitate park-lets and pedestrian plazas. (Robin Abad Ocubillo, San Francisco)

Participants suggested that PARK(ing) Day has played a role in many other projects around San Francisco. One connected PARK(ing) Day to the more recent conversion of shipping containers to form mobile miniparks with plants and seating by the Yerba Buena Arts Center. Another linked PARK(ing) Day to a range of interventions by the San Francisco Municipal Transformation Agency (SFMTrA, a play on the City's Municipal Transportation Agency, the SFMTA) to make city streets safer for cyclists and pedestrians, deploying techniques from spraypainting crosswalks to installing bollards along bike lanes, techniques that are often hard to distinguish from those of the SFMTA.

Some participants noted more direct impacts, with improvements secured or under development for the particular sites on which they built their parks. The park built by CC Puede on Cesar Chavez Street, for example, was later followed by traffic calming, turning what was a "traffic sewer" into a street that is now much safer and more pleasant for pedestrians and cyclists as well as cars. More recently, the group of businesses that installed three "parks" along Howard Street in 2016 were inspired by the event to develop a longer-term strategy for the street, and secured support from the city to progress this.

Participants in Sydney and Montréal made connections with a range of planning shifts also. In Montréal, interviewees frequently linked PARK(ing) Day to curbside "build-outs." These involve extending the curb to create more footpath space and/or garden areas, typically near intersections to increase safety and amenity for pedestrians. PARK(ing) Day was connected also to proposals for the permanent removal of many parking spaces to improve amenity for pedestrians and cyclists along Rue Saint-Catherine, the main commercial street in Montréal. Others linked PARK(ing) Day to the parklet-style timber deck installed over several hundred meters along the major commercial street Rue Saint-Denis in 2014. This was an effort (albeit not a very successful one) to improve amenity for shops, restaurants, and other businesses while extensive road works were undertaken along the street.

Participants also noted the increasing popularity of parklet-style *terrasses* installed during summer outside bars and restaurants, as well as newer *placottoirs* (explained to me as a term derived from an Italian word to describe engaging in conversation simply for the pleasure of it) installed over parking spaces by local business associations rather than one particular café (figure 7.3).

> Now, after that you have the replication of parklets everywhere in the city, you have people asking for that. The main change has been on mentalities . . . people that understand the importance of . . . greater mobility, the use of space by people who are just saying cars are not the only way to animate the city and to make it dynamic. (Félix Gravel, Montréal)

As in San Francisco, PARK(ing) Day was linked also to broader policy changes and shifts in public attitudes in Montréal. In particular, the event

Figure 7.3
Shipping container covered in bright paintwork and filled with timber seating to become a *placottoir*, a free resting space for people on Boulevard Saint-Laurent, Mile End, Montréal, 2015. Image: Amelia Thorpe.

was connected to the growing support for and greater implementation of policies reducing the availability of on-street parking. The event has gained official recognition and support in Montréal's new parking strategy, which requires the City to support and facilitate activities such as PARK(ing) Day.[10]

In Sydney, participants were more hesitant to link PARK(ing) Day to changes in the city. Several suggested that PARK(ing) Day is too tiny to achieve any lasting change.

> PARK(ing) Day was a rogue activity, four people? . . . I felt as soon as we had left, although a few people might have thought slightly differently about a parking space, in general it was exactly as it was before. . . . If I was a decision maker in council, what does a very temporary, rogue protest have, what effect does that have on my planning? Zero. None . . . it was too small to have an impact. (Eytan Rocheta, Sydney)

Concerns about the lack of consequences dissuade some people from engaging in the event. One interviewee explained that she liked the idea but didn't want to build a park herself, deciding instead to encourage a colleague to get her students involved:

> for me it was a balance of the effort required. . . . If I thought I could kill a motorway by having a parklet there for one day I'd be out there doing it every day! For what I thought I could get out of it, I wasn't putting the effort in. (Kerryn Wilmot, Sydney)

Others did find changes that could be linked to PARK(ing) Day, especially parklets and various temporary (and temporary-looking) interventions around the city. As participants in all three cities note, however, these developments cannot be traced to PARK(ing) Day alone. In considering the many urban interventions that have been linked to PARK(ing) Day, there is a problem of attribution. It is difficult to say with certainty what came out of the event, and what should more accurately be traced to other sources.

> It feels like there's a more, there's an approach to adapting to things by taking over parking that I think is influenced by PARK(ing) Day. I really do think that.
> . . . It's hard to say because there is a general trend toward more pedestrian-friendly streets, and there are a lot of things that have been done recently in New York towards that. And I mean it would be ridiculous to say that John Bela and Blaine are responsible for it. (Amy Seek, San Francisco)

Even for parklets, the story must include more than PARK(ing) Day. As one of the early organizers from the Trust for Public Land commented:

> The parklet movement I don't think began in San Francisco, although I believe there's a bit of myth that it did. But I think it absolutely gained a considerable amount of traction because of PARK(ing) Day. (Matthew Shaffer, San Francisco)

San Francisco's parklet program is part of a larger Pavement to Parks (now Groundplay) initiative. This was informed by PARK(ing) Day but also other developments, particularly the Plaza Program introduced in New York City in 2008.[11] Visits by Danish urban designer Jan Gehl and by New York Transportation Commissioner Janette Sadik-Kahn to San Francisco in 2008 provided strong encouragement for the establishment of a program within the city to improve amenity for pedestrians.[12] Other precedents are also relevant, including several already mentioned: the sidewalk plazas proposed by Public Architecture, the sidewalk landscaping permits Jane Martin and Plant*SF worked with the City of San Francisco to develop, and the street furniture installed by Steve Rasmussen Cancian and others in Oakland. Further afield, there are also many precedents that may have played some role. In Montréal, for example, local authorities have had permitting processes for the conversion of parking spaces into *terrasses* since at least 2006.[13]

Broader shifts in planning and urban design were also influential, with events such as Ciclovía, Sunday Streets, Better Block, and Critical Mass (another event originating in San Francisco that has since spread internationally) prompting a rethinking of the allocation of urban space since at least the 1990s. In Montréal, several participants cited texts such as Donald Shoup's *The High Price of Free Parking* (2005) and Charles Montgomery's *Happy City* (2013) as important drivers for their engagement in PARK(ing) Day, perhaps more important even than Rebar.[14] Daniel Bouchard, who began the CRE's PARK(ing) Day campaign, was unsure where he first heard about the idea of taking over parking spaces, but thought it probably wasn't actually PARK(ing) Day.

Planning policy and professional training in all three countries (and many others) had similarly been moving away from car-based planning to more small-scale, pedestrian-centered design with the growing popularity of new urbanism and transit-oriented development among practitioners and policymakers in planning. A greater focus on activities originating outside formal planning processes coincides also with the broader policy shifts toward participation and partnerships with the private sector in urban policy. Several participants used the term "zeitgeist" in discussing PARK(ing) Day.

> All of that contributes to the way we see our cities being different in the future. And I think PARK(ing) Day is part of that. I mean maybe it's just the zeitgeist of now, but I think people even just hearing about PARK(ing) Day or experiencing it question, you know, "Is it better for me to ride my bike or walk?" or "How do I get to work?" and "Why do I use one mode of transportation over another?" and "I might be part of some sort of better sharing of the environment." It's interesting that all of those things really didn't exist before this whole movement. (Zoee Astrachan, San Francisco)

> You know how these things become almost like part of the zeitgeist? It's just lots of people are thinking about it at the same time. So I didn't even know about PARK(ing), we were doing this and then it, it's sort of the same thing. (Sam Crawford, Sydney)

Rebar's participation in the Venice Biennale in 2008 was alongside several other designers working in comparable ways. Other projects in the US Pavilion that year included a lightweight mobile house, a public art project developed in a derelict Detroit neighborhood, and a mobile swimming pool made from a decommissioned cargo barge.[15] The Italian pavilion featured a range of design practices approaching the city in ways much like Rebar: testing regulatory niches, experimenting with small-scale, temporary interventions to catalyze broader debate. The celebration of these practices at the Biennale was itself one of many. By 2008, "DIY," "guerrilla," "adaptive," "tactical," "everyday," or "insurgent" urbanism had become the subject of much scholarly and popular attention.[16]

Many of the practices now understood as part of a "new" approach to urban design in fact have much longer histories. A wide range of practices—from street art and graffiti to food trucks and street vendors, from sit-ins and squats to "plant-ins" and community gardens—can be understood as precedents for PARK(ing) Day, and for many of the practices with which it has since been linked.

Accordingly, many of the changes linked to PARK(ing) Day in fact predate the event. This is particularly apparent in Montréal, where there is a rich tradition of citizen and community-led urban interventions. As noted above, permitting programs for parking space *terrasses* have been in existence since at least 2006; various other forms of outdoor *terrasses* have much longer histories across the city.[17] The closure of Rue Saint-Catherine through the summer started in 2008, and was preceded by temporary closures well before then.[18] Summer street closures in the Downtown area have been a regular occurrence since at least 1980, when they were undertaken as part of the Jazz Festival. Long-running precedents for the reclamation of public space can be found also in other parts of the city. These include temporary street closures, ranging from those organized over the past decade by groups such as Rue Publique to more spontaneous closures as part of block parties and neighborhood gatherings.[19] There are also precedents entailing more permanent reclamations of public space, such as the conversion of laneways into permanent *ruelles vertes* (green alleys) since at least 1999.[20]

In Sydney, participants tend to associate shifts in planning policy and practice with other trends, particularly precedents from cities at the top of various livability and innovation rankings such as Vancouver, New York, or Copenhagen (Jan Gehl, the Copenhagen-based founder of Gehl Studio, has consulted on several major projects in Sydney). Participants are more likely to trace parklets to complete streets or Better Block approaches than to PARK(ing) Day. Parklets are still relatively new in Sydney, with just a small number built on a trial basis. Only one of Sydney's councils, Waverley Council, has a process in place to allow for parklets.[21] Waverley's parklet policy was introduced as part of a broader urban interventions program, which includes public art, play spaces, and bike facilities as well as parklets and explains these as "following the Complete Streets Strategy."[22] Several parklet trials in other areas can be traced to a Better Block project along Clovelly Road, and the parklet structure built for that project.[23] One of Sydney's earliest parklets, a garden built over two parking spaces in Surry Hills by Sam Crawford Architects in 2009, was conceived and installed in response to local conditions, without any reference to parklets, PARK(ing) Day, or any other precedents.[24]

Even in San Francisco, participants in recent years had often heard about PARK(ing) Day only after hearing about parklets. Sustainability consultancy Stok, for example, heard about PARK(ing) Day after their request for permission to install a parklet was declined. Stok's participation in PARK(ing) Day was explicitly undertaken in the hope that a temporary, material transformation of the space might help to prompt a revision of that decision.

The impacts of PARK(ing) Day on urban planning and governance can also be underestimated. While New York's Pavement to Plazas program was influential in the development of San Francisco's parklet program, PARK(ing) Day may have influenced New York in its policy development (as several participants claimed). Similarly, in suggesting that parklets in Sydney should be traced to Better Block, there remains a link with PARK(ing) Day, since the Better Block approach was itself inspired at least in part by PARK(ing) Day.[25] Many of the other activities—from one-off interventions to more formal policies incorporating complete streets and creative cities approaches—can also be linked to PARK(ing) Day. The increasing circulation of images and ideas makes tracing lineages very difficult. As one participant commented with respect to a story in Sydney's tabloid, the *Daily Telegraph*, deriding participants in PARK(ing) Day as "park raving-mad" and likely to cause "traffic chaos and disruption to local businesses":[26]

> even though it was bad press, I think any press is good press. And I know a few people in the Department of Planning that saw that article that hadn't heard of PARK(ing) Day before and that then looked at PARK(ing) Day and what PARK(ing)

Day was about and they were like "Yeah, that makes sense. You know, maybe we can embed it." I think there's a whole lot of tangible and intangible things that come from something like that. You know, because it really, there is shock quality I think for some people around PARK(ing) Day and I think that stays with them for a little while. (John O'Callaghan, Sydney)

Most participants are confident that the event does have some impact. One way to understand the significance of PARK(ing) Day for the practice of city-making in this context is in terms of discourse. PARK(ing) Day provided a way to connect previously small-scale and largely unnoticed activities. In Montréal, one participant connected this visibility to shifts in the City's approach:

It's being taken up by the municipality and as well as being taken up by municipal politicians who . . . don't have a, like a profound ideological attachment to these sorts of things. But because people like it and because it's popular and because there's been a number of successful projects . . . they're willing to support this kind of project. (David Alfaro Clark, Montréal)

PARK(ing) Day cannot be credited with initiating these activities, but it did provide a useful vocabulary with which to describe them, and that in turn helped to increase their visibility. In Sydney, as noted above, Crawford Architects had not heard of PARK(ing) Day or parklets until well after they installed a garden in parking spaces in Surry Hills.

We started calling these parklets because John [O'Callaghan, who set up the Sydney PARK(ing) Day webpage, Twitter and Facebook accounts] had tweeted us something about them and called it a parklet and I thought it was a much better name than what we'd come up with. Then I later found out that parklets is a kind of a word that's used for [these]. . . . I think parklets is a really good word because it's just a little bit of green public space in a street that didn't really have any. (Sam Crawford, Sydney)

PARK(ing) Day helped draw together a diverse and disparate range of activities in a way that could be explained and understood. Importantly, PARK(ing) Day captured a range of increasingly pressing issues in a single, highly shareable image:

I just remember being struck by how brilliant that was, as a way of illustrating that streets could be used in a completely different way. . . . I was part of this group of people and we were trying to think of like "Okay, how are we going to make these points? How are we going to move policy? What kind of hundred-page research paper should we write?" And these artists in San Francisco, in just one simple, two-hour-long project and a photo, I felt like they had conveyed this entire set of ideas in such a compelling way." (Aaron Naparstek, New York)

With its strong narratives of legitimacy, PARK(ing) Day was an important factor in gaining public and policy support for the wide range of activities with which the event has been linked. For Crawford, PARK(ing) Day and, particularly, parklets proved valuable in explaining the Surry Hills intervention, and in connecting it to other events and other ideas. In 2008, John Chase, a Los Angeles urban designer who coedited the influential publication *Everyday Urbanism* in 1998, highlighted the significance of PARK(ing) Day for a much wider range of urban interventions: "the greatest boost to the importance of very small spaces since the first edition of *Everyday Urbanism* has been the phenomenon of appropriating parking spaces for temporary parks and even proposing that parking spaces be made into micro-parks."[27]

As Chase argues, PARK(ing) Day should be understood as an important contributor to the growth of temporary and bottom-up approaches in planning. PARK(ing) Day remains the most prominent example of tactical urbanism. For Merker and Bela, PARK(ing) Day remains a key initiative despite their move to Gehl Studio. While it is now part of a longer story, PARK(ing) Day is still a foundational reference in many of the office's presentations. Merker explains:

[PARK(ing) Day] stands in as the primary example of [tactical urbanism]. . . . It has allowed a lot of people who had no other reference to talk about doing that kind of thing with a very specific example . . . you know, the mayor of some town or some dorky planner or designer that's using it to show a client. Even if it doesn't really live up to all that they're saying that it does, it provides the example that they can use. So I think it's been a really useful kind of communication device in the political and design fields.

The particular contributions made by PARK(ing) Day may be hard to pinpoint, but the event should not be dismissed as without consequence. In all three cities, PARK(ing) Day has had impacts on policy, public attitudes, the physical form of the public realm, and, perhaps most significantly, on the way in which cities are imagined and discussed.

7.2 Changing one's place in the city: commoning

It changed the world [laughs]. I'm kidding, that was a joke. Well, I think it started a very important conversation in cities all over. . . . It was part of the inspiration for the creation of parklets, but my deeper hope is that it really is more about changing people's perception of what it means to be in a democratic society, to be an individual and take some responsibility and some agency and some action to live out your values. . . . Having the experience of doing it . . . changed I think all of us who were participating. The actual doing of it really made you feel like, wow, this is a powerful thing. (Matthew Passmore, San Francisco)

The shift Passmore describes, from seeing PARK(ing) Day as a way to achieve external change toward seeing PARK(ing) Day more as a source of personal reflection and inspiration, is one that emerged in many interviews. While emotional or affective impacts were less likely to be described as motivating engagement, these proved surprisingly significant for many participants.

It definitely changed your perspective on what's okay. . . . It's not necessarily changing anything in the long run to do a PARK(ing) Day parklet. It's not, I mean a lot of the benefit I see is personal benefit. (Alex Gregor, San Francisco)

Participants often began their engagement with PARK(ing) Day with a view to prompting physical and policy changes, and a lack of directly traceable, tangible outcomes was a source of regret for some.

I think that's a disappointment that people that may have participated in PARK(ing) Day, certainly I felt disappointed afterwards that there's a lack of any action or there was lack of change. . . . But actually it was more internal . . . than something physical or something on the street. (John O'Callaghan, Sydney)

Reflecting more broadly, beyond the initial goals motivating their engagement with the event, a large proportion of participants felt their involvement had a significant impact on them or their organization. PARK(ing) Day was often described as a turning point, empowering participants and starting them on a trajectory of increasingly significant contributions. The experience of building a park changed the way in which they understood their relationship to the street and the city.

I carry that I did PARK(ing) Day . . . I still sometimes walk the street and look at the street or public realm and kind of envision something else. My little planner mind totally reimagines street intersections on a daily basis. (Anais Mathez, Montréal)

What I found was it was pretty empowering if you make a big enough noise, especially given San Francisco politics, you know, you can be heard. And you can make a little bit of a difference and you can make sure that decent things happen. (Daniel Sherman, San Francisco)

In explaining these shifts, participants describe feelings of empowerment, belonging, and, particularly, feelings of ownership arising out of their contributions to PARK(ing) Day. Through the process of building a park, many participants said that their sense of ownership was strengthened.

The multiple opportunities provided in PARK(ing) Day to develop a sense of ownership are significant for the performance and evolution of legality in the event, with ownership a key predictor of responses by legal actors, and important in revealing the dynamic and co-constitutive interactions between law and society. At a more personal level, the opportunities to develop a sense of ownership through PARK(ing) Day are in many cases the most valuable aspect of the event. By strengthening participants' sense of ownership, PARK(ing) Day can have much longer-lasting impacts on participants' understandings of the city and their ability to shape it. In many cases, participants then link this shift to later involvement in related activities.

Jérôme Glad was nearing the end of his architecture studies when he participated in PARK(ing) Day in 2012. Working with a group of young designers, he installed a cinema in Old Montréal, complete with popcorn, red carpet, a high-quality sound system, and authentic vintage seats. Glad emphasized repeatedly the impact that this had on him, how he was inspired by this experience to lead a number of other temporary interventions around other parts of the city:

> I think the fact of doing the PARK(ing) Day helped me doing other projects, participation projects, and helped me discover that we could have an impact in our city. It was the first time when I built something for PARK(ing) Day that I realized that I could build things in the city. (Jérôme Glad, Montréal)

In 2013, Glad coordinated the installation of a *village éphémère* (temporary village), which he described as "a whole street of PARK(ing) Day" lasting for one day and one night. The following summer he organized a similar event, but with a six-week duration, then in 2015 and again in 2016 for the whole summer. The success of these projects led Glad to establish Pépinière & Co, a not-for-profit company dedicated to the development of events like PARK(ing) Day on a full-time basis. Focusing on neglected spaces such as laneways, unpopular public spaces, and underused infrastructure, Pépinière & Co have constructed several temporary projects enlivening and encouraging debate about various parts of the city (figure 7.4). These

Figure 7.4
Jardins Gamelin, Montréal, 2015. Parc Émilie-Gamelin had been a neglected space in downtown Montreal, until Pépinière & Co worked with urban agriculture collective Sentier Urbain to create a concert venue, public garden, and outdoor café in the square, funded by the Quartier des Spectacles. Image: Amelia Thorpe.

projects are highly regarded in Montréal, and were mentioned in many interviews as making very positive contributions to the city. Glad traced them all to PARK(ing) Day:

> For me, it was a foundational act, to do PARK(ing) Day. It activated things in my life enormously. I remember writing a very long email to a friend about, oh, now it's possible! We can do things in the city!

Similar stories can be found in all three cities. Rebar itself provides a clear example, with PARK(ing) playing a major role in the group's move from planning guerrilla installations over beers to professionals running a major design office with international recognition. There are many others. Ming Thompson and Christina Cho, two young architects who coordinated a

PARK(ing) Day installation within the architecture firm Bohlin Cywinski Jackson, were inspired by the experience to establish their own studio. Atelier Cho Thompson now focuses on public projects informed by the approach they took in PARK(ing) Day.

> I saw the fun and the potential of doing stuff like that and at some point I started something in my head, yeah. Maybe it led to that, maybe. (Mikael St-Pierre, Montréal)

In Montréal, Mikael St-Pierre and Philippe Letarte, who built a hockey rink in the downtown area in 2012, went on to found Lande, a nonprofit organization that helps communities to convert unused spaces into parks, gardens, and playgrounds. Staff at the architecture and planning office Rayside Labossière were inspired by PARK(ing) Day to design a new kind of street furniture that would provide seating and tables for a wide range of social interactions, and to work with the city to develop a permitting system to enable their installation across Montréal. For the young design studio Atelier MAP, a weekend venture squeezed in between the demands of day jobs with larger firms, PARK(ing) Day provided a valuable opportunity to test and publicize design ideas.[28] This proved fruitful, leading to further work, including an installation for the summer-length *village éphémère* in 2016.

Even in Sydney, where PARK(ing) Day has been smaller, participants have been inspired by their experience to contribute to the city in other ways. After working on PARK(ing) Day within a larger office, John O'Callaghan was inspired to start further participatory planning projects—such as Idea Bombing Sydney, an event series to engage young people in thinking about the city—and in turn to set up his own consultancy. Jonathon Carle went from PARK(ing) Day to installing a bookshare outside his home, and now sits on the board of Street Libraries Australia. Elise O'Ryan and Kris Spann went from participating in PARK(ing) Day to leading the installation of a trial parklet in the inner city suburb of Glebe, including obtaining a grant from the City of Sydney and conducting detailed evaluations to inform the development of a parklet policy for the City, and then later developing a parklet on a trailer base that could be moved quickly and easily around the city (figure 7.5). As O'Ryan explains:

Figure 7.5
Mobile parklet, developed by People Parkers to be legible as a vehicle in an effort to comply with parking regulations. Glebe, Sydney, 2017. Image: Barton Taylor.

> I've been involved in PARK(ing) Day for a number of years now and it was short-term action. Now it's just kind of heading more towards long-term change. That's kind of cool to have gone through that process.

Participation in PARK(ing) Day can be a transformative experience for groups as well as individuals. An important part of the event is the way in which it draws people together. Glad's involvement in 2012 was as part of the newly formed Association du Design Urbain du Québec (ADUQ), which has gone on to become an influential and respected organization in Mont-réal, advocating for the profession and the public realm. Another group in Montréal, the McGill Spaces Project, used PARK(ing) Day as a launch event. This was successful, as director Alan Chen explains:

> We blew up a bit after that. Our name gained a lot of traction on campus and that was a really big thing because that was our first year. From there we sort of took off so I think a lot of that success could be attributed to the amount of awareness, that exposure that we got on PARK(ing) Day.

For established institutions as well as newer organizations, PARK(ing) Day can help to strengthen relationships between and within groups. For UTS Green, the sustainability office within the University of Technology Sydney, PARK(ing) Day was helpful in developing relationships.

> [PARK(ing) Day] certainly has impacts for us on campus. There's a camaraderie between all of those who participated. Some of them already are mates before they come and participate but then by the end of the day there's a certain sort of mateship built up and I've certainly noticed just in going around the campus you know, you chat to and you acknowledge people that have participated in the event that you might not otherwise have, so there's certainly some social benefits. (Seb Crawford, Sydney)

For Safiah Moore, participating in PARK(ing) Day helped strengthen feelings of belonging and connection to Arup as an organization.

> I was probably a student or a graduate here, so trying something new was good. And the fact that we pulled it off and there was a lot of support for us to pull it off and continue to be involved, I think that impacted me in a work sense that I was in a place that supported things like PARK(ing) Day, so that kind of affirmed that I was in a good place here. (Safiah Moore, Sydney)

Perhaps most importantly, PARK(ing) Day can be significant in drawing together informal groups. Consistently, participants describe getting to know their neighbors through the event.

> Having a day where people are invited to come and be part of their street and do something and just hang out and meet each other . . . I think that's a great way to start community dialogue or bring people together. And help people feel like they own physically the space as well as be part of their community. I think the concept is so strong. (Sam George, Sydney)

PARK(ing) Day, for many participants, is valued for strengthening feelings of belonging and attachment to the local community, developing a collective as well as an individual feeling of ownership.

> I felt like it really brought a lot of people together, I met our neighbors in other office buildings who I've never talked to before. And people were coming out and introducing themselves and offering us food and . . . resources, things like that. I thought it was a really cool community bonding event, not only were we taking over the street and showing more creative uses of public space, but it was also a way to really get to know the community pretty well. We met a lot of really cool people that day. (Annalise Reichert, San Francisco)

> It was definitely a community-building exercise, and a direct result of that was getting to know some of the issues on our street and issues in our neighborhood and

the people that live here, the people that work here. So it had way far-reaching social and community benefits outside of just doing this small little installation. (Trevor Sell, San Francisco)

As an activity that nurtures collective forms of ownership, participating in PARK(ing) Day can be understood as a process of commoning. As a verb rather than a noun, commoning is less about the management of common resources,[29] and more the generative potential of commoning as a practice.[30] In the context of concerns about the enclosure, dispossession, and ecological crisis being wrought by contemporary capitalism, commoning is celebrated as "a unifying concept prefiguring the cooperative society that many are striving to create."[31]

Scholarship on commoning draws in a wide range of examples, from community gardens and housing cooperatives to more transitory and dispersed practices like ad busting and social support networks.[32] Some are explicitly counterhegemonic (the camps of the climate justice movement),[33] others are much less political (a community of mobile-home owners in New Hampshire that formed a cooperative when their landlord put the site up for sale).[34] Many don't actually identify as commons, and don't conceptualize their activities as commoning.[35]

What unifies these activities, and what prompts commentators to describe them as commoning, is "a shared interest or value that is produced through communal relations."[36] Commoning emphasizes the specific and the contextual over the universal, and prioritizes a sense of shared life and collective responsibility over instrumental, individualized rationality. The productive nature of commoning is central: commoning emphasizes sharing for the common good and building new social relationships, beyond the market form.[37] Commoning does not simply give effect to preexisting values, it "is also and most importantly *a field of production of values.*"[38]

Commoning is celebrated for the way it produces forms of ownership that are more inclusive, more open-ended, and more productive than private property. In some cases, new commons provide the basis for assertions of ownership that constrain and challenge other forms of property: claims by nearby residents and former customers of what was once a department store in Vancouver to resist its demolition and replacement by condos;[39] similar claims by residents and activists in Italy over an old cinema building.[40] Commons can be understood as thresholds, spaces that threaten dominant taxonomies in the urban order.[41] With strong parallels to Sarah Keenan's analysis of subversive property—an alternative form of property that unsettles hegemonic power relations, perhaps contributing to more equitable and sustainable futures[42]—Patrick Bresnihan and Michael Byrne argue, "the urban commons thus emerges in response to the particular circumstances not as a form of protest but as a way of materializing an alternative, thereby producing an actually existing crack in the city."[43]

The ongoing and performative aspects of the relations involved in commoning are central. In their discussion of a range of alternative social spaces in Dublin, Bresnihan and Byrne describe something very much like an informal sense of ownership, finding that the spaces "first and foremost belong to those who participate in and make use of them."[44] The work involved in maintaining these alternative spaces—gathering materials and sharing labor to repair and convert run-down buildings into useful spaces; holding dinners, markets, gigs, and other events to raise the monthly rent; participating in collective decision-making—is directly productive of ownership. As Bresnihan and Byrne explain, "all of this means that those involved in using and sustaining a given space can feel it belongs to them—a fact which is often immediately tangible."[45]

The importance of such ownership is noted by participants; many recognize that "users and participants taking ownership is a prerequisite to their survival and sustainability."[46] Participants also recognize the connection between feelings of ownership and contributions to the spaces. Accordingly, in their own experience of joining one space as new users, Bresnihan and Byrne note that they were "encouraged to transform the space, make decisions and generally take ownership of it."[47]

Commoning is an active process, requiring continued acts of renewal.[48] A sense of ownership of the social spaces of Dublin empowers the participation that is necessary for the sustainability of those spaces, and it is strengthened through the process of participation. Participation is also productive of the community spaces themselves, the object of ownership. This is consistent across the literature on new commons: in community gardens, climate camps, social spaces and makerspaces, and in many other examples, the process of "taking" and building ownership actually creates the thing that is owned. Commoning is thus significant not simply as an alternative way in which to hold a preexisting resource (collective rather than public or private property), but as a means of producing new commons.

The shared interest or value that is produced through commoning is much like the sense of ownership that so many participants describe as produced and strengthened through PARK(ing) Day: a feeling of belonging connected to identity, community, agency, and power. As in other forms of commoning, the opportunity to develop ownership by engaging in PARK(ing) Day is one of the most valuable aspects of the event.

> Being in a PARK(ing) Day installation starts to hack kind of your predisposi-tions and expectations, and so yeah, it does help foster a sense of ownership and the possibility of change, that you yourself with your neighbors can effect this change. (Robin Abad Ocubillo, San Francisco)

Personal impacts tend to come up later in the interviews than external impacts on planning, policy, or public attitudes. Personal impacts were dis-missed by some participants as less significant, at least to begin with. Eytan Rocheta, quoted above describing the lack of any lasting change resulting from the park in which he was involved, explained later in the interview that he had focused on external impacts because he assumed that was what I would be interested in. Once he realized that personal changes were also relevant, he commented:

> I might have answered some of the questions quite negatively then because it did . . . really make me engaged and you know the fact that it was small and allowed for that ownership. . . . If we're not looking at the impact it had on others, the impact it had on us was profound.

Rocheta and his friends approached PARK(ing) Day wanting to achieve a specific, tangible objective: a change to the road conditions on King Street. The fact that this was not achieved and, even worse, that the group were directed by the police to pack away their park produced a sense of failure. Yet the event was an affirmative experience in other respects, attracting very positive responses from passersby. As such it was effective in building a sense of agency and ownership that remains significant years later. Rocheta linked his experience in PARK(ing) Day to his ongoing advocacy for greater sustainability in the built environment, and to a number of recent achieve-ments in securing cycling infrastructure.

Typically groups of people (at least two or three) are involved in put-ting on a PARK(ing) Day installation, so with close to 1,000 constructed in Montréal alone in the past five years, many thousands of people have been involved.

> Every year it grows and it finds more and more hidden corners of the world and that is incredible. To see people in Kazakhstan doing PARK(ing) Days is just phenomenal. (John O'Callaghan, Sydney)

The number is much, much higher when including the people who see and perhaps engage with installations and their creators. Potentially, the event could have a very large impact on the ways in which people understand the city and their place within it.

7.3 Changing possibilities: prefigurative practices

> It kind of felt like, um, the future. This is like the future that I would like for myself and my kids. You know, it will happen slowly over time. (Jonathon Carle, Sydney)

For many participants, PARK(ing) Day is exciting because of its connection to new possibilities. Many participants approach PARK(ing) Day with specific goals in mind: securing policy or physical changes to the street or city, working toward more trees, safer bike lanes, and more lively public spaces. Through their engagement in the event, however, participants often move beyond these to consider a much wider range of possibilities.

> It's kind of freeing to be able to take over a space that's usually just used for a car to sit there all day. And it opens space you don't normally get to occupy because there's usually a barrier between you and traffic, and so you're right in the middle of the swirling cacophony of downtown San Francisco. . . . When I walk by there I still think about it that there's kind of hidden layers of potential throughout the city, including in that place. (Ming Thompson, San Francisco)

PARK(ing) Day can be understood as prefigurative. Prefiguration, a term coined by Carl Boggs, describes "the embodiment, within the ongoing political practice of a movement, of those forms of social relations, decision-making, culture, and human experience that are the ultimate goal."[49]

Prefiguration joins "ends" and "means." Instead of imagining or lobbying for the implementation of alternative urban forms, prefigurative strategies work performatively to put those alternatives into practice, "removing the temporal distinction between the struggle in the *present* and a goal in the *future*."[50] Prefiguration has gained increasing attention in conceptualizing contemporary social movement activity, particularly anarchist-inspired politics like Occupy and the alterglobalization movement, but also social centers and free spaces, municipal radicalism and environmental activism.[51]

In transforming a parking space as part of PARK(ing) Day, participants do not ask city or state authorities to rethink the space allocated for car parking, they do not seek to enter into negotiations about whether or to what extent other uses should be permitted. Participants act as if the space is available for more sociable and sustainable uses, and in doing so both challenge and remake forms of urban governance.

The merging of ends and means in prefiguration is an open-ended and experimental process. In her examination of the alterglobalization movement, Marianne Maeckelberg finds that movement actors do not seek to implement a predefined alternative.[52] Instead, they design new power structures through practice: each event is an experiment in communication, coordination, goal-setting, and decision-making within a diverse polity.

This inclusive and iterative character is particularly important, Maeckelbergh argues, given the diverse range of actors, aims, and identities involved in the movement, making prefiguration the most effective (and perhaps the only) strategy to bring about social change.[53] PARK(ing) Day is comparable to the alterglobalization movement in this respect: aside from a desire to rethink the way in which space on city streets is allocated, there is no singular objective, adversary, or identity that is shared by all participants.

The ends that are imagined are shaped and reshaped through the process of their enactment in prefigurative practices. Intended consequences may fail to eventuate, while new possibilities arise unexpectedly. Social change is cyclical rather than linear, means become ends, which in turn become the means to other ends, and so on. Prefiguration enacts an interplay between theory and practice.

The sentiment expressed by Jonathon Carle above, that participation in PARK(ing) Day felt like creating the future, is consistent with the descriptions of other participants. For many, the process of creating a pop-up park can generate new understandings of the city and its potential.

> It's quite exhilarating I think . . . because you're disrupting something out of the norm that people may not be expecting to see. (Lucinda Hartley, Melbourne)

PARK(ing) Day prompted Hartley and her collaborators in the placemaking consultancy CoDesign to look for other loopholes in the regulation of street space. Finding that licenses for the storage of refuse containers were cheap and easy to obtain, CoDesign created a more durable, but still temporary, public space inside a skip bin (prompting media reports about "skipster hipsters").[54] Carle himself moved from PARK(ing) Day to street libraries, and he continues to imagine new possibilities beyond these:

> Sometimes I think it would be good to have a pedestrian crossing, you know, at the school. I'm just going to paint one myself [laughs]. . . .
>
> I've been eyeing off . . . this super ugly traffic island . . . the idea I had would be to have a formal dinner setting with a white tablecloth and everyone wears a tuxedo. . . . You go along and you do that, and motorists drive past, they're like "what's going on?" almost like a public performance sort of thing. The other idea would be to put some beach sand down, so deckchairs and maybe like a little white picket fence around it. Yeah, I've been thinking about that.

PARK(ing) Day is embedded within and takes place in dialogue with existing conditions and concerns. Like other prefigurative practices, it both challenges those conditions and proposes new possibilities, potentially undermining the hegemony of prevailing structures by demonstrating concrete alternatives.[55] What makes it prefigurative is the way in which it "produces a 'critical distance' that denaturalises prevailing ways of doing things while simultaneously inspiring, crafting and developing alternatives."[56]

The space created by that critical distance has been productive in PARK(ing) Day. In all three cities, unintended consequences and unimagined possibilities emerge through the event. Back in 2005, Rebar expected to be challenged by the City of San Francisco, not invited to drinks by an advisor from the mayor's office. The subsequent collaboration that fed into the Pavement to Parks program was not planned or even imagined by Passmore, Merker, or Bela. The production of feelings of connection, belonging, and ownership, the development of skip bin seating or Rayside Labossière's footpath furniture, and the establishment of new organizations like Lande, Atelier Cho Thompson, and Pépinière & Co, are among many others.

Some of these are unsanctioned, like PARK(ing) Day. Several, however, work actively with city and state authorities. Most obviously, parklet policies have been developed and even led by municipal authorities in all three cities. Rayside Labossière worked with the city to seek permits for their footpath furniture installation, and to develop these for wider deployment across the city. Rue Publique went from unsanctioned transformations of streets to undertaking urban design consultancies for the city; Pépinière & Co's projects are largely funded by public grants. There is considerable variation between (and within) these collaborations, and my research did not examine any of them in depth. More research might suggest a critical appraisal, in line with concerns about co-optation and greenwashing leveled at other DIY-inspired activities.[57] Yet they could also be read in more hopeful ways, as transforming relations with city and state authorities to produce more inclusive and sustainable forms of governance.

A collaborative approach to remaking governance is apparent in the work of several scholars exploring ideas of prefiguration. Davina Cooper, for example, argues that more progressive forms of governance can potentially be developed through experimental practices.[58] Through activities ranging from British municipal radicalism in the 1980s to more recent mock parliaments, the Feminist Judgments Project, and the playful declaration of independence by Brighton and Hove in 2015, Cooper highlights the importance of performance in inspiring, legitimating, and rationalizing new imaginaries. Cooper is particularly interested in playful practices comparable to PARK(ing) Day, suggesting an important role for these in troubling existing understandings and unsettling notions of common sense: "simulation and make-believe, so often trivialized, may prove important registers for exploring what counter-states could entail."[59]

Luke Yates makes related claims in his analysis of "free spaces," autonomous social centers in Barcelona.[60] One of the key features distinguishing prefigurative practices from subcultural or countercultural groups, Yates argues, is that the orientation toward the future is not utopian or proleptic, but engaged in the world. The aim is to model and inspire wider change: "When participants said that their actions or experiments were political 'in themselves' or that 'living differently was political' per se, they nearly always added disclaimers with a pragmatic sense of political impact: they were an 'example' to be seen and communicated; people wanted to 'inspire' change and diffuse perspectives."[61]

The construction of a park for PARK(ing) Day may be a brief and small-scale intervention, but it provides an opportunity to rethink the institutions through which social life is conducted. Significantly, the event presents a different experience to those typically offered to citizens wishing to participate in shaping their cities. PARK(ing) Day suggests a more active role for citizens than as recipients of services provided by state and city authorities, subjects to be consulted in discrete, state-directed processes.

> People are not able to understand that they are in charge of the next decision by the Transport Society, the next bus line, the next, you know, the sidewalk could be wider, the sidewalk could be shallower, you can have no parking, that's

possible, streets could be green. PARK(ing) Day ignites that like, "Oh, that all happened, and it happened in 24 hours and was over. Well, what could happen?" And I think that you can't do that enough . . . [PARK(ing) Day] starts to ignite people's ideas. (Andrew Dunbar, San Francisco)

Like many prefigurative practices, PARK(ing) Day can be productive in unexpected ways. Through policy and physical shifts as well as the more personal transformations that follow from participation in the event, PARK(ing) Day can be important in changing understandings of what is possible in contemporary cities.

PARK(ing) Day does change people's perspective. . . . [People] suddenly realize they can have an impact and influence on government. (Daniel Sherman, San Francisco)

PARK(ing) Day can also bring about change even when it doesn't lead to the particular changes sought by participants. While there is still no parklet on Australia Street, Newtown, the two parks constructed there had an impact on the local council, as one council employee explained:

After that, and because of the process of co-design with the community group and what the parklet would look like, and working very closely with the community to contact the businesses and neighbors, council just went down this road of really investing in co-design, public space and doing traffic management through temporary structures, even just painting the road. So it led to quite a bit of acceptance from within the organization that you can do things differently, and we had multiple workshops when we were designing intersections. . . . So culturally it had a positive impact in our organization.

The experience of building a park can have a powerful impact on participants, and perhaps also on the state and city authorities with which they engage. PARK(ing) Day provides an opportunity to contribute directly and materially to the city, to physically enact something different, and in doing so both challenge and demonstrate alternatives to current conditions. As an open-ended, prefigurative practice, PARK(ing) Day can be productive, often in surprising ways.

7.4   Undesirable impacts?

Most critical evaluations of PARK(ing) Day center on the event's lack of direct, tangible consequences. For those who set out to achieve specific policy or planning shifts, PARK(ing) Day can be disappointing.

Some participants went further, particularly when considering the event alongside other forms of DIY urbanism. While the scale and duration of PARK(ing) Day might limit its impacts, one cannot assume that these are unquestionably positive, and certainly not for everyone. As with other DIY interventions, differences in intention and the socioeconomic position of those involved can be significant.

With greater prominence, DIY urbanism is attracting scrutiny as well as celebration.[62] The strongly unequal social and economic context in which interventions like community gardens, parklets, pop-up shops, and restaurants take place has been a key source of concern.[63] DIY and "tactical" strategies are being adopted by commercial interests, government agencies, and professional planners.[64] Instead of furthering a right to the city, the deployment of pop-ups by businesses and by cities seeking to increase their competitiveness can have the opposite effect.[65] Unsanctioned interventions, as Margit Mayer argues, can be "harnessed by clever city officials and (especially real estate) capital as branding assets that contribute to the image of 'cool cities' or 'happening places.'"[66] The effect of DIY urbanism might then be to fuel real estate speculation, further marginalizing people and places with less cultural capital.[67]

DIY urbanism can be adopted by officials in pursuit of other agendas too. With state and municipal authorities increasingly stretched after long periods of austerity, infrastructure improvements by citizens, communities, and businesses can be vital. For Fran Tonkiss, the adoption of community gardens and other grassroots initiatives as part of wider neoliberal strategies for outsourcing municipal services to private actors means that "the distance between seedbed and sellout becomes very tight indeed."[68]

Participants were not generally concerned about co-optation by commercial interests in the context of PARK(ing) Day. Rebar's prohibitions on advertising have limited the commercial use of PARK(ing) Day, but small businesses have often participated. Some larger businesses have also been involved, though less directly. In 2008, IKEA provided materials with which the lifestyle and fashion blog PopSugar constructed a park, along with a $1,000 gift certificate to be offered as a prize to PopSugar's readers.[69] Then in 2013, a park constructed entirely from IKEA products appeared as a double-page spread in its catalogue, and videos of the installation could be viewed on the IKEA website. While the catalogue did not refer to Rebar or to PARK(ing) Day, the text made a clear connection to the PARK(ing) idea.[70]

Highlighted in orange, a caption at the top reads: "Even if you live in a city, it's easy to create a great outdoor living space in an instant. Just don't forget to pay the parking fee!"

The small scale and short duration of PARK(ing) Day means that participants tend not to be troubled by this kind of engagement. Some even saw it as positive, providing much greater visibility:

> IKEA probably had a much bigger impact [than us] because it was seen by tens of millions whereas our YouTube video might be seen by a couple of thousand and you know on the street, by a few hundred or a few thousand . . . [IKEA] made more people aware of PARK(ing) Day. (Eytan Rocheta, Sydney)

In discussing the connection between PARK(ing) Day and parklets, a few participants did note that many are associated with businesses, providing extra seating for café patrons, but emphasized the requirement that parklets are public spaces that cannot be restricted to customers (and the requirement that parklets display a sign explaining this). It was this public element they linked to PARK(ing) Day, in contrast with earlier, more commercially oriented forms of outdoor seating. Participants also mentioned parklets without a commercial element: the green parklet built by 'Deep Jawa (designed by Jane Martin, and notable for its topiary dinosaur) outside his home on Valencia Street; the educational parklet built outside Buena Vista Horace Mann School by the Exploratorium and Boys and Girls Club of San Francisco, with funding from the National Science Foundation (figures 7.6 and 7.7).

Participants were more concerned about politicians and government departments using the event as a way of sidestepping their responsibilities. One of the very first parks built in 2005, after Rebar's November installation but before the development of PARK(ing) Day, was by the Santa Monica Parks and Recreation Department. For Rebar, this was problematic, as Passmore explained:

> I'm thinking, Well, isn't it your job? How can you protest not having parks when that's what you do? You know what I mean? Can you join our side and look back and go "Yeah, more parks," like who are you pointing at because isn't that supposed to be you? We're pointing at you.

Across San Francisco, Sydney, and Montréal, local and state government agencies have participated many times in subsequent years. Another participant was critical of the way that PARK(ing) Day has been supported in San Francisco:

Figure 7.6
Ciencia Publica Parklet outside Buena Vista Horace Mann School, Valencia Street, San Francisco. Image: Stella Kim, San Francisco Planning Department.

I became skeptical about it . . . it was too sanctioned by the city. . . . This is a critique. And so you can't adopt this as your project when the whole point is to make you aware that there's not enough park space in this town. And then they get the people to solve it once a year by creating these little park things, and they were just too token. . . . It just has added to the parades and the celebrations of San Francisco. (Amy Seek, San Francisco)

In Montréal, some participants worried that politicians were keen to be associated with the event, but not to undertake any substantive change.

Nothing changed. So last year I wasn't very optimistic about doing a second PARK(ing) Day event. But I've been asked . . . maybe because it's trendy, I don't know . . . from a borough to another, also there seems to have a competition. . . . [But] I don't see any evolution. The director or the politicians, they still use their cars. (Sylvain Thériault, Montréal)

Figure 7.7
Ciencia Publica Parklet (detail). Image: Stella Kim, San Francisco Planning Department.

> Politicians, they like to go in those places to show themselves and say, yeah I'm
> for viable mobility, and next day they use a car, they give money to highways . . .
> we don't want PARK(ing) Day to be just a funny moment, just greenwashing . . .
> and then it's okay, we forget all our message. (Félix Gravel, Montréal)

Concerns about who is involved in DIY urbanism extend beyond corporations and the state. Scholars including Megan LaFrombois, Kimberley Kinder, and Gordon Douglas have called for much greater attention to the range of people who participate in informal city-making practices, highlighting the degree to which DIY interventions are structured along class, race, and gender divides.[71] Much like other forms of environmental activism,[72] participants tend to come from a position of some privilege. As one participant commented:

> You know, you're probably not going to be thinking about urban design, public space improvements if your neighborhood is full of crime, if you can't even afford to live there, if your schools are bad. There's a certain way in which this type of work is a little bit of a luxury. (Aaron Naparstek, New York)

The deep entanglement of ownership with other forms of privilege means that PARK(ing) Day, like other forms of DIY urbanism, is most often undertaken by people with some form of capital—cultural if not financial—young professionals, small businesses, "could haves."

The influence of PARK(ing) Day on wider city-making processes makes the privilege of its participants an issue requiring careful consideration. If the infrastructure upgrades and policy amendments that participants secure through PARK(ing) Day are prioritized over changes in other parts of the city, might they exacerbate patterns of disadvantage and exclusion? Or might they contribute to processes of gentrification, providing a symbol or catalyst for real estate speculation while marginalizing and displacing more vulnerable residents?

There are strong parallels between these concerns and the growing literature on green gentrification.[73] Urban environmental improvements such as new and upgraded parks, bike lanes, footpaths, community gardens, and tree planting are widely understood to benefit all residents, making cities more liveable and sustainable. Increasingly, however, plans for these kinds of improvements are generating opposition. Critics have noted the class, gender, and race dimensions of city greening, highlighting the role of whiteness and other forms of privilege in determining which facilities are provided (infrastructure for commuters cycling to professional jobs in the city, for example, rather than delivery cyclists; parklets, green alleys, and curbside buildouts in areas that are already leafy).[74]

Those critiques have in turn encouraged efforts to expand the reach of greening activities, particularly into more vulnerable communities subject to the worst environmental justice concerns.[75] Yet efforts to "improve" lower-income and minority communities have also attracted opposition, with residents working actively to prevent the upgrading of amenities and infrastructure.[76] Jennifer Wolch, Jason Byrne, and Joshua Newell describe this as the "urban green space paradox": the creation of new green space to address environmental justice can make neighborhoods healthier and more attractive, but it can also increase property prices, leading to the displacement of the very residents the green space strategies were designed to benefit.[77]

Like green gentrifiers, participants in PARK(ing) Day might unintentionally (and unwittingly) be fueling processes of exclusion and displacement. While the small scale and short duration of pop-up parks limit their potential impact, PARK(ing) Day is not without consequence. Blaine Merker emphasizes the complexity of the issues involved:

> I don't even know where to start. It's just such a complex issue. I think it does have something to do with ownership, because the question is, who's exerting their claim? . . . It shows up how powerful a tool for ownership self-made projects can be, and how charged public space is with creating ownership and signifying it. . . . You just have to be pretty aware of the context as you're putting yourself out there and asserting that claim on space, that you might be asserting it in a context of other people with claims on the space too.

Despite good intentions, participants in PARK(ing) Day might be adding to the problems faced by communities they set out to assist. With PARK(ing) Day, as with other "improvements" in public space, close engagement with the local context is necessary to understand how (and whether) pop-up parks might contribute to the creation of cities that are not only more sustainable but also more just.

Privilege is perhaps even more important with respect to the less tangible impacts of PARK(ing) Day. As a practice through which personal and collective feelings of ownership, voice, and agency can be sustained and strengthened, PARK(ing) Day can work to shift perceptions about what might be possible and, perhaps most significantly, to shift participants' understandings of their capacity to effect change in the city. In contrast to official channels for participation in planning, PARK(ing) Day provides an opportunity to contribute directly and materially to the city, to propose and test new ideas instead of simply commenting on preformed proposals. In this way PARK(ing) Day opens up city-making processes, extending these to younger and less wealthy groups of people.

The importance of ownership, however, means that PARK(ing) Day opens up the planning process only so far. If PARK(ing) Day is undertaken primarily by the already empowered, or at least the already relatively empowered, then there is a danger that it might operate to further marginalize those with less ownership, voice, and agency. PARK(ing) Day might contribute to gentrification and displacement less through city greening projects, and more through the empowerment of the more privileged communities who pursue them—and the relative disempowerment of those who don't. If PARK(ing) Day can strengthen feelings of ownership, and in turn empower participants to contribute to city-making processes in larger and longer-lasting ways, might it also render those without ownership even less visible?

Building a park on PARK(ing) Day can be a moving experience, leading many participants to shift the ways in which they understand the city and their capacity to contribute to it. While participants were often disappointed that their parks failed to produce particular changes in planning policy or urban design, many felt that the event did have an impact. PARK(ing) Day can operate as a prefigurative practice, a form of commoning that nurtures shared interests and identities, opening up new and unexpected possibilities for intervention in the city. The significance of those possibilities is highly contextual, however, requiring careful attention to wider relationships of power and privilege. As in other public spaces, particularly in global and increasingly unequal cities like Sydney and San Francisco, interventions in parking spaces are not neutral. At its best, PARK(ing) Day pushes participants to reflect on the politics of public space. For at least some participants, the event provides an important opportunity to deepen their understanding of spatial politics and of their own positions. PARK(ing) Day presents a vivid example of the degree to which even tiny, temporary interventions in the street connect to wider networks of power and privilege.

Figure 8.1
PARK(ing) Day 2017, Chelsea Street, Redfern, Sydney. Image: Amelia Thorpe.

Postscript

In 2017, I built a park for PARK(ing) Day. I did this with a group of friends from my neighborhood in the inner Sydney suburb of Redfern. Our park was nothing fancy, put together by three friends in between various other commitments, and accordingly employing many of the most familiar tropes of DIY urbanism: hay bales, milk crates, macramé, and even an old pallet (figure 8.1).

Building my own park was not something I had planned on doing for this project. The collaboration came out of a post–school run coffee, during which a friend asked how my research was going. Like so many of the people I interviewed, my friends were immediately excited about PARK(ing) Day when they heard about it: we have to do it, they said. I had mixed feelings about how to contribute, whether my role would be more as an observer or an active participant. I wavered somewhere between the two, trying to see what my friends thought before offering advice based on what I had learned about other people's experiences.

We took a while to settle on the site for our park. There are not many parking spaces with meters in Redfern; those that do have meters are not on streets that we visit much, and it was hard to imagine setting up our installation in an unfamiliar place. So we decided to go with a local spot to which we felt connected. The parking space we wanted had a 15-minute time limit; we thought about doing it there anyway but, in conversation with the adjacent business, decided not to. That spot was on Bourke Street, a major pedestrian- and cyclist-friendly thoroughfare. The business is a café that we have all visited regularly for many years, one that we each pass every day when walking our kids to school. The café owner thought the cars coming and going would make it dangerous for us to sit in the parking space right outside the café (and, though he didn't say so, I suspect he was also concerned that we might annoy people wanting to park there while picking up a takeaway coffee). So we chose a parking space outside the café's other frontage, a largely residential side street where there is a two-hour parking limit.

We drew on the café to come up with a theme: the huge waste associated with takeaway coffee cups. Inspired by SJB's contribution to PARK(ing) Day in 2013, we collected around 100 used coffee cups (scavenging over a few weeks in places from meetings at work to rubbish bins outside the bakery) and grew small plants inside them. On PARK(ing) Day, we stuck hand-made posters onto the adjacent wall with information about the environmental problems of takeaway coffee (e.g., that Australians throw away one billion cups every year, and they are not recyclable), along with a print of Rebar's PARK(ing) Day logo. We gave the seedlings away to anyone who said no to a takeaway coffee cup, encouraging people to sit in our park with a ceramic cup from the café if they hadn't already brought their own reusable mug. To encourage lingering, we provided materials and invited people to sit with us and make a simple macramé holder for their seedlings.

Larger networks were important in making the park happen. Friends helped by collecting cups and growing seedlings in the weeks before the event, by parking their car in the spot the night before to make sure it would be available in the morning, and by helping us with setting up and packing away on the day.

We installed our park from 7:30 am, catching people on the way to work and school, so the turnout was good. We were joined by friends and neighbors, the school principal and several teachers came along, and we also met quite a few new people who were curious about what we were doing. When asked what was going on, my friends directed people to me as the expert, generally after a quick explanation that we were part of PARK(ing) Day, an event that has been happening in cities all around the world for more than a decade.

We didn't get any negative comments and we didn't see any police or council officers (my friends were pleased about this, though I was a little disappointed). None of us are very engaged with social media, but we sent a picture to John O'Callaghan who posted it on the Sydney PARK(ing) Day Facebook and Twitter accounts; those posts were in turn liked and retweeted by others.

At about 9 am we packed up, taking our hay bales to a couple of nearby community gardens and sharing out the leftover seedlings. We borrowed brooms and brushes from the café to clean up; sweeping away the remnants of hay took much longer than expected. Packing up and, particularly, sweeping the street turned out to be a surprisingly moving experience. I did feel more connected to the space and to the neighborhood.

Overall the event was fun, and I think it was good for the community. PARK(ing) Day got me talking to people I had seen on the street but not actually spoken to before, and it strengthened relationships with people I knew only a little. I feel pretty special when I go into the café now, and my kids still talk about taking that small space away from cars.

Despite having spent almost four years researching PARK(ing) Day, I found the experience of physically remaking the street to be a powerful one. I did feel a stronger sense of belonging and connection during and after the event. Like so many of the participants in my research, I found PARK(ing) Day to be significant in facilitating the development of ownership. PARK(ing) Day did indeed help to shape my understanding of the city and my place within it.

But if I'm more critical, I should note that the street we built our park on was already pretty safe, and already well used for walking and cycling. Bourke Street and the neighborhood around it are leafy and walkable because of deliberate decisions by the City of Sydney, our local council. Over the past two decades, traffic lanes and parking spaces in the area have been removed to make way for dedicated bike lanes, wider footpaths, shade trees and other landscaping improvements. The idea that streets can be put to better uses than car parking is far from novel in our part of the city, and certainly not something about which the council needs to be persuaded.

Socially, we are already a pretty well connected community, with high levels of ownership and engagement in both formal and informal processes. As well as the school principal, we had several other prominent community members pop in—engineers, architects, and other professionals, board members and company directors, actors and artists. Our park built on strong feelings of ownership, and these in turn built on skills, networks, and relatively high socioeconomic status. As with other examples of DIY urbanism, our park could be dismissed as superfluous. More troublingly, our self-help might be read as entrepreneurial or even libertarian, feeding into a withdrawal of the state from the provision of services and exacerbating inequality. People in my community get parks because we are able to demand them, while others are left out.

To go even further, I should note that Redfern—and particularly our part of Redfern, marketed by real estate agents as "East Redfern" to distinguish it from "The Block" and the housing commission high-rises at the other end of the suburb, and ironically referred to by some of our neighbors as "SoCle" or "EBo" (South of Cleveland St, East of Bourke St, a play on the nomenclature used for hip neighborhoods in New York)—has skyrocketed in price in recent years. Cafés and boutiques have replaced the poorer residents who historically lived in Redfern, a displacement with particular significance given Redfern's indigenous history.[1] Again, as with so many other examples of DIY urbanism, our community-building might be read as an act of gentrification, contributing not to the empowerment of the community but to its reconstitution.

The role of privilege and the implication of PARK(ing) Day in processes of gentrification and displacement are concerns that have come up increasingly in discussing my research with other scholars. If PARK(ing) Day represents a right to the city, I was asked, what about the right to the city of other more vulnerable and less privileged groups (low-income, nonwhite, immigrant, working-class)? Could PARK(ing) Day become more inclusive to include such groups?

These concerns are both overwhelming and encouraging. PARK(ing) Day was never intended as a movement, it was a playful installation that inspired others to imitate it, and to expand the idea far beyond Rebar's aims or aspirations. PARK(ing) Day's "organizers" provided information rather than coordination; the event has relied primarily on its own momentum. Certainly, participants could and should think carefully about context, the potential for unintended consequences, and how to be inclusive in their interventions. But how much can we really expect from pop-up parks? As Kimberley Kinder argues in her discussion of DIY activities in Detroit, "it would be unreasonable to expect self-provisioning alone to solve the problems that daunt policy makers, community groups, faith-based organizations, and socially conscious investors."[2] DIY interventions in Detroit were conceived not as solutions, but as temporary fixes when no other options seemed available, undertaken "with the hope that comprehensive solutions to disinvestment, racism, and vulnerability would eventually emerge."[3]

To suggest that PARK(ing) Day should do more to address wider structural issues like neoliberal enclosure, colonial dispossession or the right to the city for vulnerable groups is perhaps hopeful in suggesting that tiny, temporary interventions *could* make a difference in the face of systemic challenges such as these.

Sous les pavés, la plage!

This rallying cry from the protests of Paris in 1968 is useful in thinking about PARK(ing) Day in two respects. First, for the issues animating the event: concerns about the workings of capitalism, the frameworks for participation, and a desire for ownership, agency, and voice in the city. Second, for the form of the intervention: like the invitation to uncover the beach below the pavement, PARK(ing) Day suggests that another alternative is already available, simply by looking differently at the rules that shape the city.

PARK(ing) Day responds to widespread and deeply felt concerns about processes of enclosure in contemporary cities: the growing crisis of housing affordability, with an increasing share of the population, even the professional population, seemingly shut out from ownership for good, and the increasing erosion of public space with privatization leading to much greater control of the public realm and the publics within it. PARK(ing) Day connects also to concerns about democracy and participation in shaping the future of the city, with increasing power held by a small group of powerful interests, and the apparent disregard in their decisions for issues like climate change, public life, equality and inclusion between and within societies. PARK(ing) Day reflects a desire to access property and, perhaps even more strongly, to access the things that property provides: voice and agency, identity and community. PARK(ing) Day, like the Parisian slogan, stands as a "cry and a demand" for a right to the city.[4]

The temporary property made accessible through PARK(ing) Day is taken up enthusiastically by participants eager to express themselves and their right to the city. Participants emphasize visibility and publicity in planning their contributions, and attention and affirmation from others in evaluating their success. Participants want to be seen and acknowledged, and they want to be seen and acknowledged as part of something bigger. Just as my friends were quick to point out to passersby that our installation was part of an international and long-running event, other participants also prioritized presentation of their parks as contributing to a larger project.

Beyond personal expressions of voice and agency, PARK(ing) Day is valued for the way in which engagement allows participants to develop a sense of ownership. Significantly, PARK(ing) Day enables participants to build a sense of ownership collectively, comparable to practices through which people work to reclaim the city by commoning. PARK(ing) Day provides many opportunities to sustain and strengthen feelings of ownership: labor, self-expression, social, spatial, and material connections, possibilities for play and for pleasure.

PARK(ing) Day provides a sharp contrast to the opportunities more commonly provided for public engagement in decision-making about the built environment. While much planning is state-led, with opportunities for citizen contributions tightly scripted, PARK(ing) Day allows participants to produce tangible change with immediate feedback. PARK(ing) Day suggests a more active role for citizens.

The degree to which PARK(ing) Day can be understood as emancipatory, counterhegemonic, or challenging to neoliberal systems of governance should not be overstated. PARK(ing) Day, like the alternative social spaces leased through the private market in Dublin[5] or the co-living spaces that operate in apartments rented through AirBnb in Taipei,[6] does not completely reject the market or the commodification of public space. Participants pay the meter (at least in some cases), and they rely on this payment to justify their use of the street. As Jeffrey Hou comments in the context of Hong Kong and Taipei, these nested relationships raise important questions.[7] The initiatives Hou describes "perform all the good things that are promised in the commons literature," yet, he asks, might dependence on state and corporate resources defeat the very purpose of commoning?[8]

The meter embodies a market-based allocation of space; it also enables a privatized and individualized approach. While PARK(ing) Day can be read as an effort to resist the commodification of public space and to reclaim the commons, there is a tension in the claim that paying the meter justifies putting the space to uses other than those decided by democratically elected city governments (and often through planning processes that at least purport to be democratic, deliberative, and inclusive). Others highlight related concerns with respect to commoning practices, noting that commons can be profoundly undemocratic, and can reinforce existing exclusions and inequalities.[9]

In discussing their sense of ownership, many participants emphasize the importance of responsibility and stewardship, reflecting the need for recognition and affirmation from others. Yet participants also note the connection between a sense of ownership and privilege, emphasizing how much harder it is for some people to express ownership and to gain support for those expressions.

> I love this space and I want it to be better and I really do love the idea of making it better for everyone. But you can't talk like that unless you have a sense of "I belong here. I'm entitled to feel this way. It's my right to feel this way." All of those things are there and for me, I'm relatively well-off, and . . . it does get kind of complicated about that feeling of ownership, right? You kind of have to feel entitled to what you're doing to do it. ('Deep Jawa, San Francisco)

A sense of ownership, like more conventional forms of property, connects to power. Without some level of social or economic standing, it is much harder to feel or maintain feelings of ownership or belonging. Like other forms of commoning, PARK(ing) Day has both repressive and emancipatory potential, making it important to politicize the practices involved, "to question how and who creates what kinds of commons."[10]

PARK(ing) Day opens up ownership, but it also shows that it is not always easy to pursue those openings. Like other forms of property, a sense of ownership is performative and citational. This means that ownership can be subverted or unsettled, but it may be difficult to do so (as, for example, in the case of the park installed on King Street). Just as Sarah Keenan claims that property can be subversive, but more often tends to be (re)productive of the status quo,[11] the potential to build a sense of ownership through PARK(ing) Day is constrained by current conditions, sometimes very tightly.

How PARK(ing) Day and the ownership it produces and sustains relate to property or to wider power relations is in many ways dependent on the particular circumstances of individual parks. Who is involved, who and what do they include and exclude? What are their objectives, how do these relate to local, regional, and wider issues? Who sees and engages with them, what do they think, and does this have any lasting impact? Which issues and which perspectives are privileged, and which are obscured?

*   *   *

The idea of a beach beneath the pavement also connects to PARK(ing) Day in its claim that an alternative is there for the taking. Participants do not set out to protest or to plead for change, they do not complain about the order of things, and they do not call for reform to that order. By emphasizing the legality of their interventions, participants in PARK(ing) Day act as if the city is *already* different.

In its invocation of the lease, and of a concomitant right to contribute to shaping the parking space and the city beyond it, PARK(ing) Day makes a claim to voice and agency. This is central to the ongoing appeal of the event, and to its ability to inspire and engage so many people, in so many places, over so many years.

The lease is not the result of careful theorization or detailed legal analysis. Its value lies not in its truth, but in its power to move things along. PARK(ing) Day works as a vehicular idea: a tool to connect concerns—about ownership, legality, and agency in the city—and to offer a new perspective enabling debate to progress. It is not a solution, but a step toward one.

PARK(ing) Day can be contrasted with more explicitly and aggressively political interventions in contemporary debates about urban development and city life. Like PARK(ing) Day, interventions such as Occupy, Critical Mass, and Reclaim the Streets question who owns and uses the city, and the kinds of uses for which public space should be regulated. Unlike PARK(ing) Day, they center on resistance and dissent. While the appropriations of space in PARK(ing) Day are small, brief, neat, and often professional, the encampments of Occupy are larger, longer-lasting, often dirty and always confrontational. In Occupy, as in precursors like Reclaim the Streets and Critical Mass, participants challenge the status quo by disrupting it. Rules are deliberately broken, space is explicitly taken without any form of permission: the authority that might underpin such permission is itself challenged. Jenny Pickerill and John Krinsky argue: "in order to occupy a space it must already be owned. . . . This was, in part, the point of Occupy—to identify the need to reclaim space from corporate greed."[12]

By highlighting spaces that are off limits to most citizens, spaces that participants do *not* own, participants critique exclusion and enclosure in the city, and demand redress, reform, and perhaps revolution. PARK(ing) Day, in contrast, is playful and polite. It is this politeness that makes

PARK(ing) Day so provocative. Participants make claims that are smaller and more spatially contained: instead of broad claims about the workings of contemporary capitalism, participants make concrete demands about particular places. They draw power from this specificity, as an expression of ownership that is constructed locally and relationally. By installing a pop-up park on the street, participants do not challenge the social consensus: they invoke it.

PARK(ing) Day goes well beyond Rebar's initial claims about the property rights obtainable by paying a parking meter. Through its performance over the years in cities far from San Francisco, the event reveals a deeper contingency within the regulation of the built environment, and regulation more generally. Consistent with the analyses of Fuller, Hartog, and Cover, PARK(ing) Day provides a vivid demonstration of the fluid and ambiguous nature of legality, its intimate entanglement with other sources of meaning. No matter how stable or dominant it appears, any legal system "is constantly having to accommodate, and in certain cases appropriate, a vast array of legal meanings, logics, values, identities and cultural contexts emerging inside and outside established jurisdictional lines."[13]

As the varied reactions from passersby, police, and other officials in all three cities suggest, formal laws are both constrained and constituted by the networks in which they are embedded. PARK(ing) Day succeeds when it engages with local understandings of legality, showing that these are not separate from the law but integral to its application. PARK(ing) Day reveals the degree to which regulations rely on normative values, not just for their legitimacy but for their content. In highlighting the crucial role of social understandings, PARK(ing) Day shows the ongoing potential for the meanings of rules and regulations to be shifted. PARK(ing) Day thus opens up the city for participants, and for the many others with whom they engage.

Coupled with its role in developing a sense of ownership, this shift in understandings of legality can be transformative, empowering participants to make more substantial and enduring contributions to the city. Among others, these range from new organizations (Atelier Cho Thompson, Lande, Pépinière & Co), to new legal frameworks (parklet permitting processes, the San Francisco ordinance for temporary interventions), to material interventions in the built environment (parklets, community gardens, festivals, plazas, and public spaces).

While PARK(ing) Day relies on preexisting understandings of legality, it can also remake them. The installation of a pop-up park can sustain and strengthen understandings of law, ownership, and property; it can also shift such understandings, opening up new perspectives on the regulation of the built environment and with these new possibilities to play a role in shaping it. PARK(ing) Day highlights the multiplicity of interpretive possibilities and the crucial role of social practice in choosing among these. By enacting particular interpretations of law, and by drawing in people, places, and things to support those enactments, participants work to bring purported legalities into being. In PARK(ing) Day, the performance of law can be productive.

Notes

Except where otherwise noted, quotations from participants are taken from interviews with the author. Translations from the French are by the author. Wherever possible, webpages referenced have been archived at web.archive.org.

Introduction

1. "BIG Loves in a Tiny Space: PARK(ing) Day Wedding Vow Renewal Ceremonies," *Quelcy*, October 1, 2015, http://quelcy.com/2015/10/01/big-loves-in-a-tiny-space -parking-day-wedding-vow-renewal-ceremonies/.

2. Kenneth Lim, "Lots of Fun, Food and Art for PARK(ing) Day 2015," *Channel NewsAsia*, September 18, 2015, https://www.channelnewsasia.com/news/singapore/ lots-of-fun-food-and-art-for-park-ing-day-2015-8234902; Urban Redevelopment Authority, "PARK(ing) Day SG," 2018, https://www.ura.gov.sg/Corporate/Get -Involved/Enliven-Public-Spaces/Parking-Day-SG.

3. "El Park(ing) Day de Los Coles STARS," *STARS Madrid*, September 30, 2015, http:// eustarsmadrid.blogspot.com.au/2015/09/el-parking-day-de-los-coles-stars.html.

4. Mariya Sharova, "First Parking Day in Almaty: How Else Can One Use Parking Space?," *UNDP Kazakhstan*, October 5, 2015, http://www.kz.undp.org/content/ kazakhstan/en/home/ourperspective/-11.html.

5. Alex Bohmer, "How to Turn a Parking Bay into a Public Space?," *Future Cape Town*, October 1, 2015, http://futurecapetown.com/2015/10/future-cape-town-parking-bays -are-not-only-meant-for-cars/.

6. Peter Newman and Jeffrey R. Kenworthy, *Sustainability and Cities: Overcoming Automobile Dependence* (Washington, DC: Island Press, 1999); Donald C. Shoup, *The High Cost of Free Parking* (Chicago: Planners Press, American Planning Association, 2004); Charles Montgomery, *Happy City: Transforming Our Lives through Urban Design* (New York: Farrar, Straus and Giroux, 2013); Zack Furness, *One Less Car: Bicycling*

and the Politics of Automobility (Philadelphia: Temple University Press, 2010); Elly Blue, *Bikenomics: How Bicycling Can Save the Economy*, 2nd ed. (Portland, OR: Microcosm Publishing, 2016); Jane Holtz Kay, *Asphalt Nation: How the Automobile Took over America, and How We Can Take It Back* (Berkeley: University of California Press, 1998); John Urry, "The 'System' of Automobility," *Theory, Culture and Society* 21, no. 4–5 (2004): 25–39; Steffen Böhm, Campbell Jones, Chris Land, and Matthew Paterson, eds., *Against Automobility* (Malden, MA: Blackwell, 2006); Peter D. Norton, *Fighting Traffic: The Dawn of the Motor Age in the American City* (Cambridge, MA: MIT Press, 2011); David Prytherch, *Law, Engineering, and the American Right-of-Way: Imagining a More Just Street* (London: Palgrave Macmillan, 2018); Nicole Foletta and Jason Henderson, *Low Car(bon) Communities: Inspiring Car-Free and Car-Lite Urban Futures* (London: Routledge, 2016); Janette Sadik-Khan and Seth Solomonow, *Streetfight: Handbook for an Urban Revolution* (New York: Penguin Books, 2017); Tim Cresswell and Peter Merriman, eds., *Geographies of Mobilities: Practices, Spaces, Subjects* (Farnham, UK: Ashgate, 2011); Margaret J. Douglas, Stephen J. Watkins, Dermot R. Gorman, and Martin Higgins, "Are Cars the New Tobacco?," *Journal of Public Health* 33, no. 2 (2011): 160–169.

7. Transport is the second biggest emitter of greenhouse gases, accounting for 23% of global emissions. Road vehicles are the primary source of transport emissions (72%). Intergovernmental Panel on Climate Change, "Climate Change 2014: Mitigation of Climate Change. Contribution of Working Group III to the Fifth Assessment Report of the IPCC," 2014, 606.

8. Road accidents account for 1.35 million deaths each year worldwide, and are now the leading killer of people aged between five and 29. Injury and death rates are far higher among vulnerable groups (children, pedestrians, cyclists, and motorcyclists) and in low- and middle-income countries. World Health Organization, "Global Status Report on Road Safety 2018," 2019, https://www.who.int/violence_injury _prevention/road_safety_status/2018/en/.

9. Vehicle emissions are a major source of local air pollution, linked to asthma, heart disease, cancer, and other chronic diseases. In a review of recent literature, Frederica Perera concludes that pollution from fossil fuel combustion is the biggest threat to children's health and equity worldwide. Frederica Perera, "Pollution from Fossil-Fuel Combustion is the Leading Environmental Threat to Global Pediatric Health and Equity: Solutions Exist," *International Journal of Environmental Research and Public Health* 15, no. 1 (2017): 16–32. Reliance on cars instead of more active transport compounds those health impacts, contributing to a growing obesity epidemic, particularly among children. Dustin T. Duncan and Ichirō Kawachi, eds., *Neighbourhoods and Health*, 2nd ed. (Oxford: Oxford University Press, 2018); Mia A. Papas, Anthony J. Alberg, Reid Ewing, Kathy J. Helzlsouer, Tiffany L. Gary, and Ann C. Klassen, "The Built Environment and Obesity," *Epidemiologic Reviews* 29, no. 1 (2007): 129–143.

10. The space required to accommodate cars is enormous, with roads and parking covering more than half the urban area of many cities. These paved expanses displace more productive, interactive, and desirable uses, exacerbate biodiversity loss, water pollution, and other environmental pressures, and add significantly to the cost of housing. Donald C. Shoup, *The High Cost of Free Parking*, 2nd ed. (Chicago: Planners Press, American Planning Association, 2011); Donald C. Shoup, ed., *Parking and the City* (New York: Routledge, 2018); Todd Litman, "Transportation Cost and Benefit Analysis Techniques, Estimates and Implications" (Victoria, BC: Victoria Transportation Policy Institute, 2016); Amélie Y. Davis, Bryan C. Pijanowski, Kimberly Robinson, and Bernard Engel, "The Environmental and Economic Costs of Sprawling Parking Lots in the United States," *Land Use Policy* 27, no. 2 (2010): 255–261; Michael Manville, "Parking Requirements and Housing Development: Regulation and Reform in Los Angeles," *Journal of the American Planning Association* 79, no. 1 (2013): 49–66; Elizabeth Jean Taylor, "Who's Been Parking on My Street? The Politics and Uneven Use of Residential Parking Space," *Land Use Policy* (2018).

11. These range from impacts associated with the manufacture (mining and production of steel, rubber, glass, plastics, paints; energy production and consumption), use (mining and burning of fossil fuels; pollution of air, water, and soils by brake dust, oil, and tire particles), and disposal (particularly of plastics and batteries) of cars, to the construction of roads and other infrastructure to support them, and the sprawling urban development that they enable (loss of agricultural land and greenspace; fragmentation and destruction of habitat; energy and water consumption; heat island effects; noise, air, and water pollution). Litman, "Transportation Cost and Benefit Analysis Techniques, Estimates and Implications," Artem Korzhenevych, Nicola Dehnen, Johannes Bröcker, Michael Holtkamp, Henning Meier, Gena Gibson, Adarsh Varma, and Victoria Cox, *Update of the Handbook on External Costs of Transport*, Report for the European Commission DG Move no. Ricardo-AEA/R/ ED57769, 2014. When the full range of externalities are considered, car use is subsidized to a far higher extent than public transport. Gary Glazebrook, "Taking the Con Out of Convenience: TheTrue Cost of Transport Modes in Sydney," *Urban Policy and Research* 27, no. 1 (2009): 5–24.

12. The young, the elderly, the poor, members of minority groups, and people with disabilities are more vulnerable to accidents and injuries, and more likely to suffer from community severance and displacement by road projects, from air, noise, and other pollution, from long communtes, and from social isolation and a lack of mobility because of an inability to drive, or to cover the cost of driving. Robert D. Bullard, Glenn S. Johnson, and Angel O. Torres, eds., *Highway Robbery: Transportation Racism and New Routes to Equity* (Cambridge, MA: South End Press, 2004); Gregg Culver, "Death and the Car: On (Auto)Mobility, Violence, and Injustice," *ACME: An International Journal for Critical Geographies* 17, no. 1 (2018): 144–170; Stephen Zavestoski and Julian Agyeman, eds., *Incomplete Streets: Processes, Practices, and Possibilities* (Abingdon, UK: Routledge, 2015).

13. Culver, "Death and the Car," 145.

14. A planning and development approach centered on walkable blocks and streets, housing and shopping in close proximity, and accessible public spaces. Peter Katz, *The New Urbanism: Toward an Architecture of Community* (New York: McGraw-Hill, 1994).

15. The creation of compact, pedestrian-oriented, mixed-use communities around high-quality train systems. Hank Dittmar and Gloria Ohland, eds., *The New Transit Town: Best Practices in Transit-Oriented Development* (Washington, DC: Island Press, 2004).

16. Streets designed to allow pedestrians, cyclists, motorists and transit users of all ages and abilities to share the space safely. Barbara McCann, *Completing Our Streets: The Transition to Safe and Inclusive Transportation Networks* (Washington, DC: Island Press, 2013).

17. An international road safety initiative, originally from Sweden, which aims to eliminate deaths and serious injuries from traffic accidents. Matts-Åke Belin, Per Tillgren, and Evert Vedung, "Vision Zero—a Road Safety Policy Innovation," *International Journal of Injury Control and Safety Promotion* 19, no. 2 (2012): 171–179.

18. Monthly events in which cyclists temporarily take over the streets by riding together. Chris Carlsson, ed., *Critical Mass: Bicycling's Defiant Celebration* (Edinburgh, UK: AK Press, 2002).

19. Marches and events through which participants reclaim public spaces, often connected to other political causes, and sometimes resulting in the creation of Temporary Autonomous Zones. Amory Starr, *Global Revolt: A Guide to the Movements against Globalization* (London: Zed Books, 2013).

20. The closure of streets to cars, usually on Sundays or holidays, to allow for cycling, play and performances. Ciclovía began in Bogotá, Colombia in 1974, and has inspired related events in many other cities, often referred to as Sunday Streets. Sergio Montero, "Worlding Bogotá's Ciclovía: From Urban Experiment to International 'Best Practice,'" *Latin American Perspectives* 44, no. 2 (2017): 111–131.

21. Temporary projects aiming to demonstrate the benefits of interventions like bike lanes, café seating, trees, plants, pop-up businesses, and lighting. Andrew Howard and Susan McLaughlin, "Interim Design/Tactical Urbanism: A New Civic Engagement Approach in Action," *ITE Journal* 85, no. 3 (March 2015): 12–16.

22. Norton, *Fighting Traffic*; John A. Jakle and Keith A. Sculle, *Lots of Parking: Land Use in a Car Culture* (Charlottesville: University of Virginia Press, 2004).

23. Norton, *Fighting Traffic*; Ryan J. Westrom, Chris Shaheen, and Rebecca Schwartzman, "Parking Is for People: A History of Public Parking in Washington, D.C. (and

Implications for Transportation Design Today)," *Transportation Research Record: Journal of the Transportation Research Board* 2672, no. 13 (2018): 50–59; Clay McShane, *Down the Asphalt Path: The Automobile and the American City* (New York: Columbia University Press, 1994); Graeme Davison, *Car Wars: How the Car Won our Hearts and Conquered our Cities* (Sydney: Allen and Unwin, 2004).

24. Norton, *Fighting Traffic*; Jakle and Sculle, *Lots of Parking*.

25. Jakle and Sculle, *Lots of Parking*, 244.

26. Terry Schwarz, Steve Rugare, David Jurca, and Gauri Torgalkar, *Pop Up City* (Cleveland: Cleveland Urban Design Collaborative, College of Architecture and Environmental Design, Kent State University, 2009); Jeffrey Hou, ed., *Insurgent Public Space: Guerrilla Urbanism and the Remaking of Contemporary Cities* (New York: Routledge, 2010); Peter Bishop and Lesley Williams, *The Temporary City* (London: Routledge, 2012); Philipp Oswalt, Klaus Overmeyer, and Philipp Misselwitz, eds., *Urban Catalyst: The Power of Temporary Use* (Berlin: DOM Publishers, 2013); Jeroen Beekmans and Joop de Boer, *Pop-Up City: City-Making in a Fluid World* (Amsterdam: BIS, 2014); Jeffrey Hou, Benjamin Spencer, Thaisa Way, and Ken Yocom, *Now Urbanism: The Future City Is Here* (Abingdon, UK: Routledge, 2015).

27. Jay Walljasper and Project for Public Spaces, *The Great Neighborhood Book: A Do-It-Yourself Guide to Placemaking* (Gabriola Island, BC: New Society Publishers, 2007); Mike Lydon and Anthony Garcia, *Tactical Urbanism* (Washington, DC: Island Press, 2015).

28. Michel de Certeau, *The Practice of Everyday Life*, 2nd ed. (Berkeley: University of California Press, 2013); Henri Lefebvre, *Writings on Cities* (Cambridge, MA: Blackwell, 1996); James C. Scott, *Seeing Like a State: How Certain Schemes to Improve the Human Condition Have Failed* (New Haven: Yale University Press, 1998).

29. Hou, *Insurgent Public Space*; Kurt Iveson, "Cities within the City: Do-It-Yourself Urbanism and the Right to the City," *International Journal of Urban and Regional Research* 37, no. 3 (2013): 941–956.

30. Gordon C. C. Douglas, *The Help-Yourself City: Legitimacy and Inequality in DIY Urbanism* (New York: Oxford University Press, 2018); Megan Heim LaFrombois, *Reframing the Reclaiming of Urban Space: A Feminist Exploration into Do-It-Yourself Urbanism in Chicago* (Lanham, MD: Lexington Books, 2018).

31. Ann Deslandes, "Exemplary Amateurism: Thoughts on DIY Urbanism," *Cultural Studies Review* 19, no. 1 (2013): 216–227; Lee Stickells, "Beyond the Pop-Up: Art and Urban Regeneration," *Christchurch Art Bulletin* 171 (2013): 48–51; Johannes Novy and Claire Colomb, "Struggling for the Right to the (Creative) City in Berlin and Hamburg: New Urban Social Movements, New 'Spaces of Hope'?: Debates and Developments," *International Journal of Urban and Regional Research* 37, no. 5 (2013): 1816–1838.

32. Margit Mayer, "First World Urban Activism: Beyond Austerity Urbanism and Creative City Politics," *City* 17, no. 1 (2013): 5–19; Fran Tonkiss, "Austerity Urbanism and the Makeshift City," *City* 17, no. 3 (June 2013): 312–324; Claire Colomb, "Pushing the Urban Frontier: Temporary Uses of Space, City Marketing, and the Use of the Creative City Discourse in 2000s Berlin," *Journal of Urban Affairs* 34, no. 2 (2012): 131–152.

33. Patsy Healey, *Collaborative Planning: Shaping Places in Fragmented Societies* (Basingstoke, UK: Macmillan, 1997); John Forester, *The Deliberative Practitioner: Encouraging Participatory Planning Processes* (Cambridge, MA: MIT Press, 1999); Judith Innes, *Planning with Complexity: An Introduction to Collaborative Rationality for Public Policy* (Abingdon, UK: Routledge, 2010); Ruth Fincher and Kurt Iveson, *Planning and Diversity in the City: Redistribution, Recognition and Encounter* (Basingstoke, UK: Palgrave Macmillan, 2008); Susan S. Fainstein, *The Just City* (Ithaca: Cornell University Press, 2010); Ben Clifford and Mark Tewdwr-Jones, *The Collaborating Planner? Practitioners in the Neoliberal Age* (Bristol, UK: Policy Press, 2013).

34. Sue Brownill and Juliet Carpenter, "Increasing Participation in Planning: Emergent Experiences of the Reformed Planning System in England," *Planning Practice and Research* 22, no. 4 (2007): 619–634; Andy Inch, "Creating 'a Generation of NIMBYs'? Interpreting the Role of the State in Managing the Politics of Urban Development," *Environment and Planning C: Government and Policy* 30, no. 3 (2012): 520–535; Susan E. Owens, *Land and Limits: Interpreting Sustainability in the Planning Process*, 2nd ed. (Abingdon, UK: Routledge, 2011).

35. Clifford and Tewdwr-Jones, *The Collaborating Planner?*

36. When I asked if she had ever participated in any form of planning before, Elyse replied: "I'm not specialized. . . . *Ça prend des gens, des urbanistes . . . je sais pas à quel point je pourrait être* [it takes people, urbanists . . . I'm not sure at which point I could be] . . . involved in it. I would be interested to, to tell my idea, but I'm not qualified."

37. M. J. Dear, *Not on Our Street: Community Attitudes to Mental Health Care* (London: Pion, 1982); Leonie Sandercock, "When Strangers Become Neighbours: Managing Cities of Difference," *Planning Theory and Practice* 1, no. 1 (2000): 13–30; Brendan Gleeson, *Geographies of Disability* (London: Routledge, 1999); Richard E. Foglesong, *Planning the Capitalist City: The Colonial Era to the 1920s* (Princeton: Princeton University Press, 1986); Susan S. Fainstein, *The City Builders: Property Development in New York and London, 1980–2000*, 2nd ed. (Lawrence: University Press of Kansas, 2001); Leonie Sandercock, *Cities for Sale: Property, Politics, and Urban Planning in Australia* (Carlton, Vic: Melbourne University Press, 1975); David Harvey, *Social Justice and the City* (Athens: University of Georgia Press, 2009); Neil Brenner, Peter Marcuse, and Margit Mayer, *Cities for People, Not for Profit: Critical Urban Theory and the Right to the City* (London: Routledge, 2012).

38. "Nous on s'est installé sur la plaza parce que on aimait déjà la plaza . . . it's really a part of the Montréal story. Ouais ça fait partie de notre, de notre culture. . . . C'est pour ça aussi qu'on veut la faire revivre . . . c'est comme sauver un vieux couple qui était déjà en amoureux et puis on essaye de retrouver les, les premières années? Ouais, c'est un peu ça aussi notre sens d'appartenance, c'est de faire revivre cet espèce de, cet artère commerciale."

39. Sarah Wright, "More-than-Human, Emergent Belongings: A Weak Theory Approach," *Progress in Human Geography* 39, no. 4 (2015): 391–411; Marco Antonsich, "Searching for Belonging—An Analytical Framework," *Geography Compass* 4, no. 6 (2010): 644–659; Lynne Manzo and Patrick Devine-Wright, eds., *Place Attachment: Advances in Theory, Methods, and Applications* (London: Routledge, 2014).

40. Ananya Roy and Nezar AlSayyad, eds., *Urban Informality: Transnational Perspectives from the Middle East, Latin America, and South Asia* (Lanham, MD: Lexington Books, 2004); Libby Porter, Melanie Lombard, Margo Huxley, Aslı Kıyak Ingin, Tolga Islam, John Briggs, Deden Rukmana, Ryan Devlin, and Vanessa Watson, "Informality, the Commons and the Paradoxes for Planning: Concepts and Debates," *Planning Theory and Practice* 12, no. 1 (2011): 115–153; Ryan Devlin, "'An Area That Governs Itself': Informality, Uncertainty and the Management of Street Vending in New York City," *Planning Theory* 10, no. 1 (2011): 53–65; Annette M. Kim, "The Mixed-Use Sidewalk: Vending and Property Rights in Public Space," *Journal of the American Planning Association* 78, no. 3 (2012): 225–238.

41. Kevin J. Gray and Susan Francis Gray, *Land Law*, 5th ed. (Oxford: Oxford University Press, 2007); Margaret Davies, *Property: Meanings, Histories and Theories* (Abingdon, UK: Routledge-Cavendish, 2007); Gregory S. Alexander and Eduardo M. Peñalver, *An Introduction to Property Theory* (Cambridge: Cambridge University Press, 2012).

42. Carol Rose, *Property and Persuasion: Essays on the History, Theory, and Rhetoric of Ownership* (Boulder, CO: Westview Press, 1994); Davies, *Property: Meanings, Histories and Theories*; Kevin Gray and Susan Francis Gray, "The Idea of Property in Land," in *Land Law: Themes and Perspectives*, ed. Susan Bright and John Dewar (Oxford: Oxford University Press, 1998), 15–51; Nicholas Blomley, *Unsettling the City: Urban Land and the Politics of Property* (New York: Routledge, 2004).

43. Gregory S. Alexander, Eduardo M. Peñalver, Joseph William Singer, and Laura S. Underkuffler, "A Statement of Progressive Property," *Cornell Law Review* 94 (2008): 743–744.

44. Robert C. Ellickson, *Order without Law: How Neighbors Settle Disputes* (Cambridge, MA: Harvard University Press, 1991).

45. Veronica Strang and Mark Busse, eds., *Ownership and Appropriation* (Oxford: Berg Publishers, 2011); Marilyn Strathern, *Property, Substance and Effect: Anthropological*

Essays on Persons and Things (London: Athlone Press, 1999); Sarah Keenan, *Subversive Property: Law and the Production of Spaces of Belonging* (Abingdon, UK: Routledge, 2014); Kevin Gray, "Property in a Queue," in *Property and Community*, ed. Gregory S. Alexander and Eduardo M. Peñalver (Oxford: Oxford University Press, 2009), 165–196; Susan S. Silbey, "J. Locke, Op. Cit.: Invocations of Law on Snowy Streets," *Journal of Comparative Law* 5, no. 2 (2010): 66–91; Davina Cooper, "Opening Up Ownership: Community Belonging, Belongings, and the Productive Life of Property," *Law and Social Inquiry* 32, no. 3 (2007): 625–664.

46. Rose, *Property and Persuasion.*

47. Nicholas Blomley, "Flowers in the Bathtub: Boundary Crossings at the Public-Private Divide," *Geoforum* 36, no. 3 (2005): 281–296; Nicholas Blomley, "Making Private Property: Enclosure, Common Right and the Work of Hedges," *Rural History* 18, no. 1 (2007): 1–21; Nicholas Blomley, *Law, Space, and the Geographies of Power* (New York: Guilford Press, 1994); Blomley, *Unsettling the City.*

48. Blomley, *Unsettling the City*, xvi.

49. Nicholas Blomley, "Performing Property: Making the World," *Canadian Journal of Law and Jurisprudence* 26, no. 1 (2013): 23–48.

50. Cooper, "Opening Up Ownership"; Davies, *Property: Meanings, Histories and Theories*; Keenan, *Subversive Property*; Davina Cooper, *Everyday Utopias: The Conceptual Life of Promising Spaces* (Durham: Duke University Press, 2014).

51. Blomley, *Unsettling the City*; Peter Burdon, *Earth Jurisprudence: Private Property and the Environment* (Abingdon, UK: Routledge, 2015); Davies, *Property: Meanings, Histories and Theories*; Nicole Graham, *Lawscape: Property, Environment, Law* (Abingdon, UK: Routledge, 2011).

52. Davies, *Property: Meanings, Histories and Theories.*

53. A. J. Van der Walt, *Property in the Margins* (Oxford: Hart Pub, 2009).

54. John Law and John Urry, "Enacting the Social," *Economy and Society* 33, no. 3 (2004): 390–410.

55. J. K. Gibson-Graham and Gerda Roelvink, "An Economic Ethics for the Anthropocene," *Antipode* 41 (2010): 324.

56. J. K. Gibson-Graham, "Diverse Economies: Performative Practices for 'Other Worlds,'" *Progress in Human Geography* 32, no. 5 (2008): 613–632; Kurt Iveson, "Some Critical Reflections on Being Critical: Reading for Deviance, Dominance or Difference?," *City* 14, no. 4 (2010): 434–441; Blomley, "Performing Property."

57. Iveson, "Some Critical Reflections on Being Critical," 434.

58. Gibson-Graham, "Diverse Economies," 623.

59. Nicholas Blomley, "The Boundaries of Property: Complexity, Relationality, and Spatiality," *Law and Society Review* 50, no. 1 (2016): 225.

60. George E. Marcus, "Ethnography in/of the World System: The Emergence of Multi-Sited Ethnography," *Annual Review of Anthropology* (1995): 95–117; Eve Darian-Smith, "Ethnographies of Law," in *The Blackwell Companion to Law and Society*, ed. Austin Sarat (Oxford, UK: Blackwell, 2004), 545–568.

61. Blomley, "Flowers in the Bathtub"; Patricia Ewick and Susan S. Silbey, *The Common Place of Law: Stories from Everyday Life* (Chicago: University of Chicago Press, 1998); Simon Halliday and Patrick D. Schmidt, *Conducting Law and Society Research: Reflections on Methods and Practices* (Cambridge: Cambridge University Press, 2009); Irus Braverman, "Who's Afraid of Methodology? Advocating a Methodological Turn in Legal Geography," in *The Expanding Spaces of Law: A Timely Legal Geography*, ed. Irus Braverman, Nicholas Blomley, David Delaney, and Alexandre (Sandy) Kedar (Stanford: Stanford University Press, 2014), 120–142.

62. Benjamin F. Crabtree and William L. Miller, eds., *Doing Qualitative Research*, 2nd ed. (Thousand Oaks, CA: Sage, 1999); Malcolm Parlett and David Hamilton, "Evaluation as Illumination: A New Approach to the Study of Innovatory Programs," in *Beyond the Numbers Game: A Reader in Educational Evaluation*, ed. David Hamilton (Berkeley, CA: McCutchan, 1977), 6–22.

63. Kathy Charmaz, *Constructing Grounded Theory*, 2nd ed. (Thousand Oaks, CA: Sage, 2014); David A. Snow, Calvin Morrill, and Leon Anderson, "Elaborating Analytic Ethnography Linking Fieldwork and Theory," *Ethnography* 4, no. 2 (2003): 181–200.

64. Braverman, "Who's Afraid of Methodology?"; Caroline Brettell, ed., *When They Read What We Write: The Politics of Ethnography* (Westport, CT: Bergin and Garvey, 1996).

65. Sarah Pink, *Doing Visual Ethnography*, 3rd ed. (Thousand Oaks, CA: Sage, 2013).

66. Darian-Smith, "Ethnographies of Law," 552–553.

67. Blomley, "Flowers in the Bathtub"; Ewick and Silbey, *The Common Place of Law*.

68. Gregor McLennan and Thomas Osborne, "Contemporary 'Vehicularity' and 'Romanticism': Debating the Status of Ideas and Intellectuals," *Critical Review of International Social and Political Philosophy* 6, no. 4 (2003): 51–66.

69. Jacques Rancière, *Dissensus: On Politics and Aesthetics*, trans. Steve Corcoran (London: Continuum, 2010).

70. Robert M. Cover, "The Supreme Court, 1982 Term—Foreword: Nomos and Narrative," *Harvard Law Review* 97 (1983): 16.

71. Paul Chatterton, "Seeking the Urban Common: Furthering the Debate on Spatial Justice," *City* 14, no. 6 (2010): 625–628; Christian Borch and Martin Kornberger, eds., *Urban Commons: Rethinking the City* (Abingdon, UK: Routledge, 2015), 1–21.

Chapter 1

1. Rebar, "PARK(ing) Day Assembly Manual and Streetscape Intervention Toolkit," 2008, 4. PARK(ing) ran from 12 to 2 pm on Wednesday, November 16.

2. The filing cabinet would be covered on three sides by a mound of earth and native plants. Passmore explained this in his letter: "The idea is to make it look like the cabinet grew naturally out of the landscape; as if, in Cabinetlandia, cabinets are naturally occurring elements of the ecosystem." Sina Najafi, "Cabinetlandia: Update No. 1," *Cabinet*, Fall/Winter 2003.

3. Matthew Passmore, "Building the Cabinet National Library," *Cabinet*, Winter 2005.

4. Matthew Passmore, interview, November 10, 2016.

5. Blaine Merker, interview, October 28, 2016.

6. Rebar, "PARK(ing) Day Assembly Manual and Streetscape Intervention Toolkit," 3.

7. John Bela, "User-Generated Urbanism and the Right to the City," in *Now Urbanism: The Future City Is Here*, ed. Jeffrey Hou, Benjamin Spencer, Thaisa Way, and Ken Yocom (Abingdon, UK: Routledge, 2015), 150. For more on Matta-Clark, see chapter 4.

8. Blaine Merker, interview, October 24, 2014.

9. Matthew Passmore, interview, November 10, 2016.

10. Ibid.

11. Rebar, "PARK(ing) Day Assembly Manual and Streetscape Intervention Toolkit," 4.

12. Ryan Blitstein, "Space, the Final Frontier," *SF Weekly*, May 22, 2006.

13. Bela, "User-Generated Urbanism and the Right to the City," 150.

14. Rebar, "PARK(ing) Day Assembly Manual and Streetscape Intervention Toolkit," 4.

15. Blaine Merker, interview, October 28, 2016.

16. Blitstein, "Space, the Final Frontier."

17. "Park(ing)," Architecture+DesignScotland, 2006, https://www.ads.org.uk/parking/.

18. Blaine Merker, interview, October 28, 2016.

19. Matthew Passmore, interview, November 10, 2016; Matthew Shaffer, interview, September 30, 2016.

20. Matthew Shaffer, interview, September 30, 2016.

21. Matthew Passmore, interview, November 10, 2016.

22. "National Park(ing) Day Returns September 19," Trust for Public Land, June 26, 2008, http://www.tpl.org/media-room/national-parking-day-returns-september-19.

23. Blaine Merker, interview, October 28, 2016.

24. "Frequently Asked Questions," Park(ing) Day, 2012, http://parkingday.org/frequently-asked-questions/.

25. Matthew Shaffer, interview, September 30, 2016.

26. Rebar, "PARK(ing) Day 2006—Trailer," 2006, https://www.youtube.com/watch?v=6zvG-ay7k5c.

27. "Park(ing) Day Sites," Community Walk, 2006, http://www.communitywalk.com/parking.

28. Rebar, "PARK(ing) Day 2006—Trailer." Parks were installed on Friday, September 21 in San Francisco, Berkeley, Manhattan, Milwaukee, Cleveland, Manhattan, Manchester, London, and Rio de Janiero.

29. Rebar, "PARK(ing) Day 2006—Trailer."

30. "Park(ing) Day Sites," Community Walk, 2006.

31. Clarence Eckerson Jr., "PARK(ing) Day Was Streetfilms First Big Hit in 2006!!," September 17, 2014, http://www.streetfilms.org/parking-day-was-streetfilms-first-big-hit-in-2006/.

32. James E. Claffey, "Anti-Immigrant Violence in Suburbia," *Social Text* 24, no. 3 (2006): 73–80; Susanne Jonas, "Reflections on the Great Immigration Battle of 2006 and the Future of the Americas," *Social Justice* 33, no. 1 (2006): 6–20; Carol Cleaveland and Leo Pierson, "Parking Lots and Police: Undocumented Latinos' Tactics for Finding Day Labor Jobs," *Ethnography* 10, no. 4 (2009): 515–533.

33. A short video documenting this can be viewed at https://www.youtube.com/watch?v=1cRM6-eJgs4.

34. "PARK(ing) Day Archive," http://parkingday.org/archive/.

35. Rebar, "PARK(ing) Day Assembly Manual and Streetscape Intervention Toolkit," 5.

36. "On PARK(ing) Day, People Demand More Parks, Less Parking," Institute for Transportation and Development Policy, February 25, 2008, https://www.itdp.org/on-parking-day-people-demand-more-parks-less-parking/.

37. Black Rock Arts Foundation, "2007 Grant Recipients," Black Rock Arts Foundation, 2007, http://blackrockarts.org/projects/grantee-projects/2007-grant-recipients; Rebar, "Parkcycle," Rebar Art & Design Studio, 2008, http://rebargroup.org/parkcycle/. A short video can be viewed at https://www.youtube.com/watch?v=ZR7Qhvq0xAQ.

38. "Paraformance [06] The Nappening," *Southern Exposure*, https://www.soex.org/events/paraformance-06-nappening.

39. "Panhandle Bandshell," Rebar Art & Design Studio, http://rebargroup.org/panhandle-bandshell/.

40. Rebar, "Bushwaffle," Rebar Art & Design Studio, http://rebargroup.org/bushwaffle/.

41. "Venice Biennale," Rebar Art & Design Studio, 2008, http://rebargroup.org/venice-biennale.

42. John King, "Civic Adventures with Rebar Design Collective," *SF Gate*, September 9, 2008, http://www.sfgate.com/entertainment/article/Civic-adventures-with-Rebar-design-collective-3196123.php.

43. PARK(ing) Day Philadelphia, http://www.parkingdayphila.org/about.

44. "Rethink Parking Usage at UQ PARK(ing) Day," *UQ News*, University of Queensland, September 16, 2010, https://www.uq.edu.au/news/article/2010/09/rethink-parking-usage-uq-parking-day.

45. Brisbane PARK(ing) Day, http://brisbaneparkingday.blogspot.com.au.

46. Meghan McClosky, "From Parking to Parks," *San Francisco Bay Guardian*, September 24, 2008, http://www.sfbg.com/print/2008/09/24/parking-parks.

47. "2008 National Park(ing) Day," https://www.google.com/maps/d/viewer?ll=37.804901%2C-122.27015&spn=0.027228%2C0.040684&hl=en&msa=0&z=15&ie=UTF8&mid=199PAnQHJAIJumPlzPfAQDivEV9o.

48. "Popsugar 2008_Park(ing) Day 10 Hints for Your Own Park," *PopSugar*, September 24, 2008, http://www.popsugar.com/home/Parking-Day-10-Hints-Your-Own-Park-2058326#photo-2058326.

49. Rebar, "PARK(ing) Day T-Shirt Design Contest!," PARK(ing) Day Network, http://my.parkingday.org/page/parking-day-tshirt-design; Rebar, "Announcing the Winning PARK(ing) Day T-Shirt Design!," *PARK(ing) Day DIY Planning Network*, http://my.parkingday.org/profiles/blogs/announcing-the-winning-parking.

50. Rebar, "Resources," PARK(ing) Day DIY Planning Network, http://my.parkingday.org/page/resources-1.

51. "ITDP Celebrates Park(ing) Day with Events in 8 Countries around the World," Institute for Transportation and Development Policy, September 16, 2011, https://www.itdp.org/wp-content/uploads/2014/07/231.-091611_ParkingDay_ITDP.pdf.

52. *Adelaide PARK(ing) Day*, www.adelaideparkingday.com.

53. Woods Bagot, "Augmented Reality at Adelaide PARK(ing) Day 2013," Woods Bagot, 2013, http://www.woodsbagot.com/news/augmented-reality-at-adelaide-parking -day-2013.

54. "PARK(ing) Day Returns to Singapore for Its Third Run," Channel NewsAsia, July 22, 2015, http://www.channelnewsasia.com/news/singapore/park-ing-day-returns-to/ 1999890.html; "Have a Play Date with Park(ing) Day 2016," Sioux City Iowa, July 8, 2016, https://www.sioux-city.org/press-releases/4449-have-a-play-date-with-parking-day -2016; "Parking Day 2016 Registration Due," City of Cambridge, Massachusetts, May 1, 2016, https://www.cambridgema.gov/citycalendar/View?guid=%7B8E48FEC9-6C88 -4C92-9A49-22ADB1554454%7D&start=20160501T170000&end=20160501T170000; City of Fremantle, "2015 PARK(ing) Day Takes Back the Streets," City of Fremantle, August 25, 2015, http://www.fremantle.wa.gov.au/parkingday2015.

55. "Frequently Asked Questions."

56. Matthew Passmore, interview, November 10, 2016.

57. Mike Lydon and Anthony Garcia, *Tactical Urbanism* (Washington, DC: Island Press, 2015), 134.

58. Robin Abad Ocubillo, "Experimenting with the Margin: Parklets and Plazas" (master's thesis, University of Southern California, 2012), 45.

59. Robert Emmett Smith, "The Development and Impact of the Parking Meter before World War II" (master's thesis, Oklahoma State University, 1968), 1.

60. Jeff Ferrell, *Tearing Down the Streets: Adventures in Urban Anarchy* (New York: Palgrave, 2001), 92.

61. Tooker Gomberg, "So-Far . . . So Good!," *Car Busters*, July 1999.

62. Constance M. Lewallen, "A Larger Stage," in Constance M. Lewallen and Karen Moss, *State of Mind: New California Art circa 1970* (Berkeley: University of California Press, 2011); Pierre-François Galpin, "Cultivating the Human & Ecological Garden: A Conversation with Bonnie Ora Sherk, October 5, 2013," Independent Curators International, December 16, 2013, https://curatorsintl.org/posts/ cultivating-the-human-ecological-garden-a-conversation-with-bonnie-ora-sher.

63. Lewallen and Moss, *State of Mind*, 171.

64. "Portable Parks IV.: Past, Present, Future," *Pacific Standard Time*, 2012, http:// pacificstandardtimefestival.org/events/portable-parks-iv-past-present-future-a-l-l-by -bonnie-ora-sherk/.

65. Lewallen and Moss, *State of Mind*; Carl E. Loeffler and Darlene Tong, eds., *Performance Anthology: Source Book of California Performance Art*, updated edition (San Francisco: Last Gasp Press: Contemporary Arts Press, 1989).

66. Brenda Richardson, "Bay Area Survey: The Myth of Neo-Dada," *Arts Magazine* 44, no. 8 (1970): 44.

67. David Engwicht, *Street Reclaiming: Creating Livable Streets and Vibrant Communities* (Philadelphia: New Society, 1999).

68. David Engwicht, *Mental Speed Bumps: The Smarter Way to Tame Traffic* (Annandale: Envirobook, 2005).

69. "Parking Meter Party!," *Transportation for Liveable Communities*, July 9, 2001, http://tlchamilton.blogspot.com.au/2001/07/parking-meter-party.html.

70. "Sod It," *Transportation for Liveable Communities*, July 16, 2001, http://tlchamilton.blogspot.com.au/2001/07/sod-it.html.

71. Ruth Keffner, "DIY Urbanism," *The Urbanist*, September 2010, http://www.spur.org/publications/urbanist-article/2010-09-01/diy-urbanism.

72. Ibid.

73. Ibid.

74. Ted Dewan, "The Road Witch Trail," *Road Witch*, http://www.wormworks.com/roadwitch.

75. Ted Dewan, "Living Room," *Road Witch*, http://www.wormworks.com/roadwitch/pages/livingroom.htm.

76. Jane Marie Francis Martin, interview, November 4, 2016.

77. Abad Ocubillo, "Experimenting with the Margin," 60.

78. Michael Rakowitz, "(P)LOT Proposition I," accessed August 24, 2016, http://www.michaelrakowitz.com/plot-proposition-i/.

79. Ibid.

80. Transportation Alternatives, "Transportation Alternatives' Parking Spot Squat," 2005, http://transalt.org/sites/default/files/news/streetbeat/e-bulletin/2005/Nov/bedford_photoessay.html.

81. Melanie Colavito, "(PARK)ing Day 2009," *Bike Shop Hub*, September 18, 2009, http://www.bikeshophub.com/blog/2009/09/18/parking-day-2009/.

82. Aaron Naparstek, "Parking It in the Slope," *Streetsblog NYC*, May 12, 2006, https://nyc.streetsblog.org/2006/05/12/parking-it-in-the-slope/; Aaron Naparstek, "Why Is There a Picnic in My Parking Spot," *Streetsblog NYC*, September 21, 2007, https://nyc.streetsblog.org/2007/09/21/why-is-there-a-picnic-in-my-parking-spot/.

83. Napartsek, "Parking It in the Slope."

84. Ibid.; Colavito, "(PARK)ing Day 2009."

85. Eytan Rocheta, interview, November 24, 2015.

86. This can be viewed at https://www.youtube.com/watch?v=fC_5A55vAP4

87. Dan Hill, "PARKing Day Sydney 2008" *City of Sound*, September 20, 2008, https://www.cityofsound.com/blog/2008/09/parking-day-syd.html.

88. Safiah Moore, "PARK(ing) and Housing," *Inside*, September 22, 2016, https://www.arup.com/perspectives/parking-and-housing.

89. Harriet Watts, "PARK I PARK," Cargo Collective, 2011, http://cargocollective.com/harrietwatts/PARK-PARK; "PARK(ing) Day at Gaffa Gallery," *Australian Design Review*, September 21, 2010, https://www.australiandesignreview.com/news/1628-parking-day-at-gaffa-gallery.

90. Peta Mount, "Call for Action," PARK(ing) Day Network—Sydney, 2010, http://my.parkingday.org/group/parkingdaysydney.

91. Hilary Best, "Park(ing) Day!," *Spacing Montreal*, September 16, 2011, http://spacing.ca/montreal/2011/09/16/parking-day/; Agriurbain, "Parking Day (Rue St-Viateur)," Ning, September 23, 2011, http://agriurbain.ning.com/photo/parking-day-rue-st-viateur?context=album&albumId=3832755%3AAlbum%3A21289.

92. Transport Canada, "En ville, sans ma Voiture!," Études de Cas sur les Transports Durables, May 2005, http://publications.gc.ca/pub?id=9.603762&sl=0.

93. Ibid.

94. "Mission," Association du Design Urbain du Québec, http://aduq.ca/aduq/mission/.

95. "Concours Park(ing) Day," Association du Design Urbain du Québec, 2012, http://aduq.ca/concours/concours-parking-day/.

96. Daniel Bouchard, Abdoulaye Diallo, and Aurore Tanier, "Bilan 2012 du PARK(ing) Day Montréal," Conseil Régional de l'Environnement de Montréal, October 2012, parkingdaymontreal.org.

97. Daniel Bouchard, Maxence Ponche, Catherine Louchou Berthiaume, and Aurore Tanier, "Bilan PARK(ing) Day à Montréal 2013," Conseil Régional de l'Environnement de Montréal, 2013, http://parkingdaymontreal.org/2013.

98. Félix Gravel and Raphaëlle Cayla, "Bilan PARK(ing) Day à Montréal 2014," Conseil Régional de l'Environnement de Montréal, December 4, 2014, http://parkingdaymontreal.org/2014.

99. Félix Gravel and Julie Richard, "Bilan PARK(ing) Day à Montréal 2015," Conseil Régional de l'Environnement de Montréal, May 2016, http://parkingdaymontreal.org/2015.

100. Conseil Régional de l'Environnement de Montréal, "2016," Park(ing) Day Montréal, http://parkingdaymontreal.org/2016.

101. Conseil Régional de l'Environnement de Montréal, "PARK(ing) Day Montréal," PARK(ing) Day Montréal, 2018, http://parkingdaymontreal.org/.

102. Conseil Régional de l'Environnement de Montréal, "PARK(ing) Day 2018: Merci à tous!," PARK(ing) Day Montréal, http://parkingdaymontreal.org/.

103. "PARK(ing) Day Archive."

104. Conseil Régional de l'Environnement de Montréal, "2016."

105. Lydon and Garcia, *Tactical Urbanism*; Kylie Legge, *Future City Solutions* (Sydney: Place Partners, 2013); Mahyar Arefi and Conrad Kickert, eds., *The Palgrave Handbook of Bottom-Up Urbanism* (Cham, Switzerland: Palgrave Macmillan, 2018); Anastasia Loukaitou-Sideris, Madeline Brozen, and Colleen Callahan, "Reclaiming the Right of Way: A Toolkit for Creating and Implementing Parklets" (UCLA Complete Streets Initiative, Luskin School of Public Affairs, 2012).

106. Alissa Walker, "Why We Don't Need PARK(ing) Day Anymore," *Gizmodo*, September 21, 2013, https://www.gizmodo.com.au/2013/09/why-we-dont-need -parking-day-anymore/. Walker provides eight arguments to support this claim: PARK(ing) Day is dangerous, it's not always city-appropriate, it's not original, it's illegal, it's show-off time for architects, it's already worked, it's wasteful, and it's time better spent working on an actual park.

Chapter 2

1. Mario Diani, "The Concept of Social Movement," *Sociological Review* 40, no. 1 (1992): 3.

2. Zygmunt Bauman, *Legislators and Interpreters: On Modernity, Post-Modernity, and Intellectuals* (Cambridge, UK: Polity Press, 1987).

3. Thomas Osborne, "On Mediators: Intellectuals and the Ideas Trade in the Knowledge Society," *Economy and Society* 33, no. 4 (2004): 430–447; Gregor McLennan, "Travelling with Vehicular Ideas: The Case of the Third Way," *Economy and Society* 33, no. 4 (2004): 484–499; Gregor McLennan and Thomas Osborne, "Contemporary 'Vehicularity' and 'Romanticism': Debating the Status of Ideas and Intellectuals," *Critical Review of International Social and Political Philosophy* 6, no. 4 (2003): 51–66.

4. Osborne, "On Mediators."

5. McLennan and Osborne, "Contemporary 'Vehicularity' and 'Romanticism.'"

6. Osborne, "On Mediators"; McLennan, "Travelling with Vehicular Ideas."

7. Helen Carr and Dave Cowan, "Labelling: Constructing Definitions of Anti-Social Behaviour?," in *Housing, Urban Governance and Anti-Social Behaviour: Perspectives, Policy and Practice*, ed. John Flint (Bristol, UK: Policy Press, 2006), 57–78.

8. Cristina Temenos and Eugene McCann, "The Local Politics of Policy Mobility: Learning, Persuasion, and the Production of a Municipal Sustainability Fix," *Environment and Planning A* 44, no. 6 (2012): 1389–1406.

9. Jamie Peck, "Recreative City: Amsterdam, Vehicular Ideas and the Adaptive Spaces of Creativity Policy," *International Journal of Urban and Regional Research* 36, no. 3 (2012): 462–485.

10. Cass R. Sunstein, "Incompletely Theorized Agreements," *Harvard Law Review* 108, no. 7 (1995): 1733.

11. Robert Emmett Smith, "The Development and Impact of the Parking Meter before World War II" (master's thesis, Oklahoma State University, 1968).

12. Kerry Segrave, *Parking Cars in America, 1910–1945: A History* (Jefferson, NC: McFarland, 2012); Eric Gregory Klocko, "The Public-Private City: Automobile Parking and the Control of Urban Space in San Francisco, 1920–1959" (PhD diss., University of California, Berkeley, 2006); Smith, "The Development and Impact of the Parking Meter before World War II."

13. McLennan, "Travelling with Vehicular Ideas," 485.

14. Peck, "Recreative City," 480.

15. Osborne, "On Mediators," 441.

16. McLennan, "Travelling with Vehicular Ideas," 485.

17. For more on the legal rules applicable to PARK(ing) Day, see chapter 3.

18. Jamie Peck and Nik Theodore, "Mobilizing Policy: Models, Methods, and Mutations," *Geoforum* 41, no. 2 (2010): 169–174.

19. W. Lance Bennett and Alexandra Segerberg, "The Logic of Connective Action: Digital Media and the Personalization of Contentious Politics," *Information, Communication and Society* 15, no. 5 (2012): 739–768. See also Engin Isin discussing a shift from "we, the people" to "we, the connected": Engin Isin, *Citizens without Frontiers* (New York: Continuum International, 2012).

20. Bennett and Segerberg, "The Logic of Connective Action," 743.

21. Ibid., 752.

22. McLennan, "Travelling with Vehicular Ideas," 494.

23. Peck and Theodore, "Mobilizing Policy."

24. Ibid., 171.

25. San Francisco has consistently appeared near the top of A. T. Kearney's Global Cities Report, for example, which compares global standing, influence, and potential for future importance—including three years as number one on this list. A. T. Kearney, "2019 Global Cities Report," 2019, https://www.atkearney.com/global-cities.

26. Richard Florida, "Where the Streets Are Paved with Ideas," *Nature* 550, no. 7676 (2017): S172. San Francisco received $6.47 billion in 2012, well above second-place San Jose's $4.18 billion.

27. Richard Barbrook and Andy Cameron, "The Californian Ideology," *Science as Culture* 6, no. 1 (1996): 44–45.

28. Justin McGuirk and Brendan McGetrick, eds., *California: Designing Freedom* (London: Phaidon Press, 2017).

29. McLennan, "Travelling with Vehicular Ideas," 488 (original emphasis).

30. "Parking Meter Party!," *Transportation for Liveable Communities*, July 9, 2001, http://tlchamilton.blogspot.com.au/2001/07/parking-meter-party.html.

31. Donald C. Shoup, *The High Cost of Free Parking* (Chicago: Planners Press, American Planning Association, 2004); Peter Newman and Jeffrey R. Kenworthy, *Sustainability and Cities: Overcoming Automobile Dependence* (Washington, DC: Island Press, 1999).

32. Jacques Rancière, *Dissensus: On Politics and Aesthetics*, trans. Steve Corcoran (London: Continuum, 2010).

33. Ibid., 37.

34. Ibid.

35. Paul Bowman and Richard Stamp, "Introduction: A Critical Dissensus," in *Reading Rancière: Critical Dissensus* (London: Bloomsbury, 2011), xii.

36. Jacques Rancière, "The Aesthetic Dimension: Aesthetics, Politics, Knowledge," *Critical Inquiry* 36, no. 1 (2009): 8.

37. Rancière, *Dissensus*, 37 (original emphasis).

38. Rancière, "The Aesthetic Dimension," 3.

39. Ibid., 19.

40. Ibid., 8.

41. Ibid.

42. Blaine Merker, "Taking Place: Rebar's Absurd Tactics in Generous Urbanism," in *Insurgent Public Space: Guerrilla Urbanism and the Remaking of Contemporary Cities*, ed. Jeffrey Hou (New York: Routledge, 2010), 45–58.

43. Rebar, "PARK(ing) Day Assembly Manual and Streetscape Intervention Toolkit," 2008, 5.

44. Rancière, "The Aesthetic Dimension," 8.

45. Merker, "Taking Place," 49.

46. Jacques Rancière, *Disagreement: Politics and Philosophy* (Minneapolis: University of Minnesota Press, 1999), 31.

47. Rebar, "PARK(ing) Day Assembly Manual and Streetscape Intervention Toolkit," 5.

48. Rebar, "PARK(ing) Day Manual," 2011, 11 (original emphasis).

Chapter 3

1. San Francisco Transportation Code, art. 7.2.23.

2. By-Law Concerning Traffic and Parking, C-4.1, Ville de Montréal, section III.

3. "Road Rules 2014," Part 12, Division 7. Made under the Road Transportation Act 2013 (NSW).

4. Rebar, "PARK(ing) Day Assembly Manual and Streetscape Intervention Toolkit," 2008, 13.

5. Lon L. Fuller, "Positivism and Fidelity to Law: A Reply to Professor Hart," *Harvard Law Review* 71, no. 4 (1968): 663.

6. Ibid., 665–666.

7. Ibid., 663.

8. Eric Gregory Klocko, "The Public-Private City: Automobile Parking and the Control of Urban Space in San Francisco, 1920–1959" (PhD diss., University of California, Berkeley, 2006); Smith, "The Development and Impact of the Parking Meter before World War II"; Marion Allen Grimes, "The Legality of Parking Meter Ordinances and Permissible Use of Parking Meter Funds," *California Law Review* (1947): 235–251; Kerry Segrave, *Parking Cars in America, 1910–1945: A History* (Jefferson, NC: McFarland, 2012).

9. Stanford Anderson, ed., *On Streets* (Cambridge, MA: MIT Press, 1991).

10. Klocko, "The Public-Private City."

11. (1812) 3 Camp 224, at 227.

12. Rachel Vorspan, "'Freedom of Assembly' and the Right to Passage in Modern English Legal History," *San Diego Law Review* 34 (1997): 927. It was not until the eighteenth and in some cases the nineteenth century that highways became publicly

owned land. See also Nicholas Blomley, *Rights of Passage: Sidewalks and the Regulation of Public Flow* (London: Routledge, 2011).

13. Vorspan, "'Freedom of Assembly' and the Right to Passage in Modern English Legal History," 929–934.

14. Ibid.

15. Blomley, *Rights of Passage*, chap. 6.

16. DPP v Jones [1999] 2 AC 240. A group of 21 protesters had been charged under s 14B(2) of the Public Order Act 1986, for trespassory assembly. The protestors' appeals to the Salisbury Crown Court succeeded, but their convictions were reinstated on appeal to the Divisional Court. It was not disputed that the grassy verge on which the protestors gathered was part of the highway; the questions before the House of Lords centered on the scope of the right of access to the public highway at common law, and the purposes for which the public has a right to use the highway.

17. DPP v Jones [1999] 2 AC 240, at 255.

18. DPP v Jones [1999] 2 AC 240, at 256.

19. Michelle Watts, *Urban Park(ing) Day Newtown (Sydney, Australia) 2008* (Sydney, NSW, 2008), https://www.youtube.com/watch?v=fC_5A55vAP4.

20. Roads Act 1993 (NSW), s 107.

21. Local Government Act 1993 (NSW), s 680A(1).

22. Local Government Act 1993 (NSW), s 125.

23. Law Enforcement (Powers and Responsibilities) Act 2002 (NSW), s 197(1).

24. Criminal Code ss 175(1)(c), 180(1)(a).

25. By-Law Concerning the Prevention of Breaches of the Peace, Public Order and Safety, and the Use of Public Property, R.B.C.M. P-6, Ville de Montréal

26. San Francisco Police Code, s 22.

27. California Penal Code, Title 10, s 372

28. San Francisco Transportation Code, Article 6; Section 904.

29. San Francisco Public Works Code, ss 416, 703.1, 706, 708, and 724.2; Robin Abad Ocubillo, interview, October 17, 2016.

30. San Francisco Public Works Code, s 176.1

31. City of San Francisco, Ordinance no. 224-16, October 2016.

32. "Le placottoir est une aire de détente et de rencontre, ouvert à tous, aménagé sur la chaussée devant un établissement. Il s'agit d'un aménagement de

l'espace public, construit en plateforme, installé en continuité et au même niveau que le trottoir. Tous ses éléments doivent être fixés à la structure (bancs, supports à vélo ou autre). La vente et le service y sont interdits. Il n'y a aucun frais d'occupation du domaine public." Le Plateau-Mont-Royal Montréal, "Aménagement d'un placottoir," Ville de Montréal, http://ville.montreal.qc.ca/portal/page? _pageid=7297,129877587&_dad=portal&_schema=PORTAL.

33. Le Plateau-Mont-Royal, "Guide d'aménagement d'un placottoir sur le domaine public," 2017, 6.

34. Roads Act 1993 (NSW), ss 125, 139A, 144.

35. Roads Act 1993 (NSW), dictionary.

36. Roads Act 1993 (NSW), s 139A.

37. Roads Act 1993 (NSW), s 144.

38. Roads Act 1993 (NSW), ss 138, 139.

39. The court takes a purposive approach in determining whether something constitutes a structure, referring to the purpose of the legislation to determine whether something should be included. In a case before the NSW Court of Appeal concerning the characterization of gates, Mahoney JA explained: "It may perhaps be a permissible application of the purposive approach to construction to determine whether a thing or operation is within the statutory provision by considering, not whether it is of a kind which could carry out the statutory purpose, but whether, in the particular case, it could be or would be of assistance in achieving that purpose. On that view, a sculpture consisting of a structure of several parts would be a structure if set up in the garden but not if set up inside the house in a place where it could have no conceivable relationship to the environment." *Mulcahy v Blue Mountains CC* (1993) 81 LGERA 302, at 308.

40. Environmental Planning and Assessment Act 1979 (NSW), s 76A.

41. State Environmental Planning Policy (Exempt and Complying Development Codes) 2008, cll 2.108, 2.119, 2.123, 4A.5–8.

42. Karen Profilio, interview, October 28, 2015.

43. Félix Gravel, interview, August 6, 2015.

44. Félix Gravel, interview, November 16, 2016.

45. Ibid.

46. Ville de Montreal, "Politique de Stationnement," June 2016, 56, http://ville .montreal.qc.ca/pls/portal/docs/page/proj_urbains_fr/media/documents/politique _de_stationnement_v2.pdf.

47. John Stephens, "PARK(ing) Day Event—Marion Street Carpark, Leichhardt" (Leichhardt Municipal Council, Infrastructure and Service Delivery Division, September 9, 2013).

48. Anonymous Sydney participant A, interview, November 7, 2016.

49. Peta Mount, "Call for Action," PARK(ing) Day Network—Sydney, 2010, http://my.parkingday.org/group/parkingdaysydney; Seb Crawford, interview, November 3, 2015.

50. Bonnie Parfit and Kate Sayeg, interview, November 17, 2015.

51. Mount, "Call for Action."

52. Summary Offences Regulation 2015, Schedule 1 (Clause 13(1)).

53. Section 23 provides that a public assembly is an authorized public assembly if notice in writing, in the prescribed form giving the required particulars, is served on the Commissioner at least seven days before the event and the Commissioner has not notified the organizers that the Commissioner opposes the holding of the public assembly.

54. Summary Offences Act 1988 (NSW), s 24.

55. Hendrik Hartog, "Pigs and Positivism," *Wisconsin Law Review* (1985): 925.

56. Ibid.

57. Ibid., 933.

58. Sally Engle Merry, "Legal Pluralism," *Law and Society Review* 22, no. 5 (1988): 869–896.

59. Boaventura de Sousa Santos, "Law: A Map of Misreading. Toward a Postmodern Conception of Law," *Journal of Law and Society* (1987): 279–302.

60. Margaret Davies, *Law Unlimited* (Abingdon, UK: Routledge, 2017), 30.

61. Martha-Marie Kleinhans and Roderick Macdonald, "What Is a Critical Legal Pluralism?," *Canadian Journal of Law and Society* 12 (1997): 39.

62. Ibid., 42.

63. Robert C. Ellickson, *Order without Law: How Neighbors Settle Disputes* (Cambridge, MA: Harvard University Press, 1991); Austin Sarat, ed., *Law in Everyday Life* (Ann Arbor: University of Michigan Press, 1995); Patricia Ewick and Susan S. Silbey, *The Common Place of Law: Stories from Everyday Life* (Chicago: University of Chicago Press, 1998); Simon Halliday and Bronwen Morgan, "I Fought the Law and the Law Won? Legal Consciousness and the Critical Imagination," *Current Legal Problems* 66, no. 1 (2013): 1–32.

64. Ewick and Silbey, *The Common Place of Law*.

65. Ibid., 32.

66. Robert M Cover, "The Supreme Court, 1982 Term—Foreword: Nomos and Narrative," *Harvard Law Review* 97 (1983): 4–68.

67. Ibid., 7, 41.

68. Ibid., 18.

69. Ibid., 16.

70. Ewick and Silbey, *The Common Place of Law*, 46 (emphasis in original).

71. This distinction is well established for San Francisco (California: Nahas v. Local 905, Retail Clerks Assn., 144 Cal. App. 2d 808, 302 P.2d 829 (2d Dist. 1956)), and for Sydney (Western Australia v Ward (2002) 213 CLR 1; 76 ALJR 1098; [2002] HCA 28, McHugh J at [504]). It can be traced back to the seventeenth-century decision in *Thomas v Sorrell* where it was stated that a license "passeth no interest, nor alters or transfers property in anything, but only makes an action lawful which without it, had been unlawful; as, a license . . . to hunt in a man's park, to come into his house, are only actions which, without license, had been unlawful": [1673] EWHC KB J85 (1673) Vaugh 330; 124 ER 1098–1113. The civil law system in Quebec means that a lease is not a proprietary right in Montréal.

72. New South Wales: Radaich v Smith (1959) 101 CLR 209; Lewis v Bell (1985) 1 NSWLR 731.

73. In San Francisco, parking meters are provided by the San Francisco Municipal Transportation Authority. Their website explains: "Parking meters are used to maintain parking availability in high demand areas," suggesting not a grant of possession, but a management of permissions to use the land ("Parking Meters," San Francisco Municipal Transportation Agency, 2016, https://www.sfmta.com/getting-around/parking/meters). The very short duration of times purchasable from a parking meter (typically two hours) and the prohibition on extension (adding coins to extend the time beyond the original two-hour limit is not allowed) provide further challenges for establishing a lease, and further confirmation that the right in question is a mere license. The San Francisco Municipal Transportation Code similarly suggests that payment of a parking meter creates a license rather than a lease. The Code defines a parking meter as "any device, including any electronic pay station, that, upon payment, registers the amount of time for which a vehicle is authorized to Park in a particular Parking Space" (Art 1, definitions).

74. A lease of the roadway cannot be granted by any authority other than the Department of Roads and Maritime Services, except with the approval of the Secretary of the Department of Planning (Roads Act 1993 (NSW), s 149). Since parking

meters are managed by local councils in Sydney, no leases can be implied with payments for parking.

75. Mariana Valverde, *Everyday Law on the Street: City Governance in an Age of Diversity* (Chicago: University of Chicago Press, 2012).

76. "Frequently Asked Questions," Park(ing) Day, 2012, http://parkingday.org/frequently-asked-questions/ (original emphasis).

77. Ibid.

78. John Langshaw Austin, *How to Do Things with Words* (Oxford: Oxford University Press, 1962).

79. Judith Butler, *Excitable Speech: A Politics of the Performative* (New York: Routledge, 1997).

80. Austin distinguished illocutionary and perlocutionary performatives: the first bring about certain effects (such as judicial decisions), the second do so only when certain other kinds of conditions are in place. Michel Callon argues that this distinction should be understood as one of degree, and that perlocution is the more fundamental and general condition. Illocution, Callon explains, can be seen as an extreme case of perlocution, characterized by the fact that the (material and institutional) conditions for success are met. Michel Callon, "Performativity, Misfires and Politics," *Journal of Cultural Economy* 3, no. 2 (2010): 163–169.

81. Judith Butler, "Performative Agency," *Journal of Cultural Economy* 3, no. 2 (2010): 153 (original emphasis).

82. Judith Butler, *Bodies That Matter: On the Discursive Limits of "Sex"* (New York: Routledge, 1993), 2.

83. Judith Butler, *Notes toward a Performative Theory of Assembly* (Cambridge, MA: Harvard University Press, 2015), 9.

84. Judith Butler, "Restaging the Universal: Hegemony and the Limits of Formalism," in *Contingency, Hegemony, Universality: Contemporary Dialogues on the Left*, ed. Judith Butler, Ernesto Laclau, and Slavok Žižek (London: Verso, 2000), 11–43.

85. Judith Butler and Athena Athanasiou, *Dispossession: The Performative in the Political* (Malden, MA: Polity, 2013), 196.

86. Butler, "Performative Agency," 150.

87. Michel Callon, "What Does It Mean to Say that Economics Is Performative?," in *How Economists Make Markets*, ed. Donald MacKenzie, Fabian Muniesa, and Lucia Siu (Princeton: Princeton University Press, 2007), 311–357.

88. Bruno Latour, "On Using ANT for Studying Information Systems: A (Somewhat) Socratic Dialogue," in *The Social Study of Information and Communication Study*, ed.

Chrisianti Avgerou, Claudio Ciborra, and Frank Land (Oxford: Oxford University Press, 2004), 63.

89. Callon, "Performativity, Misfires and Politics," 165.

90. Bruno Latour, *Reassembling the Social: An Introduction to Actor-Network Theory* (Oxford: Oxford University Press, 2005).

91. Bruno Latour, *The Making of Law: An Ethnography of the Conseil d'Etat* (Cambridge, UK; Malden, MA: Polity, 2010).

92. Noortje Marres, "Why Political Ontology Must Be Experimentalized: On Eco-Show Homes as Devices of Participation," *Social Studies of Science* 43, no. 3 (2013): 434.

93. Robert M. Cover, "Violence and the Word," *Yale Law Journal* 95, no. 8 (1986): 1065.

Chapter 4

1. Margaret Davies, *Property: Meanings, Histories and Theories* (Abingdon, UK: Routledge-Cavendish, 2007), 9.

2. Kevin Gray and Susan Francis Gray, "The Idea of Property in Land," in *Land Law: Themes and Perspectives*, ed. Susan Bright and John Dewar (Oxford: Oxford University Press, 1998), 15.

3. Kevin Gray and Susan Francis Gray, *Elements of Land Law*, 4th ed. (Oxford: Oxford University Press, 2005); Davies, *Property: Meanings, Histories and Theories*; Gregory S. Alexander and Eduardo Moisés Peñalver, *An Introduction to Property Theory* (Cambridge: Cambridge University Press, 2012).

4. This variability prompted Bruce Ackerman's famous characterization of property as a "laundry list" composed of rights with limitless permutations, subject to policy-guided tinkering. Bruce Ackerman, *Private Property and the Constitution* (New Haven: Yale University Press, 1977).

5. Margaret Davies, "Persons, Property, and Community," *Feminists@ Law* 2, no. 2 (2012), https://journals.kent.ac.uk/index.php/feministsatlaw/article/view/37.

6. James Penner, *The Idea of Property in Law* (Oxford: Clarendon Press, 1997); Michael Heller, "The Boundaries of Private Property," *Yale Law Journal* (1999): 1163–1223; Thomas Merrill and Henry Smith, "What Happened to Property in Law and Economics?," *Yale Law Journal* 111 (2001): 357–398.

7. Henry Smith, "Exclusion versus Governance: Two Strategies for Delineating Property Rights," *Journal of Legal Studies* 31, no. S2 (2002): S453–487.

8. Larissa Katz, "Exclusion and Exclusivity in Property Law," *University of Toronto Law Journal* 58, no. 3 (2008): 275–315.

9. These include legislative and court-imposed limitations on the ability of private owners to restrict access to hotels, transport, and various other businesses open to the public, to beaches and other natural areas in private ownership, to shopping malls and other quasi-public spaces, to rental accommodation, and even, in certain circumstances, to private businesses normally closed to the public. Joseph William Singer, *Entitlement: The Paradoxes of Property* (New Haven: Yale University Press, 2000); Hanoch Dagan, *Property: Values and Institutions* (Oxford: Oxford University Press, 2011); Eric T. Freyfogle, *On Private Property: Finding Common Ground on the Ownership of Land* (Boston: Beacon Press, 2007). As Hanoch Dagan argues, there are so many exceptions to exclusion that it is "condescending" and "also probably mistaken" to suggest that this is how property is popularly understood. Dagan, *Property: Values and Institutions*, 40.

10. Margaret Jane Radin, "Property and Personhood," *Stanford Law Review* 34, no. 5 (1982): 957–1015; Georg Wilhelm Friedrich Hegel, *Elements of the Philosophy of Right*, ed. Allen W. Wood and Hugh Barr Nisbet (Cambridge: Cambridge University Press, 2011). Theories of property based on personhood are discussed further in chapter 5.

11. Alexander and Peñalver, *An Introduction to Property Theory*.

12. Dagan, *Property: Values and Institutions*.

13. Kevin Gray, "Equitable Property," *Current Legal Problems* 47, no. 2 (1994): 157–214; Davies, *Property: Meanings, Histories and Theories*; Alexander and Peñalver, *An Introduction to Property Theory*.

14. Singer, *Entitlement*; Gray and Gray, "The Idea of Property in Land"; Freyfogle, *On Private Property*.

15. Davina Cooper, "Opening Up Ownership: Community Belonging, Belongings, and the Productive Life of Property," *Law and Social Inquiry* 32, no. 3 (2007): 628.

16. Jennifer Nedelsky, "Law, Boundaries and the Bounded Self," *Representations* 30 (1990): 162–189; Jennifer Nedelsky, "Reconceiving Rights as Relationship," *Review of Constitutional Studies* 1, no. 1 (1993): 1–26; Cooper, "Opening Up Ownership"; Davina Cooper, *Everyday Utopias: The Conceptual Life of Promising Spaces* (Durham: Duke University Press, 2014); Nicholas Blomley, "The Borrowed View: Privacy, Propriety, and the Entanglements of Property," *Law and Social Inquiry* 30, no. 4 (2005): 617–661; Nicholas Blomley, "Performing Property: Making the World," *Canadian Journal of Law and Jurisprudence* 26, no. 1 (2013): 23–48.

17. Carol Rose, *Property and Persuasion: Essays on the History, Theory, and Rhetoric of Ownership* (Boulder, CO: Westview Press, 1994).

18. Gray and Gray, "The Idea of Property in Land," 15, 19.

19. As William Swadling proclaimed: "Despite what the layman might think, there is no concept of ownership in English law." William Swadling, "Unjust Delivery,"

in *Mapping the Law: Essays in Memory of Peter Birks*, ed. Andrew Burrows and Alan Rodger (Oxford: Oxford University Press, 2006), 281.

20. I thank Mariana Valverde for helpful assistance on this point: property and ownership mean substantially the same thing, indicative of Anglo-Saxon and Latin origins rather than any clear or consistent semantic distinction.

21. Mark Busse and Veronica Strang, "Introduction: Ownership and Appropriation," in *Ownership and Appropriation*, ed. Veronica Strang and Mark Busse (Oxford: Berg, 2011), 4.

22. Jon L. Pierce, Tatiana Kostova, and Kurt T. Dirks, "The State of Psychological Ownership: Integrating and Extending a Century of Research," *Review of General Psychology* 7, no. 1 (2003): 86.

23. Pierce, Kostova, and Dirks, "The State of Psychological Ownership"; Graham Brown, Jon L. Pierce, and Craig Crossley, "Toward an Understanding of the Development of Ownership Feelings," *Journal of Organizational Behavior* 35, no. 3 (2014): 318–338.

24. Pierce, Kostova, and Dirks, "The State of Psychological Ownership," 86.

25. It is important to note that this literature is based primarily on studies of Western societies. The "need" for ownership is not necessarily universal, and may be shaped to a large extent by cultural factors.

26. Grant McCracken, "Culture and Consumption: A Theoretical Account of the Structure and Movement of the Cultural Meaning of Consumer Goods," *Journal of Consumer Research* (1986): 71–84; Amitai Etzioni, "The Socio-Economics of Property," *Journal of Social Behavior and Personality* 6, no. 6 (1991): 465–468; Pierce, Kostova, and Dirks, "The State of Psychological Ownership"; Linn Van Dyne and Jon L. Pierce, "Psychological Ownership and Feelings of Possession: Three Field Studies Predicting Employee Attitudes and Organizational Citizenship Behavior," *Journal of Organizational Behavior* 25, no. 4 (2004): 439–459.

27. McCracken, "Culture and Consumption."

28. Marco Antonsich, "Searching for Belonging—An Analytical Framework," *Geography Compass* 4, no. 6 (2010): 644–659; Kathleen Mee and Sarah Wright, "Geographies of Belonging," *Environment and Planning A* 41, no. 4 (2009): 772–779.

29. Elspeth Probyn, for example, describes the first as belonging, the second as longing; Nira Yuval-Davis discusses place-belongingness and politics of belonging; John Crowley and Catherine Veninga each distinguish ownership and membership aspects. Elspeth Probyn, *Outside Belongings* (New York: Routledge, 1996); Nira Yuval-Davis, "Belonging and the Politics of Belonging," *Patterns of Prejudice* 40, no. 3 (2006): 197–214; Tovi Fenster, "Gender and the City: The Different Formations of Belonging," in *A Companion to Feminist Geography*, ed. Lise Nelson and Joni Seager (Malden,

MA: Blackwell, 2005), 242–256; Antonsich, "Searching for Belonging"; Kathleen Mee, "A Space to Care, a Space of Care: Public Housing, Belonging, and Care in Inner Newcastle, Australia," *Environment and Planning A* 41, no. 4 (2009): 842–858; John Crowley, "The Politics of Belonging: Some Theoretical Considerations," in *The Politics of Belonging: Migrants and Minorities in Contemporary Europe*, ed. Andrew Geddes and Adrian Favell (Aldershot, UK: Ashgate, 1999), 15–41; Catherine Veninga, "Road Scholars: School Busing and the Politics of Integration in Seattle" (PhD diss., Department of Geography, University of Washington, 2005), cited in Richard H. Schein, "Belonging through Land/Scape," *Environment and Planning A* 41, no. 4 (2009): 813.

30. Probyn, *Outside Belongings*; Anne-Marie Fortier, "Re-Membering Places and the Performances of Belonging(s)," *Theory, Culture and Society* 16, no. 2 (1999): 41–64; Yuval-Davis, "Belonging and the Politics of Belonging"; Vicki Bell, "Performativity and Belonging: An Introduction," *Theory, Culture and Society* 16, no. 2 (1999): 1–10.

31. Yuval-Davis, "Belonging and the Politics of Belonging," 198.

32. bell hooks, *Belonging: A Culture of Place* (New York: Routledge, 2009).

33. Angelique Harris, Juan Battle, Antonio Pastrana Jr., and Jessie Daniels, "Feelings of Belonging: An Exploratory Analysis of the Sociopolitical Involvement of Black, Latina, and Asian/Pacific Islander Sexual Minority Women," *Journal of Homosexuality* 62, no. 10 (2015): 1374–1397; Antonsich, "Searching for Belonging"; Elaine Stratford, "Belonging as a Resource: The Case of Ralphs Bay, Tasmania, and the Local Politics of Place," *Environment and Planning A* 41, no. 4 (2009): 796–810; Tim McCreanor, Liane Penney, Victoria Jensen, Karen Witten, Robin Kearns, and Helen Moewaka Barnes, "'This Is Like My Comfort Zone': Senses of Place and Belonging within Oruāmo/Beachhaven, New Zealand," *New Zealand Geographer* 62, no. 3 (December 2006): 196–207; David R. Dodman, "Feelings of Belonging? Young People's Views of Their Surroundings in Kingston, Jamaica," *Children's Geographies* 2, no. 2 (2004): 185–198; Schein, "Belonging through Land/Scape"; Tovi Fenster, "The Right to the Gendered City: Different Formations of Belonging in Everyday Life," *Journal of Gender Studies* 14, no. 3 (2005): 217–231.

34. Stratford, "Belonging as a Resource," 797.

35. Julian Rappaport, "Terms of Empowerment/Exemplars of Prevention: Toward a Theory for Community Psychology," *American Journal of Community Psychology* 15, no. 2 (1987): 122. See also Paul W. Speer and Joseph Hughey, "Mechanisms of Empowerment: Psychological Processes for Members of Power-Based Community Organizations," *Journal of Community and Applied Social Psychology* 6, no. 3 (1996): 177–187, who examine empowerment as a matter of social relationships between individuals and organizations.

36. Carol M. Rose, "Several Futures of Property: Of Cyberspace and Folk Tales, Emission Trades and Ecosystems," *Minnesota Law Review* 83 (1998): 129.

37. Richard A. Epstein, "The Allocation of the Commons: Parking on Public Roads," *Journal of Legal Studies* 31, no. S2 (2002): S515–544.

38. Susan S. Silbey, "J. Locke, Op. Cit.: Invocations of Law on Snowy Streets," *Journal of Comparative Law* 5, no. 2 (2010): 66–91.

39. A sense of ownership could be likened to the right not to be excluded proposed by C. B. Macpherson. C. B. Macpherson, "The Meaning of Property," in *Property: Mainstream and Critical Positions* (Toronto: University of Toronto Press, 1978), 1–13.

40. Davina Cooper, *Governing Out of Order: Space, Law, and the Politics of Belonging* (London: Rivers Oram Press, 1998); Cooper, "Opening Up Ownership"; Cooper, *Everyday Utopias*.

41. Cooper, *Everyday Utopias*, 161–167. In earlier work, Cooper conceptualized belonging as having two dimensions; proper attachment was added later.

42. Cooper, *Governing out of Order*; Cooper, "Opening Up Ownership"; Cooper, *Everyday Utopias*.

43. Cooper, *Everyday Utopias*, 161–163.

44. Ibid., 162.

45. Ibid., 163.

46. Rebar, "PARK(ing) Day Assembly Manual and Streetscape Intervention Toolkit," 2008, 2, 5.

47. Pamela M. Lee, *Object to Be Destroyed: The Work of Gordon Matta-Clark* (Cambridge, MA: MIT Press, 2001).

48. Nancy Spector, "Reality Properties: Fake Estates," Guggenheim Collection Online, https://www.guggenheim.org/artwork/5210.

49. *Odd Lots: Revisiting Gordon Matta-Clark's "Fake Estates"* (New York: Cabinet Books, in conjunction with the Queens Museum of Art and White Columns, 2005).

50. The Universal Declaration of Human Rights provides that "everyone has the right to own property alone as well as in association with others. No one shall be arbitrarily deprived of his property" (Art 17).

51. Jeremy Waldron, "Community and Property—for Those Who Have Neither," *Theoretical Inquiries in Law* 10 (2009): 161.

52. Reflecting the contemporary resurgence of interest in property and its accessibility, a shot-for-shot remake of the *Bosom Buddies* credits was aired in 2014 as part of the satirical documentary series *The Greatest Event in Television History*.

53. Neil Brenner, Peter Marcuse, and Margit Mayer, *Cities for People, Not for Profit: Critical Urban Theory and the Right to the City* (London: Routledge, 2012); David

Harvey, *Rebel Cities: From the Right to the City to the Urban Revolution* (New York: Verso, 2012); Susan S. Fainstein, *The Just City* (Ithaca: Cornell University Press, 2010); Edward W. Soja, *Seeking Spatial Justice* (Minneapolis: University of Minnesota Press, 2010).

54. Eduardo Peñalver and Sonia Katyal, *Property Outlaws: How Squatters, Pirates, and Protesters Improve the Law of Ownership* (New Haven: Yale University Press, 2010), 14.

55. Ibid., 17.

56. Margaret Jane Radin, "Time, Possession, and Alienation," *Washington University Law Quarterly* 64 (1986): 739.

57. C. B. Macpherson, ed., *Property: Mainstream and Critical Positions* (Toronto: University of Toronto Press, 1978).

58. In recent changes to electoral laws in the cities of Sydney and Melbourne, for example, arguments for increasing the number of votes allocated to businesses made use of property claims. "Proposal to Give City of Sydney Businesses Extra Votes," *RN Breakfast* (Radio National, August 15, 2014), http://www.abc.net.au/radionational/programs/breakfast/proposal-to-give-city-of-sydney-businesses-extra-votes/5672598.

59. Patrick McAuslan, *The Ideologies of Planning Law* (Oxford: Pergamon Press, 1980); Philip Booth, "From Property Rights to Public Control: The Quest for Public Interest in the Control of Urban Development," *Town Planning Review* 73, no. 2 (2002): 153–170; Susan S. Fainstein, *The City Builders: Property Development in New York and London, 1980–2000*, 2nd ed. (Lawrence: University Press of Kansas, 2001); Leonie Sandercock, *Cities for Sale: Property, Politics, and Urban Planning in Australia* (Carlton, Vic: Melbourne University Press, 1975).

60. Defined by Michael Dear as "the protectionist attitudes of and oppositional tactics adopted by community groups facing an unwelcome development in their neighbourhood." M. J. Dear, *Not on Our Street: Community Attitudes to Mental Health Care* (London: Pion, 1982).

61. Leonie Sandercock, "When Strangers Become Neighbours: Managing Cities of Difference," *Planning Theory and Practice* 1, no. 1 (2000): 13–30; Laura Beth Bugg, "Religion on the Fringe: The Representation of Space and Minority Religious Facilities in the Rural-Urban Fringe of Metropolitan Sydney, Australia," *Australian Geographer* 43, no. 3 (2012): 273–289.

62. Fainstein, *The City Builders*; Fainstein, *The Just City*; Jerold S. Kayden, *Privately Owned Public Space: The New York City Experience* (New York: John Wiley, 2000); David Harvey, "The Art of Rent: Globalisation, Monopoly and the Commodification of Culture," *Socialist Register* 38, no. 38 (2009); Peter Marcuse, James Connolly, Johannes Novy, Ingrid Olivio, Cuz Potter, and Justin Steil, *Searching for the Just City: Debates in Urban Theory and Practice* (London: Routledge, 2011); Brenner, Marcuse, and Mayer, *Cities for People, Not for Profit*.

63. Chris McGrath, "Myth Drives Australian Government Attack on Standing and Environmental 'Lawfare,'" *Environmental and Planning Law Journal* (2016): 3–20; Estair Van Wagner, "Putting Property in Its Place: Relational Theory, Environmental Rights and Land Use Planning," *Revue générale de droit* 43 (2013): 275–315.

64. Alan W. Evans, *Economics and Land Use Planning* (Oxford: Blackwell, 2004).

65. Ryan Devlin, "'An Area That Governs Itself': Informality, Uncertainty and the Management of Street Vending in New York City," *Planning Theory* 10, no. 1 (2011): 53–65; Annette M. Kim, "The Mixed-Use Sidewalk: Vending and Property Rights in Public Space," *Journal of the American Planning Association* 78, no. 3 (July 2012): 225–238.

66. Amnon Lehavi, "Mixing Property," *Seton Hall Law Review* 38 (2008): 196.

67. Stuart Hodkinson, "The New Urban Enclosures," *City* 16, no. 5 (2012): 500–518; Massimo De Angelis, *The Beginning of History: Value Struggles and Global Capital* (London: Pluto, 2007).

68. Soja, *Seeking Spatial Justice*, 42–43.

69. Harvey, "The Art of Rent"; Harvey, *Rebel Cities*.

70. Stephanie Farmer, "Cities as Risk Managers: The Impact of Chicago's Parking Meter P3 on Municipal Governance and Transportation Planning," *Environment and Planning A: Economy and Space* 46, no. 9 (2014): 2160–2174; Mariana Valverde, Fleur Johns, and Jennifer Raso, "Governing Infrastructure in the Age of the 'Art of the Deal': Logics of Governance and Scales of Visibility," *PoLAR: Political and Legal Anthropology Review* 41, no. S1 (2018): 118–132; Ellen Dannin, "Crumbling Infrastructure, Crumbling Democracy: Infrastructure Privatization Contracts and Their Effects on State and Local Governance," *Northwestern Journal of Law and Social Policy* 6 (2011): 47–105; Peter Williams, "The 'Panelization' of Planning Decision-Making in Australia," *Planning Practice and Research* 29, no. 4 (2014): 426–447; Graeme A. Hodge and Carsten Greve, "Public-Private Partnerships: An International Performance Review," *Public Administration Review* 67, no. 3 (May 2007): 545–558.

71. "About Us," https://righttothecity.org/

72. Henri Lefebvre, *Writings on Cities* (Cambridge, MA: Blackwell, 1996).

73. Ibid., 174.

74. Ibid., 154–158, 174.

75. David Harvey, "The Right to the City," *New Left Review* 53 (2008): 23–40; Mark Purcell, "Excavating Lefebvre: The Right to the City and Its Urban Politics of the Inhabitant," *GeoJournal* 58, no. 2–3 (2002): 99–108; Kurt Iveson, "Social or Spatial Justice? Marcuse and Soja on the Right to the City," *City* 15, no. 2 (2011): 250–259; Lee Stickells, "The Right to the City: Rethinking Architecture's Social Significance,"

Architectural Theory Review 16, no. 3 (2011): 213–227; Harvey, *Rebel Cities*; Brenner, Marcuse, and Mayer, *Cities for People, Not for Profit*; Chris Butler, *Henri Lefebvre: Spatial Politics, Everyday Life and the Right to the City* (Abingdon, UK: Routledge, 2012); Fenster, "The Right to the Gendered City"; Don Mitchell, *The Right to the City: Social Justice and the Fight for Public Space* (New York: Guilford Press, 2003); Carolyn Whitzman, ed., *Building Inclusive Cities: Women's Safety and the Right to the City* (New York: Routledge, 2013); Mark Purcell, "Possible Worlds: Henri Lefebvre and the Right to the City," *Journal of Urban Affairs* 36, no. 1 (2014): 141–154; Andy Merrifield, "The Right to the City and Beyond: Notes on a Lefebvrian Re-Conceptualization," *City* 15, no. 3–4 (2011): 473–481; Łukasz Stanek, *Henri Lefebvre on Space: Architecture, Urban Research, and the Production of Theory* (Minneapolis: University of Minnesota Press, 2011).

76. Lefebvre, *Writings on Cities*, 179.

77. Yasminah Beebeejaun, "Gender, Urban Space, and the Right to Everyday Life," *Journal of Urban Affairs* 39, no. 3 (2017): 323–334; Fenster, "The Right to the Gendered City"; Brenner, Marcuse, and Mayer, *Cities for People, Not for Profit*; Gareth Millington, *"Race," Culture and the Right to the City: Centres, Peripheries and Margins* (Basingstoke, UK: Palgrave Macmillan, 2011).

78. Harvey, *Rebel Cities*.

79. Ibid., 4.

80. Joni Taylor, *D.I.Y. Urbanism—Right to the City* (Sydney: Magic Bag Productions, 2011), 4, https://issuu.com/magicbag85/docs/diyurbanism; "Creative Public Spaces Bring Life to Streets on PARK(ing) Day 2017," Singapore Urban Redevelopment Authority, September 13, 2017, https://www.ura.gov.sg/Corporate/Media-Room/Media-Releases/pr17-60; (Park)ing Day Johannesburg 2013 collective, "Time to Re-Think the Parking Bay?," *UrbanAfrica.Net*, September 16, 2013, https://www.urbanafrica.net/urban-voices/time-re-think-parking-bay/; Rebel Metropolis, "PARK(ing) Day PDX Reclaims the Streets," September 23, 2013, http://rebelmetropolis.org/parking-day-pdx-reclaims-the-streets-video-hart-noecker/; Mimi Zeiger, "The Interventionist's Toolkit: 3 Our Cities, Ourselves," *Places Journal*, September 12, 2011, https://placesjournal.org/article/the-interventionists-toolkit-our-cities-ourselves/.

81. Stickells, "The Right to the City: Rethinking Architecture's Social Significance"; Margit Mayer, "First World Urban Activism: Beyond Austerity Urbanism and Creative City Politics," *City* 17, no. 1 (2013): 5–19; Kurt Iveson, "Cities within the City: Do-It-Yourself Urbanism and the Right to the City," *International Journal of Urban and Regional Research* 37, no. 3 (2013): 941–956; Donovan Finn, "DIY Urbanism: Implications for Cities," *Journal of Urbanism: International Research on Placemaking and Urban Sustainability* (2014): 1–18.

82. Lusi Morhayim, "Fixing the City in the Context of Neoliberalism: Institutionalized DIY," in *Incomplete Streets: Processes, Practices, and Possibilities*, ed. Stephen Zavestoski and Julian Agyeman (Abingdon, UK: Routledge, 2015), 230.

83. Judith Innes, *Planning with Complexity: An Introduction to Collaborative Rationality for Public Policy* (Abingdon, UK: Routledge, 2010); John Forester, *The Deliberative Practitioner: Encouraging Participatory Planning Processes* (Cambridge, MA: MIT Press, 1999); Patsy Healey, *Collaborative Planning: Shaping Places in Fragmented Societies* (Basingstoke, UK: Macmillan, 1997); Patsy Healey, *Making Better Places: The Planning Project in the Twenty-First Century* (Basingstoke, UK: Palgrave Macmillan, 2010); Ben Clifford and Mark Tewdwr-Jones, *The Collaborating Planner? Practitioners in the Neoliberal Age* (Bristol, UK: Policy Press, 2013).

84. Sherry R. Arnstein, "A Ladder of Citizen Participation," *Journal of the American Institute of Planners* 35, no. 4 (1969): 216–224.

85. Philip Allmendinger and Graham Haughton, "Post-Political Spatial Planning in England: A Crisis of Consensus?," *Transactions of the Institute of British Geographers* 37, no. 1 (2012): 89–103; Andy Inch, "Creating 'a Generation of NIMBYs'? Interpreting the Role of the State in Managing the Politics of Urban Development," *Environment and Planning C: Government and Policy* 30, no. 3 (2012): 520–535; Erik Swyngedouw, "Governance Innovation and the Citizen: The Janus Face of Governance-beyond-the-State," *Urban Studies* 42, no. 11 (2005): 1991–2006; Erik Swyngedouw, "Apocalypse Forever? Post-Political Populism and the Spectre of Climate Change," *Theory, Culture and Society* 27, no. 2–3 (2010): 213–232.

86. Homeownership rates in Montreal are low compared to both provincial and national averages, but not that low. The 2016 national census gave a homeownership rate for the city of just over 40 percent. Statistics Canada, "Census Profile, 2016 Census, Montréal and Quebec," Statistics Canada, http://www12.statcan.gc.ca/census-recensement/2016/dp-pd/prof/details/page.cfm?B1=All&Code1=2440&Code2=24&Data=Count&Geo1=ER&Geo2=PR&Lang=E&SearchPR=01&SearchText=Montr%EF%BF%BDal&SearchType=Begins&TABID=1.

Chapter 5

1. John Locke, "Of Property," in *Property: Mainstream and Critical Positions*, ed. C. B. Macpherson (Toronto: University of Toronto Press, 1978), 15–27.

2. Ibid., sec. 26.

3. Ibid., sec. 27.

4. Ibid., sec. 28.

5. Ibid., sec. 30.

6. Robert Nozick, *Anarchy, State, and Utopia* (New York: Basic Books, 1974); Gregory S. Alexander and Eduardo Moisés Peñalver, *An Introduction to Property Theory* (Cambridge: Cambridge University Press, 2012); Margaret Davies, *Property: Meanings,*

Histories and Theories (Abingdon, UK: Routledge-Cavendish, 2007); Barbara Arneil, *John Locke and America: The Defence of English Colonialism* (Oxford: Clarendon Press, 1996); David Armitage, "John Locke, Carolina, and the Two Treatises of Government," *Political Theory* 32, no. 5 (2004): 602–627; C. B. Macpherson and Frank Cunningham, *The Political Theory of Possessive Individualism: Hobbes to Locke* (Don Mills, ON: Oxford University Press, 2011).

7. Nozick, *Anarchy, State, and Utopia*; Jeremy Waldron, *The Right to Private Property* (Oxford: Clarendon Press, 1990); Lawrence C. Becker, *Property Rights: Philosophic Foundations* (London: Routledge and K. Paul, 1977); Stephen R. Munzer, *A Theory of Property* (New York: Cambridge University Press, 1990); Stephen Buckle, *Natural Law and the Theory of Property: Grotius to Hume* (Oxford: Clarendon Press, 1991).

8. Davies, *Property: Meanings, Histories and Theories*, 87.

9. Anders Corr, *No Trespassing! Squatting, Rent Strikes, and Land Struggles Worldwide* (Cambridge, MA: South End Press, 1999).

10. Nicholas Blomley, *Unsettling the City: Urban Land and the Politics of Property* (New York: Routledge, 2004), 95–96.

11. Davina Cooper, *Everyday Utopias: The Conceptual Life of Promising Spaces* (Durham: Duke University Press, 2014), 246.

12. Richard A. Epstein, "The Allocation of the Commons: Parking on Public Roads," *Journal of Legal Studies* 31, no. S2 (2002): S529; Susan S. Silbey, "J. Locke, Op. Cit.: Invocations of Law on Snowy Streets," *Journal of Comparative Law* 5, no. 2 (2010): 66–91.

13. During a visit to Australia, Silbey commented to me that this paper has been by far her most popular, continuing to generate invitations to speak all around the world years after its publication—a very significant achievement given the rest of her work.

14. Silbey, "J. Locke, Op. Cit.," 67.

15. Munzer, *A Theory of Property*, 283.

16. Silbey, "J. Locke, Op. Cit.," 90.

17. Among the quotes provided by Silbey, for example, are "If you diligently shovel out a spot *in front to your house* and want to trade, that's fair. Stealing my diligently cleared out spot because you failed to shovel out is not"; "Regards, *A homeowner* with a sore back from shoveling so much snow!!!"; and *"residents have a right* to stake their claims" (emphases added).

18. Epstein, "The Allocation of the Commons," 531.

19. Ibid.

20. Georg Wilhelm Friedrich Hegel, *Elements of the Philosophy of Right*, ed. Allen W. Wood and Hugh Barr Nisbet (Cambridge: Cambridge University Press, 2011).

21. Ibid., sec. 41.

22. Ibid., sec. 46.

23. Ibid., 57 (original emphasis).

24. Ibid., sec. 46.

25. Ibid., sec. 45 (original emphasis).

26. Ibid., sec. 44.

27. Ibid., sec. 64.

28. Margaret Jane Radin, "Property and Personhood," *Stanford Law Review* 34, no. 5 (1982): 957–1015; Margaret Jane Radin, "Time, Possession, and Alienation," *Washington University Law Quarterly* 64 (1986).

29. Radin, "Property and Personhood," 960.

30. Jon L. Pierce, Tatiana Kostova, and Kurt T. Dirks, "The State of Psychological Ownership: Integrating and Extending a Century of Research," *Review of General Psychology* 7, no. 1 (2003); Graham Brown, Jon L. Pierce, and Craig Crossley, "Toward an Understanding of the Development of Ownership Feelings," *Journal of Organizational Behavior* 35, no. 3 (2014): 318–338.

31. Pierce, Kostova, and Dirks, "The State of Psychological Ownership," 92–97.

32. Carol Rose, "Possession as the Origin of Property," *University of Chicago Law Review* 52, no. 1 (1985): 79 (emphasis in original).

33. Hegel, *Elements of the Philosophy of Right*, 93, sec. 64–65.

34. Radin, "Property and Personhood," 968.

35. Michael Salter, "Justifying Private Property Rights: A Message from Hegel's Jurisprudential Writings," *Legal Studies* 7, no. 3 (1987): 258.

36. Pierce, Kostova, and Dirks, "The State of Psychological Ownership," 96–97.

37. Ibid., 96.

38. Davies, *Property: Meanings, Histories and Theories*; Davies, "Persons, Property, and Community"; Estair Van Wagner, "Putting Property in Its Place: Relational Theory, Environmental Rights and Land Use Planning," *Revue générale de droit* 43 (2013): 275–315; Nicholas Blomley, "The Boundaries of Property: Complexity, Relationality, and Spatiality," *Law and Society Review* 50, no. 1 (2016): 225; Sarah Keenan, *Subversive Property: Law and the Production of Spaces of Belonging* (Abingdon, UK: Routledge, 2014).

39. Jennifer Nedelsky, "Law, Boundaries and the Bounded Self," *Representations* 30 (1990): 162–189; Jennifer Nedelsky, "Reconceiving Rights as Relationship," *Review of Constitutional Studies* 1, no. 1 (1993): 1–26.

40. Jennifer Nedelsky, "Law, Boundaries and the Bounded Self," 177.

41. Ibid.

42. Joseph William Singer, *Entitlement: The Paradoxes of Property* (New Haven: Yale University Press, 2000); Gregory S. Alexander, Eduardo M. Peñalver, Joseph William Singer, and Laura S. Underkuffler, "A Statement of Progressive Property," *Cornell Law Review* 94 (2008): 743–744.

43. Davies, "Persons, Property, and Community," 14.

44. Eric T. Freyfogle, "Context and Accommodation in Modern Property Law," *Stanford Law Review* (1989): 1529–1556.

45. Rose, "Possession as the Origin of Property," 81.

46. Nicholas Blomley, "Performing Property: Making the World," *Canadian Journal of Law and Jurisprudence* 26, no. 1 (2013): 23–48; Nicholas Blomley, "Disentangling Property, Performing Space," in *Performativity, Politics, and the Production of Social Space*, ed. Michael R. Glass and Reuben Rose-Redwood (New York: Routledge, 2014), 147–175.

47. Blomley, "Performing Property," 33.

48. Pierce, Kostova, and Dirks, "The State of Psychological Ownership."

49. Personhood theory has even been critiqued, particularly as expressed by Radin, for overemphasizing the degree to which people define themselves through property, in turn fostering an atomistic, alienated society. Jeanne Schroeder, "Virgin Territory: Margaret Radin's Imagery of Personal Property as the Inviolate Feminine Body," *Minnesota Law Review* 79, no. 1 (1994): 55–171; Davies, *Property: Meanings, Histories and Theories*, 102.

50. Hegel, *Elements of the Philosophy of Right*, sec. 51. This provides an important distinction from Locke, who suggests that appropriation can be undertaken in isolation: there is no requirement for consent, and the property becomes owned as soon as the labor is mixed with it.

51. Hegel, *Elements of the Philosophy of Right*, sec. 71. As Radin argues, "though he speaks of the person in the sphere of abstract right only in the Kantian sense of abstract rationality, he implicitly claims that personhood in the richer sense of self-development and differentiation presupposes the context of human community." Radin, "Property and Personhood," 977.

52. Hegel, *Elements of the Philosophy of Right*, sec. 51.

53. Ibid., sec. 71 (original emphasis).

54. Salter, "Justifying Private Property Rights," 257. Lisa Austin argues that community relations and social networks depend, to a significant extent, on the kinds of interactions made possible by access to public spaces, and thus that personhood provides a strong basis to argue for the protection of such spaces. Lisa M. Austin, "Person, Place or Thing? Property and the Structuring of Social Relations," *University of Toronto Law Journal* 60, no. 2 (2010): 445–465. Carpenter, Katyal, and Riley develop Radin's theory in the context of lands, resources, and expressions that are integral to group identity and to the cultural survival of indigenous peoples. Kristen A. Carpenter, Sonia K. Katyal, and Angela R. Riley, "In Defense of Property," *Yale Law Journal* (2009): 1022–1125; Kristen A. Carpenter, Sonia K. Katyal, and Angela R. Riley, "Clarifying Cultural Property," *International Journal of Cultural Property* 17, no. 3 (2010): 581–598. See also Peter G. Stillman, "Property, Freedom and Individuality in Hegel's and Marx's Political Thought," in *Property*, ed. J. Roland Pennock and John W. Chapman (New York: New York University Press, 1980), 143; Alan Ryan, "Self-Ownership, Autonomy, and Property Rights," *Social Philosophy and Policy* 11, no. 2 (1994): 241–258.

55. Salter, "Justifying Private Property Rights," 257.

56. Marco Antonsich, "Searching for Belonging—An Analytical Framework," *Geography Compass* 4, no. 6 (2010): 649.

57. Sheila L. Croucher, *Globalization and Belonging: The Politics of Identity in a Changing World* (Lanham, MD: Rowman and Littlefield, 2004), 41; Zlatko Skrbiš, Loretta Baldassar, and Scott Poynting, "Introduction—Negotiating Belonging: Migration and Generations," *Journal of Intercultural Studies* 28, no. 3 (2007): 261–262; Kathleen Mee, "A Space to Care, a Space of Care: Public Housing, Belonging, and Care in Inner Newcastle, Australia," *Environment and Planning A* 41, no. 4 (2009): 844.

58. Cooper, *Everyday Utopias*, 163.

59. Keenan, *Subversive Property*, 72. See below for a fuller discussion of Keenan's approach.

60. John Bela, "User-Generated Urbanism and the Right to the City," in *Now Urbanism: The Future City Is Here*, ed. Jeffrey Hou, Benjamin Spencer, Thaisa Way, and Ken Yocom (Abingdon, UK: Routledge, 2015), 150.

61. Blomley, "Disentangling Property, Performing Space"; Keenan, *Subversive Property*; Emilie Cloatre and Dave Cowan, "Legalities and Materialities," in *Routledge Handbook of Legal Theory*, ed. A. Philippopoulos-Mihalopoulos (Abingdon, UK: Routledge, 2019).

62. Gopal Sreenivasan, *The Limits of Lockean Rights in Property* (New York: Oxford University Press, 1995).

63. Keenan, *Subversive Property*.

64. Doreen B. Massey, *For Space* (Thousand Oaks, CA: Sage, 2005).

65. Keenan, *Subversive Property*, 80.

66. Ibid.

67. Irus Braverman, *Planted Flags: Trees, Land, and Law in Israel/Palestine* (New York: Cambridge University Press, 2009).

68. Nicholas Blomley, "Making Private Property: Enclosure, Common Right and the Work of Hedges," *Rural History* 18, no. 1 (2007): 1–21.

69. Dave Cowan, Helen Carr, and Alison Wallace, *Ownership, Narrative, Things* (London: Palgrave Macmillan, 2018).

70. Pierce, Kostova, and Dirks, "The State of Psychological Ownership," 94. Attributes such as attractiveness, accessibility, openness, and manipulability render a target more or less subject to psychological ownership.

71. Bruno Latour, *Reassembling the Social: An Introduction to Actor-Network Theory* (Oxford: Oxford University Press, 2005); Jane Bennett, *Vibrant Matter: A Political Ecology of Things* (Duke University Press, 2009); Dan Hicks and Mary Carolyn Beaudry, eds., *The Oxford Handbook of Material Culture Studies* (Oxford: Oxford University Press, 2010); Diana H. Coole and Samantha Frost, eds., *New Materialisms: Ontology, Agency, and Politics* (Durham: Duke University Press, 2010); Andrew Barry, *Political Machines: Governing a Technological Society* (London: Athlone Press, 2001).

72. Noortje Marres, "Why Political Ontology Must Be Experimentalized: On Eco-Show Homes as Devices of Participation," *Social Studies of Science* 43, no. 3 (2013): 434.

73. The development of ideas following on from PARK(ing) Day is discussed in more detail in Chapter 7.

74. Lisa Peattie, "Convivial Cities," in *Cities for Citizens: Planning and the Rise of Civil Society in a Global Age*, ed. Mike Douglass and John Friedmann (Chichester, UK: John Wiley, 1999), 247–253.

75. Ibid., 253.

76. Karen A. Franck and Quentin Stevens, *Loose Space: Possibility and Diversity in Urban Life* (London: Routledge, 2007); Quentin Stevens, *The Ludic City: Exploring the Potential of Public Spaces* (London: Routledge, 2007).

77. Gavin Brown and Jenny Pickerill, "Space for Emotion in the Spaces of Activism," *Emotion, Space and Society* 2, no. 1 (2009): 24–35.

78. Davina Cooper, "Enacting Counter-States through Play," *Contemporary Political Theory* 15, no. 4 (2016): 453–461.

79. Brown and Pickerill, "Space for Emotion in the Spaces of Activism."

80. Mark Purcell, *The Down-Deep Delight of Democracy* (Chichester, UK: John Wiley, 2013).

81. Ibid., 119.

82. Sam Halvorsen, "Taking Space: Moments of Rupture and Everyday Life in Occupy London," *Antipode* 47, no. 2 (2015): 401–417; Brown, Pierce, and Crossley, "Toward an Understanding of the Development of Ownership Feelings"; Pierce, Kostova, and Dirks, "The State of Psychological Ownership."

Chapter 6

1. Jane Jacobs, *The Death and Life of Great American Cities* (Harmondsworth, UK: Penguin, 1972).

2. Ibid., 50.

3. Oscar Newman, *Defensible Space: Crime Prevention through Urban Design* (New York: Collier Books, 1978).

4. Newman's ideas about defensible space have been extremely influential, with Crime Prevention Through Environmental Design (CPTED or "Designing Out Crime") strategies now widely adopted. CPTED has also been subject to critique. Paul Cozens and Terence Love, "A Review and Current Status of Crime Prevention through Environmental Design (CPTED)," *Journal of Planning Literature* 30, no. 4 (2015): 393–412.

5. Paul Lachapelle, "A Sense of Ownership in Community Development: Understanding the Potential for Participation in Community Planning Efforts," *Community Development* 39, no. 2 (2008): 52–59.

6. Janette Hartz-Karp, "A Case Study in Deliberative Democracy: Dialogue with the City," *Journal of Public Deliberation* 1, no. 1 (2005): 1–15.

7. Ibid., 11.

8. Emma Rees-Raaijmakers, interview, June 2015.

9. Dave Meslin, "Urban Conversation" (June 20, 2013), https://www.youtube.com/watch?v=XoTVw9o9XAo&index=4&list=PLjdGX64tXQMHsdQ3L9EBdbvcXlZC_GXH3.

10. Don Vandewalle, Lyn Van Dyne, and Tatiana Kostova, "Psychological Ownership: An Empirical Examination of Its Consequences," *Group and Organization Studies* 20, no. 2 (1995): 210–226; Graham Brown, Jon L. Pierce, and Craig Crossley, "Toward an Understanding of the Development of Ownership Feelings," *Journal of Organizational Behavior* 35, no. 3 (2014): 318–338.

11. I also came across a third group that created a similar park without challenge. As described in chapter 1, Studio O+A set up an office outside their building on Howard Street in San Francisco for PARK(ing) Day in 2016. Howard Street, unlike Rue Ontario and unlike Oxford Street, is less contested: it is a one-way street with four lanes of traffic, so that the loss of a parking space had little impact on traffic conditions.

12. Stine Ejsing-Dunn, "Participatory Urbanism: Making the Stranger Familiar and the Familiar Strange," in *Citizen Media and Public Spaces*, ed. Mona Baker and Bolette B. Blaagaard (Abingdon, UK: Routledge, 2016), 155–171.

13. Ibid., 165.

14. Aileen Moreton-Robinson, *The White Possessive: Property, Power, and Indigenous Sovereignty* (Minneapolis: University of Minnesota Press, 2015), 18.

15. Gordon C. C. Douglas, *The Help-Yourself City: Legitimacy and Inequality in DIY Urbanism* (New York: Oxford University Press, 2018); Megan Heim LaFrombois, *Reframing the Reclaiming of Urban Space: A Feminist Exploration into Do-It-Yourself Urbanism in Chicago* (Lanham, MD: Lexington Books, 2018); Ann Deslandes, "Exemplary Amateurism: Thoughts on DIY Urbanism," *Cultural Studies Review* 19, no. 1 (2013): 216–227.

16. Adonia E. Lugo, *Bicycle / Race: Transportation, Culture, and Resistance* (Portland, OR: Microcosm Publishing, 2018).

17. Libby Porter, *Unlearning the Colonial Cultures of Planning* (Farnham, UK: Ashgate, 2010); Moreton-Robinson, *The White Possessive*; Brenna Bhandar, *Colonial Lives of Property: Law, Land, and Racial Regimes of Ownership* (Durham: Duke University Press, 2018).

18. Sarah Keenan, "Subversive Property: Reshaping Malleable Spaces of Belonging," *Social and Legal Studies* 19, no. 4 (2010): 433.

19. The development of parklets is discussed in chapter 7.

20. Wendy Brown argues that "democratic self-rule must be consciously valued, cultured, and tended by people seeking to practice it and that it must vigilantly resist myriad economic, social, and political forces threatening to deform or encroach upon it." Wendy Brown, *Undoing the Demos: Neoliberalism's Stealth Revolution* (New York: Zone Books, 2015), 11.

Chapter 7

1. Matthew Passmore, interview, November 10, 2016.

2. John Bela, "User-Generated Urbanism and the Right to the City," in *Now Urbanism: The Future City Is Here*, ed. Jeffrey Hou, Benjamin Spencer, Thaisa Way, and Ken Yocom (Abingdon, UK: Routledge, 2015).

3. Erin Feher, "Citizen's Rest," *California Home + Design*, June 2010, 50.

4. Michelle Birdsall, "Parklets: Providing Space for People to Park . . . Themselves," *Institute of Transportation Engineers. ITE Journal* 83, no. 5 (2013): 37.

5. "San Francisco Parklet Manual Version 2.2" (San Francisco Planning Department, Spring 2015).

6. Parfit and Sayeg, interview; Anonymous Sydney participant A, interview, November 7, 2016; Gehl Studio San Francisco, "Planning by Doing: How Small, Citizen-Powered Projects Inform Large Planning Decisions," 2016.

7. Robin Abad Ocubillo, "Experimenting with the Margin: Parklets and Plazas" (master's thesis, University of Southern California, 2012); Anonymous Sydney participant A, interview; Parfit and Sayeg, interview; Gehl Studio San Francisco, "Planning by Doing."

8. Liza Pratt, "Parklet Impact Study" (San Francisco Great Streets, April 2011), http://nacto.org/docs/usdg/parklet_impact_study_sf_planning_dept.pdf; Abad Ocubillo, "Experimenting with the Margin," 33; Claire Martin, "When the Parking Space Becomes a Park," *New York Times*, November 1, 2015.

9. John Bela, "Hacking Public Space with the Designers who Invented Park(ing) Day," *Next City*, September 18, 2015, https://nextcity.org/daily/entry/hacking-public-space-designers-parking-day.

10. Ville de Montreal, "Politique de Stationnement," June 2016, 56, http://ville.montreal.qc.ca/pls/portal/docs/page/proj_urbains_fr/media/documents/politique_de_stationnement_v2.pdf.

11. Molly Freedenberg and Steven T. Jones, "Seizing the Streets: How Some Artsy San Francisco Renegades Reignited a Movement to Reclaim Urban Environments," *San Francisco Bay Guardian*, November 18, 2009; Bela, "User-Generated Urbanism and the Right to the City"; Feher, "Citizen's Rest"; Abad Ocubillo, "Experimenting with the Margin."

12. Abad Ocubillo, "Experimenting with the Margin"; Bela, "User-Generated Urbanism and the Right to the City."

13. Susan Semenak, "Terrasses and Montreal's al Fresco Culture," *Montreal Gazette*, May 21, 2013, http://www.montrealgazette.com/life/terrasses+montreal+fresco+culture/8403332/story.html.

14. Donald C. Shoup, *The High Cost of Free Parking* (Chicago: Planners Press, American Planning Association, 2004); Charles Montgomery, *Happy City: Transforming Our Lives through Urban Design* (New York: Farrar, Straus and Giroux, 2013).

15. "Participants," Into the Open Official U.S. Representation at La Biennale di Venezia, 2008, http://intotheopen.org/project.php.

16. John Chase, Margaret Crawford, and John Kaliski, eds., *Everyday Urbanism,* expanded ed. (New York: Monacelli Press, 2008); John Chase, Margaret Crawford, and John Kaliski, eds., *Everyday Urbanism* (New York: Monacelli Press, 1999); Karen A. Franck and Quentin Stevens, *Loose Space: Possibility and Diversity in Urban Life* (London: Routledge, 2007); Sophie Watson, *City Publics: The (Dis)Enchantments of Urban Encounters* (London: Routledge, 2006).

17. Semenak, "Terrasses and Montreal's al Fresco Culture."

18. Donald W. Hinrichs, *Montreal's Gay Village: The Story of a Unique Urban Neighborhood through the Sociological Lens* (iUniverse, 2012).

19. Rue Publique, "Rue Publique," n.d., https://www.facebook.com/ruepublique/.

20. Pierre-Yves Comtois, "Les Ruelles Vertes, un Guide Pratique," Éco-quartier Plateau-Mont-Royal, 2008, https://ruelleverte23.files.wordpress.com/2009/11/guide-ruelle-verte-plateau1.pdf.

21. Waverley Council, "Urban Interventions," https://www.waverley.nsw.gov.au/building/major_projects/streets_and_public_places/urban_interventions.

22. Ibid.

23. Sam George, interview, August 18, 2016; Elise O'Ryan, Kris Spann, and Sam George, interview, November 7, 2015.

24. Sam Crawford, interview, November 3, 2015.

25. Blaine Merker, interview, October 23, 2014. Merker said that Jason Roberts told him that PARK(ing) Day was the inspiration for Better Block.

26. "They're Park Raving Mad—International PARK(ing) Day Planned for September 20," *Daily Telegraph,* August 29, 2013, https://www.dailytelegraph.com.au/news/nsw/they8217re-park-raving-mad-international-parking-day-planned-for-september-20/news-story/7db97f4bdd8dcd8057409d15c390c1f5.

27. John Chase, "The Space Formerly Known as Parking," in Chase, Crawford, and Kaliski, *Everyday Urbanism,* expanded ed., 195.

28. Carlo Tadeo and Jean-Philippe Di Marco, interview, August 20, 2015.

29. Commons are perhaps best known through the work of Garrett Hardin (as natural resources doomed to overuse, degradation, and destruction) and Elinor Ostrom (who countered Hardin's "tragedy" by documenting common pool resources managed effectively through self-governing strategies that minimize opportunities for free-riding). Garrett Hardin, "The Tragedy of the Commons," *Science* 162, no. 3859 (1968): 1243–1248; Elinor Ostrom, *Governing the Commons: The Evolution of Institutions for Collective Action* (Cambridge: Cambridge University Press, 1990). More recently, this literature has expanded beyond natural resources such as forests and

fisheries to consider new forms of common pool resources such as the internet. Charlotte Hess and Elinor Ostrom, *Understanding Knowledge as a Commons: From Theory to Practice* (Cambridge, MA: MIT Press, 2011).

30. Paul Chatterton, "Seeking the Urban Common: Furthering the Debate on Spatial Justice," *City* 14, no. 6 (2010): 625–628; Martin Kornberger and Christian Borch, "Introduction: Urban Commons," in *Urban Commons: Rethinking the City*, ed. Christian Borch and Martin Kornberger (Abingdon, UK: Routledge, 2015), 1–21; David Bollier and Silke Helfrich, eds., *The Wealth of the Commons: A World beyond Market and State* (Amherst, MA: Levellers Press, 2012); Burns H. Weston and David Bollier, *Green Governance: Ecological Survival, Human Rights, and the Law of the Commons* (New York: Cambridge University Press, 2014); Peter Linebaugh, *The Magna Carta Manifesto: Liberties and Commons for All* (Berkeley: University of California Press, 2009).

31. Silvia Federici, "Feminism and the Politics of the Commons," in Bollier and Helfrich, *The Wealth of the Commons*.

32. Chatterton, "Seeking the Urban Common"; Amanda Huron, "Theorising the Urban Commons: New Thoughts, Tensions and Paths," *Urban Studies* 54, no. 4 (2017): 1062–1069; Leila Dawney, "Making Common Worlds: An Ethos for Participation," in *Problems of Participation: Reflections on Authority, Democracy, and the Struggle for Common Life*, ed. Tehseen Noorani, Claire Blencowe, and Julian Brigstocke (Lewes, UK: ARN Press, 2013), 147–151.

33. Paul Chatterton, David Featherstone, and Paul Routledge, "Articulating Climate Justice in Copenhagen: Antagonism, the Commons, and Solidarity," *Antipode* 45, no. 3 (2013): 602–620.

34. Elsa Noterman, "Beyond Tragedy: Differential Commoning in a Manufactured Housing Cooperative," *Antipode* 48, no. 2 (2016): 433–452.

35. Ibid.; Huron, "Theorising the Urban Commons."

36. Chatterton, Featherstone, and Routledge, "Articulating Climate Justice in Copenhagen," 611.

37. Jeffrey Hou, "Urban Commoning in Cities Divided: Field Notes from Hong Kong and Taipei," in *Perspecta 50: Urban Divides*, ed. Meghan McAllister and Mahdi Sabbagh (Cambridge, MA: MIT Press, 2017), 292–301.

38. Massimo De Angelis, "The Production of Commons and the 'Explosion' of the Middle Class," *Antipode* 42, no. 4 (2010): 958 (original emphasis).

39. Nicholas Blomley describes that claim as "based upon and enacted through sustained patterns of local use and collective habitation, through ingrained practices of appropriation and 'investment'" and, Blomley argues, as giving rise to a "legitimate property interest" sufficient to challenge and constrain the developer's plans.

Nicholas Blomley, "Enclosure, Common Right and the Property of the Poor," *Social and Legal Studies* 17, no. 3 (2008): 320.

40. Maria Marella describes how the Cinema Palazzo building was claimed as a commons by residents and activists after the cinema closed down, giving rise to rights that were recognized by the court in a challenge by the developer. Maria Rosaria Marella, "The Commons as a Legal Concept," *Law and Critique* 28, no. 1 (2017): 61–86.

41. Stavros Stavrides, "Emerging Common Spaces as a Challenge to the City of Crisis," *City* 18, no. 4–5 (2014): 546–550.

42. Sarah Keenan, *Subversive Property: Law and the Production of Spaces of Belonging* (Abingdon, UK: Routledge, 2014).

43. Patrick Bresnihan and Michael Byrne, "Escape into the City: Everyday Practices of Commoning and the Production of Urban Space in Dublin," *Antipode* 47, no. 1 (2015): 48.

44. Ibid., 44.

45. Ibid.

46. Ibid.

47. Ibid.

48. Ash Amin, *Land of Strangers* (Cambridge: Polity, 2012), 80.

49. Carl Boggs, "Marxism, Prefigurative Communism and the Problem of Workers' Control," *Radical America* 6 (Winter 1977): 100.

50. Marianne Maeckelbergh, "Doing Is Believing: Prefiguration as Strategic Practice in the Alterglobalization Movement," *Social Movement Studies* 10, no. 1 (2011): 4 (original emphasis).

51. Maeckelbergh, "Doing Is Believing"; Luke Yates, "Rethinking Prefiguration: Alternatives, Micropolitics and Goals in Social Movements," *Social Movement Studies* 14, no. 1 (2015): 1; Davina Cooper, "Prefiguring the State," *Antipode* 49, no. 2 (2017): 335; Francesca Polletta, "'Free Spaces' in Collective Action," *Theory and Society* 28, no. 1 (1999): 1; Guiomar Rovira Sancho, "Networks, Insurgencies, and Prefigurative Politics: A Cycle of Global Indignation," *Convergence: The International Journal of Research into New Media Technologies* 20, no. 4 (2014): 387; Kelvin Mason, "Becoming Citizen Green: Prefigurative Politics, Autonomous Geographies, and Hoping against Hope," *Environmental Politics* 23, no. 1 (2014): 140.

52. Maeckelbergh, "Doing Is Believing," 13. Maeckelberg's research is based on participation in a series of anti-summit mobilizations in parallel with meetings of the G8, WTO, NATO, and UNFCCC between 1999 and 2009, and work in the offices of the European Social Forum and the World Social Forum.

53. Maeckelbergh, "Doing Is Believing," 3.

54. Simon Leo Brown, "Neighbourhood Project Studio behind Melbourne Skip Park Takes Aim at Council Red Tape," *ABC News*, May 24, 2016, http://www.abc.net.au/news/2016-05-24/studio-behind-melbourne-skip-park-takes-aim-at-council-red-tape/7437814.

55. Maeckelbergh, "Doing Is Believing," 14.

56. Cooper, "Prefiguring the State," 335.

57. Fran Tonkiss, "Austerity Urbanism and the Makeshift City," *City* 17, no. 3 (June 2013): 312–324; Margit Mayer, "First World Urban Activism: Beyond Austerity Urbanism and Creative City Politics," *City* 17, no. 1 (2013): 5–19.

58. Davina Cooper, "Transformative State Publics," *New Political Science* 38, no. 3 (2016): 315–334; Cooper, "Prefiguring the State"; Davina Cooper, "Enacting Counter-States through Play," *Contemporary Political Theory* 15, no. 4 (2016): 453–461.

59. Cooper, "Enacting Counter-States through Play," 459.

60. Yates, "Rethinking Prefiguration," 19.

61. Ibid.

62. Jacqueline Groth and Eric Corijn, "Reclaiming Urbanity: Indeterminate Spaces, Informal Actors and Urban Agenda Setting," *Urban Studies* 42, no. 3 (2005): 503–526; Ryan Thomas Devlin, "A Focus on Needs: Toward a More Nuanced Understanding of Inequality and Urban Informality in the Global North," *Journal of Cultural Geography* 36, no. 2 (2019): 121–143; Megan Heim LaFrombois, *Reframing the Reclaiming of Urban Space: A Feminist Exploration into Do-It-Yourself Urbanism in Chicago* (Lanham, MD: Lexington Books, 2018).

63. Ann Deslandes, "Exemplary Amateurism: Thoughts on DIY Urbanism," *Cultural Studies Review* 19, no. 1 (2013): 216–227; Nina Martin, "Food Fight! Immigrant Street Vendors, Gourmet Food Trucks and the Differential Valuation of Creative Producers in Chicago," *International Journal of Urban and Regional Research* 38, no. 5 (2014): 1867–1883.

64. Claire Colomb, "The Trajectory of Berlin's 'Interim Spaces': Tensions and Conflicts in the Mobilisation of 'Temporary Uses' of Urban Space in Local Economic Development," in *Transience and Permanence in Urban Development*, ed. John Hennebury (Chichester, UK: John Wiley, 2017), 131–149; Deslandes, "Exemplary Amateurism"; Amelia Thorpe, Timothy Moore, and Lee Stickells, "Pop-Up Justice? Reflecting on Relationships in the Temporary City," in Hennebury, *Transience and Permanence in Urban Development*, 151–169.

65. Richard L. Florida, *The Rise of the Creative Class: Revisited* (New York: Basic Books, 2012); Jamie Peck, "Struggling with the Creative Class," *International Journal of Urban and Regional Research* 29, no. 4 (2005): 740–770.

66. Mayer, "First World Urban Activism," 11.

67. Thorpe, Moore, and Stickells, "Pop-Up Justice?"; Katherine Burnett, "Commodifying Poverty: Gentrification and Consumption in Vancouver's Downtown Eastside," *Urban Geography* 35, no. 2 (2014): 157–176; Deslandes, "Exemplary Amateurism"; Libby Porter and Kate Shaw, eds., *Whose Urban Renaissance? An International Comparison of Urban Regeneration Strategies* (London: Routledge, 2009).

68. Tonkiss, "Austerity Urbanism and the Makeshift City," 318.

69. "Win a $1,000 Gift Card From Ikea!," *PopSugar*, September 30, 2008, http://www.popsugar.com/home/Win-1000-Gift-Card-From-Ikea-2028900; "Popsugar 2008 _Park(ing) Day 10 Hints for Your Own Park."

70. Interestingly, despite their clear borrowing of Rebar's idea, IKEA would not grant permission for images of their pop-up park to be included in this book.

71. LaFrombois, *Reframing the Reclaiming of Urban Space*; Gordon C. C. Douglas, *The Help-Yourself City: Legitimacy and Inequality in DIY Urbanism* (New York: Oxford University Press, 2018); Kimberley Kinder, *DIY Detroit: Making Do in a City without Services* (Minneapolis: University of Minnesota Press, 2016).

72. Karen Bell, *Environmental Classism and Working Class Environmentalism: Insults, Injuries, Resistance* (London: Palgrave Macmillan, 2019).

73. Sarah Dooling, "Ecological Gentrification: A Research Agenda Exploring Justice in the City," *International Journal of Urban and Regional Research* 33, no. 3 (2009): 621–639; Jessica Ty Miller, "Is Urban Greening for Everyone? Social Inclusion and Exclusion along the Gowanus Canal," *Urban Forestry and Urban Greening* 19 (2016): 285–294; Julian Agyeman, David Schlosberg, Luke Craven, and Caitlin Matthews, "Trends and Directions in Environmental Justice: From Inequity to Everyday Life, Community, and Just Sustainabilities," *Annual Review of Environment and Resources* 41, no. 1 (2016): 321–340; Isabelle Anguelovski, James J. T. Connolly, Melissa Garcia-Lamarca, Helen Cole, and Hamil Pearsall, "New Scholarly Pathways on Green Gentrification: What Does the Urban 'Green Turn' Mean and Where Is It Going?," *Progress in Human Geography* 42 (2018); Hamil Pearsall, "New Directions in Urban Environmental/Green Gentrification Research," in *Handbook of Gentrification Studies*, ed. Loretta Lees and Martin Phillips (Cheltenham, UK: Edward Elgar, 2018), 329–345.

74. Stephen Zavestoski and Julian Agyeman, eds., *Incomplete Streets: Processes, Practices, and Possibilities* (Abingdon, UK: Routledge, 2015); Adonia E. Lugo, *Bicycle / Race: Transportation, Culture, and Resistance* (Portland, OR: Microcosm Publishing, 2018); Melody L. Hoffmann, *Bike Lanes Are White Lanes: Bicycle Advocacy and Urban Planning* (Lincoln: University of Nebraska Press, 2016); Aaron Golub, Melody L. Hoffmann, Adonia E. Lugo, and Gerardo F. Sandoval, eds., *Bicycle Justice and Urban Transformation: Biking for All?* (Abingdon, UK: Routledge, 2018); John Stehlin, *Cyclescapes of the*

Unequal City: Bicycle Infrastructure and Uneven Development (Minneapolis: University of Minnesota Press, 2019).

75. Pearsall, "New Directions in Urban Environmental/Green Gentrification Research."

76. Miller, "Is Urban Greening for Everyone?"; Golub et al., *Bicycle Justice and Urban Transformation*.

77. Jennifer R. Wolch, Jason Byrne, and Joshua P. Newell, "Urban Green Space, Public Health, and Environmental Justice: The Challenge of Making Cities 'Just Green Enough,'" *Landscape and Urban Planning* 125 (2014): 234–244.

Postscript

1. As Kay Anderson notes, "Few urban districts occupy so prominent a place in the minds and speech of Australians as the tiny pocket of Aboriginal settlement . . . in the inner Sydney suburb of Redfern." Kay J. Anderson, "Place Narratives and the Origins of Inner Sydney's Aboriginal Settlement, 1972–73," *Journal of Historical Geography* 19, no. 3 (1993): 314. Redfern, and particularly the area at its western extent known as The Block, has been a gathering place for Aboriginal people since at least the 1930s, when structural and policy shifts forced them off Country and into the city. The site of many significant events in Australian history—foundation of the Aboriginal Legal Service and Aboriginal Medical Service in the 1970s, a landmark speech by Prime Minister Paul Keating acknowledging the devastating impacts of white settlement in 1992, race riots after a young boy died while fleeing police in 2004, to name just a few—Redfern is well known as a site of both power and disadvantage for indigenous Australians.

2. Kimberley Kinder, *DIY Detroit: Making Do in a City without Services* (Minneapolis: University of Minnesota Press, 2016), 28.

3. Ibid., 29.

4. Henri Lefebvre, *Writings on Cities* (Cambridge, MA: Blackwell, 1996), 158.

5. Patrick Bresnihan and Michael Byrne, "Escape into the City: Everyday Practices of Commoning and the Production of Urban Space in Dublin," *Antipode* 47, no. 1 (2015).

6. Jeffrey Hou, "Urban Commoning in Cities Divided: Field Notes from Hong Kong and Taipei," in *Perspecta 50: Urban Divides*, ed. Meghan McAllister and Mahdi Sabbagh (Cambridge, MA: MIT Press, 2017), 292–301.

7. Ibid., 300.

8. Ibid.

9. "Commons, and urban commons, are not just about *opposing* power and capitalism, such as the commons literature's frequent references to community gardens misleadingly suggest; all sorts of power and politics go into how commons are produced, also in ways that demonstrate that what is common is not equally common to *all*." Martin Kornberger and Christian Borch, "Introduction: Urban Commons," in *Urban Commons: Rethinking the City*, ed. Christian Borch and Martin Kornberger (Abingdon, UK: Routledge, 2015), 16 (emphasis in original, internal citations omitted). See also James McCarthy, "Commons as Counterhegemonic Projects," *Capitalism Nature Socialism* 16, no. 1 (2005): 9–24.

10. Melissa García Lamarca, "Insurgent Acts of Being-in-Common and Housing in Spain: Making Urban Commons?," in *Urban Commons: Moving Beyond State and Market*, ed. Mary Dellenbaugh, Markus Kip, Majken Bieniok, Agnes Katharina Müller, and Martin Schwegmann (Basel: Birkhäuser, 2015), 168.

11. Sarah Keenan, "Subversive Property: Reshaping Malleable Spaces of Belonging," *Social and Legal Studies* 19, no. 4 (2010): 424.

12. Jenny Pickerill and John Krinsky, "Why Does Occupy Matter?," *Social Movement Studies* 11, no. 3–4 (2012): 281.

13. Eve Darian-Smith, "Ethnographies of Law," in *The Blackwell Companion to Law and Society*, ed. Austin Sarat (Oxford, UK: Blackwell, 2004), 546.

Index

Abad Ocubillo, Robin, 52, 62, 242, 257

activism. *See also* social movements
connective action, 87
and emotion, 158, 183–190, 194–195
and ownership, 196–197, 209
and privilege, 5, 8, 194, 209–212, 252–254, 261, 263
transport activism, 52–54, 56–63, 86–87, 225–226
urban activism, 20, 144–145, 148–149, 240

actor network theory (ANT), 122–123, 179–180

Administrative Code (San Francisco), 106

adverse possession, 166

aesthetics, politics of, 79–80, 91–94

agency. *See also* empowerment; voice
development of, 234, 242, 253
of objects, 18, 97, 112, 122–128, 139–140, 158–159, 164–165, 179–182
and ownership, 2, 138–139, 197, 261
and privilege, 210, 253–254
and property, 11, 22, 131, 152–154, 261, 264

American Institute of Architects, 44

Americans with Disabilities Act (1990), 117

animals
in PARK(ing) Day, 18, 39, 45, 50, 66, 73, 126, 181, 184–185, 205
in public space, 54–55, 111–112, 118, 124, 197

apathy, 6

Arnstein, Sherry, 151

art. *See* Asco; Margolin, Reuben; Matta-Clark, Gordon; Rakowitz, Michael; Sherk, Bonnie Ora

Arup, 64–67, 69, 175, 239

Asco, 54, 56

assemblage, 18, 123–128, 179–182, 193

assembly, public, 121–122
regulation of, 103–105, 110

Association du Design Urbain du Québec (ADUQ), 73, 186, 209, 238

Austin, John, 119

Australian Institute of Landscape Architects, 47

automobiles. *See* cars

automobility, 3–4

autonomy, 11, 133, 146

Bela, John, 30–31, 34, 43, 49, 98, 224, 228, 233, 245

belonging, 2–3, 9, 86, 138, 166, 170, 204, 239, 241
dimensions of, 138, 141–142, 165, 170

belonging (cont.)
  and ownership, 22, 138–139, 157–158,
    175, 180, 194–195, 197, 209,
    212–231, 235, 241–242
  and privilege, 24, 209, 263
  and property, 22, 142, 178,
    214–215
Better Block, 4, 229, 231
bicycles, 5, 36, 41, 45, 61, 63, 64, 73, 75,
    81, 126, 175, 186, 223, 229
  infrastructure for, 5, 21, 90, 178,
    225–226, 231, 243, 252, 259
Blackstone, William, 133
Blomley, Nicholas, 10–12, 13, 19, 103,
    133, 161, 169, 177
Boggs, Carl, 243
Bosom Buddies, 52–53, 144
Bourdieu, Pierre, 30, 92
Braverman, Irus, 179
Bresnihan, Patrick, 241
Brisbane, 40, 44, 57, 64
bundle of sticks, 10, 132
Busse, Mark, 136
Butler, Judith, 119–122
By-Law Concerning the Prevention of
    Breaches of the Peace, Public Order
    and Safety, and the Use of Public
    Property (Montréal), 105
By-Law Concerning Traffic and Parking
    (Montréal), 99
Byrne, Jason, 252–253
Byrne, Michael, 241

California, influence of, 21, 89
Callon, Michel, 122–123
Cancian, Steve Rasmussen, 58,
    229
capitalism, 83, 89, 147, 149, 240, 248,
    261, 264
care, 8, 133, 176, 181, 213, 216
Carr, Helen, 179
cars, 64, 72, 75–77, 79, 86, 88, 90–91,
    224–227, 228–229, 250–251

danger created by, 3–4, 37, 109, 122,
    257
  impacts of, 3–4, 21, 57, 72, 86, 90–91,
    102, 178–179, 226
car sharing, 51, 127–128
CC Puede, 37–39, 54, 130, 176, 211, 226
Certeau, Michel de, 30
Chase, John, 233
children
  in PARK(ing) Day, 50–51, 65, 73, 175,
    184–187
  in public space, 4, 59, 61, 103, 111,
    167, 169, 187, 196, 211, 250–251
Ciclovía, 4, 229
citizenship, 138, 141, 146, 205–206,
    246, 248
citizens' relationship to the state,
    5, 6–7, 8, 13, 24, 61, 75–76, 120,
    134–136, 148–149, 151, 198–199,
    246–247, 262, 264
city greening. See greening, urban
City of San Francisco, Ordinance
    no. 224-16 (October 2016), 106,
    224–225, 265
class, 12, 93, 146, 149, 210, 251–252,
    260
climate change, 3, 13, 86, 150, 261
Cloatre, Emilie, 177
collaborative turn, 150
colonialism, 7, 10, 133, 150, 161, 211,
    261
commoning, 3, 13, 24, 240–242, 254,
    262–263
common property, 140
commons, 160–161, 164, 177, 240–241,
    263
community, 11, 91, 240
  efforts to contribute to, 8–9, 37–39,
    45–46, 152, 184, 205, 206–207, 211,
    215
  and exclusion, 37, 209, 210, 248,
    252–254, 260
  interpretive, 114

and ownership, 135–136, 138–139, 142, 159, 163, 166, 167–169, 181, 195–196, 199, 203, 204
community gardens, 10, 14, 167, 198–199, 230, 233, 236, 237, 259, 265
   as commons, 240, 241
   critiques of, 248, 252
complete streets, 4, 231
Conseil régional d'environnement de Montréal (CRE), 72–73, 75, 109, 186, 209, 229
conviviality, 188
Cooper, Davina, 22, 23, 133, 141–142, 158, 161, 165, 170, 213, 216, 246
coordination, of PARK(ing) Day, 1, 14, 33–35, 40, 43–44, 46–49, 69, 75, 82–83, 166
Corr, Anders, 161
Cover, Robert, 22, 23, 113–114, 124, 159, 193–194, 265
Cowan, Dave, 177, 199
craft, 49, 68, 159, 181
creative city policies, 84, 88, 90, 231
Creative Commons, 1, 24, 85, 93
Criminal Code (Canada), 105
Critical Mass, 4, 229, 264
critique, 12–13
critiques, of PARK(ing) Day, 12, 13, 24–25, 75–77, 247–248
cultural capital, 5, 89, 145–146, 248, 252
cycling. *See* bicycles

Darian-Smith, Eve, 19
Davies, Margaret, 168–169
democracy, 146, 148, 261, 262
   and participation, 6, 8, 86–87, 114, 136, 189, 198–199, 216, 234, 261
density, urban, 91, 178
Devlin, Ryan, 147
Dewan, Ted, 58–60
dissensus, 21, 79–80, 91–94

DIY urbanism, 4–6, 75–76, 230, 260
   critiques of, 5, 12, 24–25, 245–246, 248–253, 260
   participants in, 5, 15, 75–76, 252
documentation, of PARK(ing) Day, 1–2, 18, 31–32, 37, 41, 49, 67, 123, 172, 173–175, 258
Douglas, Gordon, 251–252
DPP v Jones [1999] 2 AC 240, 103–104
duration, of PARK(ing) Day, 20, 29, 32, 35, 214–215

éco-quartiers, 14, 70–73
effort. *See* labor
Ejsing-Dunn, Stine, 208
Ellickson, Robert, 10
emotion, 8–9, 23, 137, 158, 159, 163, 180, 183–190, 195, 226. *See also* activism: and emotion; love
empowerment, 21, 24, 120, 138–139, 141, 146, 157, 195, 234–235, 241, 253–254, 259, 265
   definition of, 138
enclosure, 8, 10, 24–25, 147–148, 177, 179, 240, 261, 264
enforcement, 13, 17, 22, 23, 94, 99–106, 110, 111–112, 115
Engwicht, David, 54–57
En Ville Sans Ma Voiture, 72
environmental justice, 3, 252–253
Environmental Planning and Assessment Act 1979 (New South Wales), 107–108
Epstein, Richard, 140, 162–163, 178
Evans, Alan, 147
everyday urbanism, 4–5, 233
Ewick, Patricia, 113–114
expertise, 6, 20, 33, 37, 38, 90, 93, 123, 148, 258
expression. *See* self-expression

feminist theory, 168, 209
Ferrell, Jeff, 52

food
    in PARK(ing) Day, 33, 37–39, 45, 51,
        57, 65, 66, 70, 71, 97, 111, 127,
        171–172, 239
    regulation of, 105, 107, 116, 199
footpaths (sidewalks)
    efforts to improve, 40, 68, 222–223,
        226, 228, 245, 252, 259
    greening of, 59–60, 231
    ownership of, 135–136, 167
    regulation of, 103, 105–106, 245
    use of in PARK(ing) Day, 1, 18, 73,
        123
Freyfogle, Eric, 169
Fuller, Lon, 22, 101–102, 112, 114,
    265

games
    in PARK(ing) Day, 1, 18, 39, 45, 51,
        69, 73, 97, 126, 127, 128, 156, 168,
        171, 176, 180, 181, 182, 187, 206,
        207, 208
    in public space, 52, 58, 59, 61, 103
Garcia, Anthony, 52, 62
gardens. See community gardens;
    footpaths; greening, urban
Gehl Architects, 49, 228, 230–231, 233
gender, 19, 119, 144
    and ownership, 210
    and participation, 15, 52, 146, 149,
        251–252
    and property, 11, 160, 164
gentrification, 5, 10, 12, 13, 24–25, 169,
    222, 252–254, 260
Gibson-Graham, J. K., 12–13
globalization, 11, 148, 243–244
governance, 79, 132, 136, 147, 188,
    231, 244, 246, 262
graffiti, 11, 73, 230
Gray, Kevin, 132–133
Gray, Susan Frances, 132–133
green alleys, 14, 230, 252
green gentrification, 252–253

greening, urban, 24, 34, 35, 40, 59–60,
    71, 72, 91, 172, 211, 230, 252–254
greenwashing, 246, 251
guerrilla gardening, 197

Hart, H. L. A., 101–102, 113
Hartog, Hendrik, 22, 111–112, 114, 124,
    159, 193–194, 265
Harvey, David, 149
Hegel, G. W. F., 164–165, 169–170
homeownership, 145, 147, 151–152,
    162, 178, 179, 195, 240
hooks, bell, 138
Hou, Jeffrey, 262
housing, 7, 67, 144–146, 147, 150,
    261
human needs, 11, 23, 37, 38, 131, 137,
    150–152, 165, 199
human rights, 144, 149

identity, 1, 9, 11, 137–139, 163–165,
    189, 242, 261
    collective, 79, 82–83, 87, 244
    relational construction of, 168–170
IKEA, 248–249
illegality, 110, 111–112, 116, 140,
    145–146, 211
images
    circulation of, 72, 86–87, 177, 180,
        231, 232, 258
    impact of, 6, 32, 71, 72, 80, 122–123,
        126–127, 184, 232–233
imagination, 6, 20, 30, 80, 112, 113,
    114, 126, 133, 171, 188, 233, 234,
    243–246, 257
immigrants, and public space, 5, 37,
    149, 211, 260
informality, 9
informal ownership. See ownership
infrastructure
    and citizenship, 134–136, 248
    for cycling (see bicycles)
Institut du Nouveau Monde, 198–199

insurance. *See* liability

international reach, of PARK(ing) Day, 1, 15, 20, 29, 34–36, 39, 40, 43, 46, 47, 48, 82–84, 89, 120, 127, 202, 224

internet. *See* social media; technology

INTERSTICE Architects, 45–47, 81, 175, 195, 220

intimacy, 163, 165, 167

Iveson, Kurt, 13

Jacobs, Jane, 196, 198

Jardins Gamelin, 16, 236

Katyal, Sonia, 145–146

Keenan, Sarah, 12, 170, 177, 178, 214–215, 241, 263

Kenworthy, Jeffrey, 90–91

Kinder, Kimberley, 251–252, 260

Kleinhans, Martha-Marie, 112

Krinsky, John, 264

labor, 37–38, 80–82, 92, 171, 187–188, 228

and identity, 163–165

as justification for property, 23, 140, 158–163

and ownership, 23, 159–166, 181, 193, 195, 197, 214, 241, 262

and relationships, 167–168, 169, 175–176

LaFrombois, Megan, 251–252

Lande, 237, 265

land use. *See* planning

Latour, Bruno, 122–123

Law, John, 12

law

interpretation of, 3, 61, 98, 101–102, 110–114, 116–117, 118

legal title, 9, 11, 116, 131, 132, 133, 136, 137, 142, 144, 147, 157, 197

loopholes, 8, 22, 30, 41, 92, 98, 110, 114, 143, 244

Law Enforcement (Powers and Responsibilities) Act 2002 (New South Wales), 105

lease

as an explanatory device, 2, 7, 8, 9, 11, 21, 22, 61, 85, 86, 87, 89, 93, 94, 97, 99, 114–116, 118, 124, 131–132, 136, 143, 146, 154, 157–158, 193, 198, 208, 214, 264

as a legal tenure, 9, 21, 86, 115–116, 132, 178, 208, 214, 262

Lefebvre, Henri, 148–149, 150

legal consciousness, 15, 19, 22, 112–114

legal geography, 15

legal pluralism, 3, 19, 22, 112–114

Lehavi, Amnon, 147

liability, 107, 108, 109, 117

licenses, 103, 115–116, 146, 244

Local Government Act 1993 (New South Wales), 104–105, 107

Locke, John, 160–161, 164, 165, 177

love

and engagement, 8–9, 178, 184–185, 189, 195

and ownership, 23, 158, 189, 195, 263

Lugo, Adonia, 210

Lydon, Mike, 52, 62, 117, 151–152, 210

Macdonald, Roderick, 112

Maeckelberg, Marianne, 244

maps, 2, 31, 67, 144

of PARK(ing) Day, 2, 35, 40, 69, 83, 173

Margolin, Reuben, 41, 43

Marres, Noortje, 124, 180

Massey, Doreen, 178

materiality

material context, 8, 9, 158, 177, 179–182, 213–214

material engagement, 2, 10, 23, 24, 124–128, 193, 231, 241, 247, 259

material turn, 179–180

Matta-Clark, Gordon, 22, 30, 41, 131, 143–144
Mayer, Margit, 248
McLennan, Gregor, 21, 79, 86
media, 44, 62, 174, 223, 231–232, 244
efforts to engage, 43, 80, 171, 173–175
Merker, Blaine, 30–31, 34, 36–37, 43, 49, 82, 93, 98, 145, 172, 189, 228, 233, 245, 253
meter maids. See ticket inspectors
Montgomery, Charles, 229
Morelab, 49
Municipal Transportation Code (San Francisco), 106

Nedelsky, Jennifer, 133, 168
neoliberalism, 11, 24, 147–149, 248, 261, 262
Newell, Joshua, 252–253
Newman, Oscar, 196
Newman, Peter, 90–91
Newsom, Gavin, 35–36
new urbanism, 4, 90, 229
New York, 61–63, 87, 98, 111–112, 116, 118, 124, 140, 143–144, 147, 161, 196, 228, 230, 231, 260
niches, 22, 30, 41, 93, 98, 101, 110, 143
NIMBY, 7, 147
North Sydney Girls High School, 69–70, 81, 82, 108
Nozick, Robert, 161, 163

objects. See agency: of objects
obstruction of the street, 102–105, 110
Occupy movement, 11, 121–122, 145, 243, 264
official responses, to PARK(ing) Day, 17, 23, 32, 35, 48, 58, 65, 97, 98–102, 104, 105–106, 108–110, 193–194, 198, 227, 265
Ogbu, Liz, 40–41, 52, 81, 126, 139, 185, 204
Osborne, Thomas, 21, 79, 86

ownership, psychological, 137–138, 157–158, 165, 167, 169, 179, 197, 214, 241, 249, 261–263

parking meter, 4, 18, 29, 92, 123–124
history of, 29, 52, 85, 102, 180
parking meter parties, 52, 56–58, 82, 90
parking meter squats, 82, 90
parklets
connection to PARK(ing) day, 14, 24, 178, 215, 222–223, 224–226, 228, 237, 265
critiques of, 248–249, 252
language, 232, 233
other precursors for, 52, 228–229, 231–232
regulation of, 106, 215, 224, 237–238, 245, 265
use of PARK(ing) Day to advocate for, 69, 231, 247
Park-O-Meter, 29, 52
participants, in PARK(ing) Day, 5–6, 9, 15, 33, 35, 46, 48, 51, 67, 73, 252
Passmore, Matthew, 30–32, 34, 38, 43, 49, 98, 123, 210, 223, 234, 245, 249
pavement. See footpaths
Peattie, Lisa, 188
Peck, Jamie, 88
Penal Code (California), 105
Peñalver, Eduardo, 145–146
performativity, 10–12, 19, 22, 118–128
personhood, 23, 133, 163–167, 169–170, 214
Philadelphia, 43–44
photographs. See images
Pickerill, Jenny, 264
place attachment, 9
placemaking, 5, 69, 76, 84, 90, 244
placottoirs, 107, 226–227
planning, 5, 86, 90–91, 93, 107–108, 172, 188, 196–198, 221, 224–233, 254

and property, 7–8, 146–154, 168–169
public participation in, 5–9, 88, 90,
138, 147, 148–152, 196–198, 237,
253–254, 262
Planning Code (San Francisco), 223
play
in PARK(ing) Day, 1, 23, 69, 73, 126,
156, 159, 171, 175, 182, 184–190,
206, 262
in public space, 52, 56, 58, 61, 102,
103, 123, 167, 211, 215, 231, 237
police, 17–18, 23, 32, 35, 54, 65, 68,
94, 98, 99–101, 104–106, 108,
110, 117–118, 126, 135, 182, 192,
198–200, 202–204, 206, 207, 208,
210, 242, 258, 265
fear of, 32, 94, 117–118, 210
Police Code (San Francisco), 105
policy transfer, 87–88
possession, 86, 115–116, 140, 161, 164
postpolitical, 151
prefiguation, 3, 13, 222, 243–247, 254
private property, 7, 19, 149, 176, 209
privilege
and ownership, 194, 209–212, 222,
252, 263
and participation, 5–6, 8, 12–13, 15,
146, 209–212, 222, 252, 253–254,
260
progressive property, 10, 168
property
definitions of, 10–11, 22, 131–133,
136, 141
folk understandings of, 23, 133, 158,
198
and inequality, 24, 144, 210
and political rights, 22, 146
and the right to exclude, 9, 10,
132–133, 140, 144
slipperiness of, 22, 131–132, 134, 137,
142–143, 154, 170
protest, 25, 30, 37, 54, 90, 93–94,
102–103, 121–122, 227, 230

Public Architecture, 34, 40–42, 52, 228
public property, 144, 241
public space
informal control of, 8, 134–136, 140,
147–150, 163, 261
regulation of, 111–112, 118, 124
vulnerable groups in, 5, 12, 37–39,
158, 176, 210, 211, 215, 222
Public Works Code (San Francisco), 106
Purcell, Mark, 189

race, 7, 10, 11, 13, 17, 19, 70, 208,
210–212
Radin, Margaret, 164–166
Rakowitz, Michael, 60–61, 90
Rancière, Jacques, 21, 79–80, 91–94
rangers, 17–18, 65, 99–101, 105, 109,
110, 117–118, 202, 203–204
Rayside Laboissière, 184–185, 205–207,
211, 213, 215–217, 237, 245
Rebar, 82
evolution of, 1, 20, 29–30, 41–43, 49,
52, 82, 236
other projects by, 29–30, 42–43,
222–223
Reclaim the Streets, 4, 264
recognition, 37, 87, 136, 137, 140, 142,
161, 163, 169–177, 187–188, 197,
198, 207, 227, 263
recycling, in PARK(ing) Day, 21, 44, 51,
73, 99, 153, 181, 258
Règlement sur l'Occupation du
Domaine Public (Montréal), 107
regulation
interpretation of, 61, 98, 101–102,
117, 118
permitting processes, 60, 61
repetition, 11, 52, 82, 119–120
right to the city, 5, 22, 148–150,
152–154, 165, 261
risk, 70, 104
Road Rules (New South Wales), 99, 110,
202

roads. *See* streets
Roads Act 1993 (New South Wales), 104, 107
road witching, 58–60, 82, 90
Rose, Carol, 10, 19, 140, 162, 165, 169
Rue Publique, 230, 245

safety, 37, 68, 104, 105, 109, 117, 180, 182, 196, 226
Salter, Michael, 170
San Francisco, influence of, 88–89, 107
San Francisco Bay Area Planning and Urban Research Association (SPUR), 45, 171–172
San Francisco Bicycle Coalition, 35, 45, 51
San Francisco State University, 47–48, 108
Santos, Boaventura de Sousa, 112
Scher, Andrea, 28, 32, 34, 52
Seek, Amy, 34, 36–37, 52, 80, 82, 157, 192, 199–201, 228, 250
self-expression, 87, 152, 163, 165–167, 177, 180, 182, 189
Sherk, Bonnie Ora, 52, 54–55, 90
Shoup, Donald, 72, 90–91, 229
sidewalks. *See* footpaths
Silbey, Susan, 113–114, 140, 162–163
SJB, 123–124, 258
snow, in parking spaces, 139–141, 162–163
social media, 19, 21, 32, 35, 80, 86–87, 173, 175, 177, 180, 258
Facebook, 19, 35, 46, 69, 73, 115, 173, 232, 258
Twitter, 19, 46, 69, 232, 258
social movements, 11, 79, 82–84, 188, 216, 243
definition of, 82
Soja, Edward, 148
SPUR. *See* San Francisco Bay Area Planning and Urban Research Association

squatting, 12, 61–63, 79, 82, 86, 90, 112, 138, 145–146, 161, 230
state. *See* citizenship
stewardship, 133, 168–169, 176, 263
Strang, Veronica, 136
street libraries, 237, 245
streets
closures to traffic, 70, 72, 135, 230
experience of sitting on, 124–126, 179, 180, 182, 184
maintenance of, 135, 136
regulation of, 102–110, 111, 116
uses of, 20, 111, 117
street vendors, 4, 137, 240
Summary Offences Act 1988 (New South Wales), 110
sustainability, 2, 7, 18, 21, 47, 70, 71, 72, 75, 84, 86, 90–91, 109, 231, 239, 241, 242, 244, 246, 252, 253. *See also* recycling

tactical urbanism. *See* DIY urbanism
technology, 4, 85, 92, 123
digital, 80, 86, 87
terrasses, 226, 229, 230
Theodore, Nik, 88
things. *See* agency: of objects
ticket inspectors, 96, 98–99, 124
time, 2, 11, 166–167, 214–215
duration of PARK(ing) Day, 6, 82, 99, 175, 202, 215, 227, 232–233, 247, 258, 259
to participate in PARK(ing) day, 49, 67, 80–81, 98, 118, 153, 159–160, 167
timing, of PARK(ing) Day, 21, 35, 70–71, 204
Tonkiss, Fran, 248
traffic, 109, 117, 125, 173, 178, 180, 182, 204, 231, 243, 245
impacts of, 37, 50, 90, 178
traffic calming, 24, 37, 56–57, 58–59, 90, 117, 226, 247, 259
Traffic Code (San Francisco), 30

transit-oriented development, 4, 90, 229
Transportation Alternatives, 61–63
Transportation for Liveable
    Communities Hamilton, 56–59
Trust for Public Land (TPL), 34–35, 40,
    43, 46, 52, 209, 228

Université du Québec à Montréal
    (UQAM), 186
University of New South Wales (UNSW),
    64, 81
University of Queensland, 44, 47
University of Technology Sydney (UTS),
    47, 69–71, 208, 239
urban agriculture, 21, 71–72, 236
urban sprawl, 7, 91
Urry, John, 12
usual suspects, 6, 199

Valverde, Mariana, 116
Van der Walt, Andres, 11
vehicular ideas, 21, 79–80, 84–89, 145
    and media, 84, 86–87
Venice Biennale, 41–43, 49, 209, 230
visibility, 176, 177, 221, 261
    of the event, 83, 166, 168, 173, 209,
        232, 249, 261
    selection of sites for, 36–37, 172–173,
        178, 201
Vision Zero, 4
voice, 9, 131, 138, 139, 140, 143, 147,
    154, 254, 261, 264
Vorspan, Rachel, 103

walklets, 223
Wallace, Alison, 179
Wolch, Jennifer, 252–253
work. *See* labor

Yates, Luke, 246

Urban and Industrial Environments

Series editor: Robert Gottlieb, Henry R. Luce Professor of Urban and Environmental Policy, Occidental College

Maureen Smith, *The U.S. Paper Industry and Sustainable Production: An Argument for Restructuring*

Keith Pezzoli, *Human Settlements and Planning for Ecological Sustainability: The Case of Mexico City*

Sarah Hammond Creighton, *Greening the Ivory Tower: Improving the Environmental Track Record of Universities, Colleges, and Other Institutions*

Jan Mazurek, *Making Microchips: Policy, Globalization, and Economic Restructuring in the Semiconductor Industry*

William A. Shutkin, *The Land That Could Be: Environmentalism and Democracy in the Twenty-First Century*

Richard Hofrichter, ed., *Reclaiming the Environmental Debate: The Politics of Health in a Toxic Culture*

Robert Gottlieb, *Environmentalism Unbound: Exploring New Pathways for Change*

Kenneth Geiser, *Materials Matter: Toward a Sustainable Materials Policy*

Thomas D. Beamish, *Silent Spill: The Organization of an Industrial Crisis*

Matthew Gandy, *Concrete and Clay: Reworking Nature in New York City*

David Naguib Pellow, *Garbage Wars: The Struggle for Environmental Justice in Chicago*

Julian Agyeman, Robert D. Bullard, and Bob Evans, eds., *Just Sustainabilities: Development in an Unequal World*

Barbara L. Allen, *Uneasy Alchemy: Citizens and Experts in Louisiana's Chemical Corridor Disputes*

Dara O'Rourke, *Community-Driven Regulation: Balancing Development and the Environment in Vietnam*

Brian K. Obach, *Labor and the Environmental Movement: The Quest for Common Ground*

Peggy F. Barlett and Geoffrey W. Chase, eds., *Sustainability on Campus: Stories and Strategies for Change*

Steve Lerner, *Diamond: A Struggle for Environmental Justice in Louisiana's Chemical Corridor*

Jason Corburn, *Street Science: Community Knowledge and Environmental Health Justice*

Peggy F. Barlett, ed., *Urban Place: Reconnecting with the Natural World*

David Naguib Pellow and Robert J. Brulle, eds., *Power, Justice, and the Environment: A Critical Appraisal of the Environmental Justice Movement*

Eran Ben-Joseph, *The Code of the City: Standards and the Hidden Language of Place Making*

Nancy J. Myers and Carolyn Raffensperger, eds., *Precautionary Tools for Reshaping Environmental Policy*

Kelly Sims Gallagher, *China Shifts Gears: Automakers, Oil, Pollution, and Development*

Kerry H. Whiteside, *Precautionary Politics: Principle and Practice in Confronting Environmental Risk*

Ronald Sandler and Phaedra C. Pezzullo, eds., *Environmental Justice and Environmentalism: The Social Justice Challenge to the Environmental Movement*

Julie Sze, *Noxious New York: The Racial Politics of Urban Health and Environmental Justice*

Robert D. Bullard, ed., *Growing Smarter: Achieving Livable Communities, Environmental Justice, and Regional Equity*

Ann Rappaport and Sarah Hammond Creighton, *Degrees That Matter: Climate Change and the University*

Michael Egan, *Barry Commoner and the Science of Survival: The Remaking of American Environmentalism*

David J. Hess, *Alternative Pathways in Science and Industry: Activism, Innovation, and the Environment in an Era of Globalization*

Peter F. Cannavò, *The Working Landscape: Founding, Preservation, and the Politics of Place*

Paul Stanton Kibel, ed., *Rivertown: Rethinking Urban Rivers*

Kevin P. Gallagher and Lyuba Zarsky, *The Enclave Economy: Foreign Investment and Sustainable Development in Mexico's Silicon Valley*

David N. Pellow, *Resisting Global Toxics: Transnational Movements for Environmental Justice*

Robert Gottlieb, *Reinventing Los Angeles: Nature and Community in the Global City*

David V. Carruthers, ed., *Environmental Justice in Latin America: Problems, Promise, and Practice*

Tom Angotti, *New York for Sale: Community Planning Confronts Global Real Estate*

Paloma Pavel, ed., *Breakthrough Communities: Sustainability and Justice in the Next American Metropolis*

Anastasia Loukaitou-Sideris and Renia Ehrenfeucht, *Sidewalks: Conflict and Negotiation over Public Space*

David J. Hess, *Localist Movements in a Global Economy: Sustainability, Justice, and Urban Development in the United States*

Julian Agyeman and Yelena Ogneva-Himmelberger, eds., *Environmental Justice and Sustainability in the Former Soviet Union*

Jason Corburn, *Toward the Healthy City: People, Places, and the Politics of Urban Planning*

JoAnn Carmin and Julian Agyeman, eds., *Environmental Inequalities Beyond Borders: Local Perspectives on Global Injustices*

Louise Mozingo, *Pastoral Capitalism: A History of Suburban Corporate Landscapes*

Gwen Ottinger and Benjamin Cohen, eds., *Technoscience and Environmental Justice: Expert Cultures in a Grassroots Movement*

Samantha MacBride, *Recycling Reconsidered: The Present Failure and Future Promise of Environmental Action in the United States*

Andrew Karvonen, *Politics of Urban Runoff: Nature, Technology, and the Sustainable City*

Daniel Schneider, *Hybrid Nature: Sewage Treatment and the Contradictions of the Industrial Ecosystem*

Catherine Tumber, *Small, Gritty, and Green: The Promise of America's Smaller Industrial Cities in a Low-Carbon World*

Sam Bass Warner and Andrew H. Whittemore, *American Urban Form: A Representative History*

John Pucher and Ralph Buehler, eds., *City Cycling*

Stephanie Foote and Elizabeth Mazzolini, eds., *Histories of the Dustheap: Waste, Material Cultures, Social Justice*

David J. Hess, *Good Green Jobs in a Global Economy: Making and Keeping New Industries in the United States*

Joseph F. C. DiMento and Clifford Ellis, *Changing Lanes: Visions and Histories of Urban Freeways*

Joanna Robinson, *Contested Water: The Struggle Against Water Privatization in the United States and Canada*

William B. Meyer, *The Environmental Advantages of Cities: Countering Commonsense Antiurbanism*

Rebecca L. Henn and Andrew J. Hoffman, eds., *Constructing Green: The Social Structures of Sustainability*

Peggy F. Barlett and Geoffrey W. Chase, eds., *Sustainability in Higher Education: Stories and Strategies for Transformation*

Isabelle Anguelovski, *Neighborhood as Refuge: Community Reconstruction, Place Remaking, and Environmental Justice in the City*

Kelly Sims Gallagher, *The Globalization of Clean Energy Technology: Lessons from China*

Vinit Mukhija and Anastasia Loukaitou-Sideris, eds., *The Informal American City: Beyond Taco Trucks and Day Labor*

Roxanne Warren, *Rail and the City: Shrinking Our Carbon Footprint While Reimagining Urban Space*

Marianne E. Krasny and Keith G. Tidball, *Civic Ecology: Adaptation and Transformation from the Ground Up*

Erik Swyngedouw, *Liquid Power: Contested Hydro-Modernities in Twentieth-Century Spain*

Ken Geiser, *Chemicals without Harm: Policies for a Sustainable World*

Duncan McLaren and Julian Agyeman, *Sharing Cities: A Case for Truly Smart and Sustainable Cities*

Jessica Smartt Gullion, *Fracking the Neighborhood: Reluctant Activists and Natural Gas Drilling*

Nicholas A. Phelps, *Sequel to Suburbia: Glimpses of America's Post-Suburban Future*

Shannon Elizabeth Bell, *Fighting King Coal: The Challenges to Micromobilization in Central Appalachia*

Theresa Enright, *The Making of Grand Paris: Metropolitan Urbanism in the Twenty-first Century*

Robert Gottlieb and Simon Ng, *Global Cities: Urban Environments in Los Angeles, Hong Kong, and China*

Anna Lora-Wainwright, *Resigned Activism: Living with Pollution in Rural China*

Scott L. Cummings, *Blue and Green: The Drive for Justice at America's Port*

David Bissell, *Transit Life: Cities, Commuting, and the Politics of Everyday Mobilities*

Javiera Barandiarán, *From Empire to Umpire: Science and Environmental Conflict in Neoliberal Chile*

Benjamin Pauli, *Flint Fights Back: Environmental Justice and Democracy in the Flint Water Crisis*

Karen Chapple and Anastasia Loukaitou-Sideris, *Transit-Oriented Displacement or Community Dividends? Understanding the Effects of Smarter Growth on Communities*

Henrik Ernstson and Sverker Sörlin, eds., *Grounding Urban Natures: Histories and Futures of Urban Ecologies*

Katrina Smith Korfmacher, *Bridging the Silos: Collaborating for Environment, Health, and Justice in Urban Communities*

Jill Lindsey Harrison, *From the Inside Out: The Fight for Environmental Justice within Government Agencies*

Anastasia Loukaitou-Sideris, Dana Cuff, Todd Presner, Maite Zubiaurre, and Jonathan Jae-an Crisman, *Urban Humanities: New Practices for Reimagining the City*

Govind Gopakumar, *Installing Automobility: Emerging Politics of Mobility and Streets in Indian Cities*

Amelia Thorpe, *Owning the Street: The Everyday Life of Property*

Tridib Banerjee, *In the Images of Development: City Design in the Global South*